AMBROSE

THE MEDIEVAL WORLD
Editor: David Bates

John Moorhead	AMBROSE
John Moorhead	JUSTINIAN
Janet Nelson	CHARLES THE BALD
Richard Abels	ALFRED THE GREAT
M.K. Lawson	CNUT
James A. Brundage	MEDIEVAL CANON LAW
John Hudson	THE FORMATION OF THE ENGLISH COMMON LAW
Lindy Grant	ABBOT SUGER OF ST-DENIS
David Crouch	WILLIAM MARSHAL
Ralph V. Turner	KING JOHN
Jim Bradbury	PHILIP AUGUSTUS
Jane Sayers	INNOCENT III
C.H. Lawrence	THE FRIARS
David Abulafia	THE WESTERN MEDITERRANEAN KINGDOMS 1200–1500
Jean Dunbabin	CHARLES I OF ANJOU
Jennifer C. Ward	ENGLISH NOBLEWOMEN IN THE LATER MIDDLE AGES
Michael Hicks	BASTARD FEUDALISM

AMBROSE

Church and Society in the Late Roman World

John Moorhead

LONGMAN
London and New York

Pearson Education Limited
Edinburgh Gate,
Harlow, Essex CM20 2JE, United Kingdom
and Associated Companies throughout the world.

Published in the United States of America by Pearson Education Inc., New York.

© Pearson Education Limited 1999

The right of John Moorhead to be identified as author of this Work has been asserted by him in accordance with the Copyright,
Designs and Patents Act 1988.

All rights reserved; no part of this publication may be reproduced, stored in any retrieval system, or transmitted in any form or by any means, electronic, mechanical, photocopying, recording, or otherwise, without either the prior written permission of the Publishers or a licence permitting restricted copying in the United Kingdom issued by the Copyright Licensing Agency Ltd, 90 Tottenham Court Road, London W1P 9HE.

First published 1999

ISBN 0–582–25112–5 CSD
ISBN 0–582–25113–3 PPR

Visit our world wide web site at http://www.awl-he.com

British Library Cataloguing in Publication Data

A catalogue entry for this title is available from the British Library

Library of Congress Cataloging-in-Publication Data

Moorhead, John, 1948–
Ambrose : church and society in the late Roman world / John Moorhead.
    p. cm. — (The medieval world)
Includes bibliographical references and index.
ISBN 0–582–25112–5 (hbk).—ISBN 0–582–25113–3 (pbk)
1. Ambrose, Saint, Bishop of Milan, d. 397. 2. Church and state—Rome—History. 3. Church history—Primitive and early church, ca. 30–600. I. Title. II. Series.
BR1720.A5M66 1999
270.2′092—dc21
[B]   99–12447
                                              CIP

Set by 35 in 11/12 pt Baskerville
Produced by Addison Wesley Longman Singapore (Pte) Ltd.,
Printed in Singapore

CONTENTS

	Editor's Preface and Acknowledgements	viii
	Abbreviations	x
	Introduction	1
CHAPTER 1	Beginnings	15
	A new bishop	15
	Ambrose	19
	Taking office	22
	Background and experience	25
	The office of bishop	30
	Death of a brother	36
CHAPTER 2	Women	40
	The two sexes	41
	The wife	43
	The virgin	51
	The senses	54
	The body	56
	Sweetness tempting men	59
	Masculinity	60
	Women pleasing themselves	62
	Virginity and society	63
	Women in private and public	68
CHAPTER 3	The Bible	71
	Ambrose's writing on the Bible	72
	Ambrose's approach to the Bible	75
	Literal interpretation	77
	Allegorical interpretation	79
	The case of David	82

	The Bible	84
	Christ in the Bible	86
	Two miracles	88
	Coming down and going up	92
	A parable	94
	Ambrose's piety	96
	Structural coherence: the case of Shechem	98
	Allegory across the centuries	100
CHAPTER 4	Church, State, Heretics and Pagans	102
	The success of the church	102
	The state	104
	The church as female	106
	Polemic against anti-Nicaeans	111
	Persecution of anti-Nicaeans	118
	Pagans	122
CHAPTER 5	The Bishop and the City	129
	Milan, sinful or Christian?	129
	A skirmish over churches	132
	Martyrdom	134
	Easter 386	137
	Music and hymns	140
	The significance of Easter	143
	Controversy with anti-Nicaeans	147
	The discovery of relics	150
	Ambrose victorious	154
	The city and its bishop	156
CHAPTER 6	On Duties	157
	The *De Officiis*	158
	The clergy	161
	Ambrose and classical thought	164
	Neoplatonism	169
	Synthesis	177
	Conclusion	180
CHAPTER 7	The Elderly Bishop	182
	The Jews	182
	Callinicum	185
	Repression at Thessaloniki	192
	Church affairs	196

	The death of Valentinian	197
	The death of Theodosius	202
	Last years	206
CHAPTER 8	Nachleben	210

Bibliography 219
Map: The late Roman world of Ambrose 228
Index 229

EDITOR'S PREFACE AND ACKNOWLEDGEMENTS

One of the four Fathers of the Catholic Church, St. Ambrose, bishop of Milan, is one of the dominant figures, not just of the late Antique Christian Church, but of the entire history of Christianity. As such, his actions and writings were constantly re-examined and reinterpreted in later historical periods. His life has acquired an aura which seems to straddle time, rather than being set in any particular historical context. Assessing Ambrose is therefore a complex matter, especially since, while Ambrose's own writings are voluminous, other relevant contemporary sources are scarce.

A member of the aristocracy of the Late Roman Empire and a man of considerable administrative experience before his somewhat unexpected elevation to the episcopate, Ambrose was intensely absorbed in all the issues and controversies of his time. Very conscious of a bishop's duty to expound Scripture to his flock and to provide pastoral guidance, he devoted a great deal of time to seeking to explain the Bible through sermons and writings. He also took it upon himself to combat heretics and pagans and, when necessary, lay authority as exalted as the Emperor Theodosius.

John Moorhead's treatment of Ambrose is notable both for the skillful way in which the historical context of the subject's life is established and for the meticulous and accessible analysis of his technically difficult writings. An emotional man capable of generosity, Ambrose was also domineering and arguably too ready to confront and to judge. Although John Moorhead himself observes that much that Ambrose did cannot be admired and that he set an authoritarian example which was not always beneficial for the Church's influence in later times, he at the same time sets out very well how the attitudes of the Late Roman aristocrat were transferred to the episcopal office. The book illustrates admirably the complexity of Ambrose's biblical exegesis, underlining the central role of analogy in his method of argument and his sensitivity to ambiguities of meaning. Out of this study of Ambrose the theologian, John Moorhead expands discussion to analyse such matters as his attitudes to female piety and participation in the Church, to doctrinal issues associated with contemporary heretical movements and to lay authority.

John Moorhead's second contribution to the *Medieval World* series is an exceptionally welcome one. As a scholar with a profound interest in the intellectual and religious world of Late Antiquity, he is superbly qualified to assess the life and importance of one of its great figures. And even if he announces that his Ambrose lacks the originality of Augustine, the clarity of Gregory the Great and the zeal of Jerome – and, indeed, the range and humanity of all three – this book takes its reader engagingly into a complex and vibrant world. A study both of an individual and of Church and society in the Late Roman Empire, it illuminates the foundations on which more than one thousand years of medieval Christian history were to build.

David Bates

It is a pleasure to thank those people who have helped in the writing of this book. Jonathan Barlow, Chris Hanlon and John Oppel supplied useful criticism of the chapters which they kindly read, while Andrew Moorhead offered very helpful responses to a draft of the whole book. Passages of it have formed the basis of papers read at meetings at Armidale, Brisbane, Christchurch, Durham and London, all of which generated fruitful discussion. With unfailing patience, Serena Bagley and Suzanne Lewis have augmented my meagre computer skills. Finally, I thank the copyeditor, Anne Henwood, for her learned and patient work, for which the book is much the better.

John Moorhead

ABBREVIATIONS

CCSL	*Corpus Christianorum Series Latina*
CIL	*Corpus Inscriptionum Latinarum*
CSEL	*Corpus Scriptorum Ecclesiasticorum Latinorum*
ep.	*epistula*
FC	*The Fathers of the Church*
HE	*Historia Ecclesiastica*
LXX	The Septuagint
MGH	*Monumenta Germaniae Historica*
AA	*Auctores Antiquissimi*
PG	*Patrologia Graeca*
PL	*Patrologia Latina*
PLRE	A.H.M. Jones, J.R. Martindale and J. Morris (eds) *The Prosopography of the Later Roman Empire* 1, Cambridge 1971.
SAEMO	*Sancti Ambrosii Episcopi Mediolanensis Opera*
SC	*Sources Chrétiennes*

Abbreviated titles of works by Ambrose can be found in the Bibliography, pages 219–221.

INTRODUCTION

As the fourth century progressed, most of its inhabitants thought the Roman empire was in good shape. The preceding century had been a time of calamities: during the period from the death of Marcus Aurelius in 180 until the accession of Diocletian in 284, thirty-four emperors had strutted upon the stage, confronting invasions and civil wars. Still visible today are the remains of a wall which was built to protect Rome itself in the 270s. Matters were taken in hand by two great reforming emperors, Diocletian and Constantine, who set the empire on a firm footing. No longer would there be a single emperor, but power would be shared among two emperors and two subordinate caesars, with responsibilities in different regions. The administration was restructured to a degree unknown for three hundred years. Henceforth, military and civil authorities were separated, while a reform of the coinage dealt with hyper-inflation. Early in the fourth century the Emperor Constantine was converted to Christianity, and went on to establish a second capital for the empire at Constantinople, the ancient Byzantium, on the Bosphorus. He left behind an empire which seemed in much better health when he died in 337, just two years before the birth of the subject of this book.

Ambrose was the son of one of the most important officials of the empire, the praetorian prefect of the Gauls. He was born in Trier, a provincial capital near the empire's frontier along the Rhine, but he did not stay there long. Like many talented people in the empire, Ambrose found his way from the periphery to the centre, and it was there that he spent most of his life. As the son of an eminent official, he was a person to whom a habit of command came naturally, although his origins were not quite such as to make him committed to the ways in which conservative Roman intellectuals saw their world. In 374 he became bishop of Milan, an office he continued to hold until his death in 397.

It was a key job in a key place. By the time Ambrose became a bishop Christianity had made great progress in the empire's major cities, and as leaders of their churches, the bishops stood at the head of groups which were increasingly coming to constitute majority opinion. As the truth-claims of Christianity were stronger than those of classical polytheism, just as its teachings were potentially more destabilizing of society, the office of bishop could be a difficult one for the structures of the Roman world to accommodate, especially if a bishop were a person of strong convictions adroit at mobilizing public opinion.

Not only was the office he held important, but Ambrose's tenure of it largely coincided with a brief period in the sun which Milan enjoyed during late antiquity. A growing uneasiness as to the security of the northern frontiers of the empire had made Rome less important to its governance. The city by the Tiber had been well placed to be the capital of an empire based on the Mediterranean, but the growth of military pressures on its northern borders made it increasingly marginal. Emperors found themselves more and more in Trier and Sirmium, towns within striking distance of the Rhine and Danube frontiers. As Milan was roughly midway between these two cities and at the centre of a network of roads, emperors concerned with the security of the northern frontiers often lived there when in Italy. This was particularly the case after Gratian became emperor in 375, so it can be said that the accession of Ambrose coincided with the birth of a capital.[1] As the importance of various churches in the empire was often seen as being related to the political importance of the places where they were located, the bishop of Milan was a major figure within the church. Hence the

---

1. Pietri (1992): 161. The change which imperial residence brought Milan is suggested by the Latin of Ambrose's biographer Paulinus. Classical authors often used the noun for 'city' (Latin *urbs*) by itself, knowing their readers would take it to refer to Rome, but Paulinus applies it to Milan when an emperor was present and does not use it of the city when an emperor was absent: *VAmb.* 21, also of Rome 27,34. Similarly, Aquileia is termed *urbs* when an emperor is present: *VAmb.* 32.

position which Ambrose occupied from 374 was one with extraordinary possibilities, in terms of both relations with the state and power within the church.

Ambrose's character, the job he held and the position of the city in which he held it ensured his importance in the history of the later Roman empire. He took a leading part in the campaign against the form of Christian belief which is generally called Arianism, engaging in activities which pointed the way towards the difficulties experienced by adherents of positions which deviated from orthodoxy in a state committed to there being one interpretation of its official religion, as was usually to be the case in Europe during the following millennium. In 384 he participated in a controversy over a non-Christian cultic object, the altar of Victory, which marked an important stage in the defeat of classical polytheism. In 386 he was involved in a bitter battle with the government over the use of church buildings in Milan. Two public clashes between Ambrose and the Emperor Theodosius I followed, one arising from the burning down of a synagogue in 388 and the other from a massacre which occurred in Thessaloniki in 390. These have widely been seen as marking important victories of the church over the state. Such activities, and the powerful expression which Ambrose gave to his convictions concerning them, guarantee him an important place in the long story of relations between church and state which has been so much a part of western history.

A book on Ambrose could easily be structured around these themes, and they will claim our attention in this book. But the most straightforward way of approaching him is by means of his writings. It was on the basis of these that scholars of the middle ages saw him as one of the four great fathers of the western church, symbolized at the beginning of the Bible by the four rivers which watered the Garden of Eden. At first glance, one may doubt whether Ambrose belongs in such noble company, lacking as he does the scholarship of Jerome, the mental fire-power of Augustine, and the benign user-friendliness later generations were to find in Gregory. But Ambrose's chief concern, the interpreting of the Bible, has been central to the western intellectual tradition. While his works may seem baffling, when approached with sympathy they not only help one understand the Christian church at one of the most important stages of its history, when a religion which saw itself as having been fertilized by the blood of martyrs was speedily becoming part of the establishment, but suggest key points of fracture with the classical world which were then becoming apparent. They also open the door on a mental universe based on principles completely different from those which dominate modern western thought.

While not all Ambrose's works survive,[2] those at our disposal constitute a formidable corpus. He devoted most of his energies to discussions of various books of the Bible which we may loosely call commentaries, although they tend to be responses to the text which often sit lightly on it rather than attempts to elucidate what its authors had in mind. While Ambrose may have come relatively late in his life to a deep study of the Bible, he appears from his works as, essentially, a man of this one text. He saturated himself in its language, to the extent that a few words in one part of it would immediately call to his mind any number of verbally similar passages in other parts.[3] Much of his reading beyond the Bible was of commentaries on it written by earlier Jewish and Christian scholars, which he studied to help him understand the Scriptures better. He also wrote on topics other than the Bible. Books on virginity, widowhood and the duties of the clergy were addressed to different groups in society; expositions of the Creed, sacraments and penitence sought to explain difficult concepts to a wide public; a group of works in which Ambrose discusses the faith, the Holy Spirit and the incarnation of Christ, is more strictly theological; while he wrote four orations to commemorate his brother and two emperors. Yet even his books which take as their starting point a definite topic rarely cover the ground in a systematic fashion. They generally proceed by discussing what Ambrose thought were relevant passages of the Bible.

We therefore possess a large body of material written by Ambrose related to the Bible. It is, as we shall see, full of

2. We only have fragments of his commentary on Isaiah and his work 'On the sacrament of regeneration or philosophy', which are edited in *CCSL* 14 and *CSEL* 11 respectively.
3. Ambrose's peculiar sensitivity to words has led me often to use his own words rather than paraphrases, and to supply the Latin forms of important terms. This has not been done to intimidate readers whose Latin may be rusty, but to provide insight into the workings of Ambrose's mind.

interest and capable of engaging modern readers of the Bible, although in ways they may not expect.[4] But it is not easy to move from such material to an understanding of its author. Most of his works are commentaries, and while it is true that commentators often reveal much of themselves, at the very least the kind of writing which Ambrose found most congenial was such as to force him to focus on and expand the thoughts of other people rather than give direct expression to his own ideas. Moreover, much of what he says in the commentaries is borrowed, sometimes *in extenso* and almost always without acknowledgment, from earlier commentators, and, while he sometimes shows originality in the way he develops and alters the material presented by his predecessors, we are not given direct access to Ambrose's own mind. Some of his borrowings are disconcerting. On two occasions Ambrose states that he had seen a poor man putting his children up to auction to pay his debts (*Nab.* 5.21; *Tob.* 8.29). But he copied this incident from the Greek writer Basil, who states that he had seen this incident occur, and while it has been urged in Ambrose's defence that it is possible that he saw it with his own eyes, as it stands the story seems purely literary.[5] Further, Ambrose's response to biblical texts often takes the form of allegorizing them, which can lend his writings an air of abstraction and unreality, and one of his most fixed habits of mind, that of developing arguments by the use of images which imply the basic structures of his thought rather than by the explicit assertion of them, can make his ideas hard to establish.

All in all, it may be thought, much of Ambrose's writing almost serves to conceal its author. Yet in some ways its nature opens doors. Although he sometimes develops themes in ways that can appear inconsequential and self-indulgent, this allows his own preoccupations to emerge. Further, his

---

4. In the hope that some readers of this book will be moved to test Ambrose's understanding of the Bible against their own, I have often supplied references to passages he discusses. Ambrose numbered the psalms according to a system different from that generally used now; hence, his long commentary on what he thought of as psalm 118 deals with that now usually numbered 119. My references are to the modern enumeration; those who seek to verify them in the Septuagint or Vulgate will therefore find they do not always work.
5. Basil: *PG* 29:277B. See the discussion in *SAEMO* 6:225n.1.

writing is often based on material recycled from sermons, and so illustrates concerns Ambrose had at the time of delivery. Whereas modern scholars in universities who write on the Bible can usually, if they wish, do so while detached from their immediate surroundings, Ambrose found himself having to relate passages of the Bible read out during the liturgy on a particular day to whatever themes were foremost in his mind on that day.[6] So it was that the biblical text was often used as a springboard to the expression of thoughts on contemporary issues rather than commented on in its own right.

Furthermore, many of his works are of uncertain date, more than is the case with the works of his slightly younger contemporary Augustine. Connections between the works of Ambrose and the events going on around him have therefore to be suggested more tentatively than would be possible if the works were securely dated. Yet this is less of a loss than it could have been, for Ambrose's thought was largely static and displays no marked evolution.[7] To be sure, we can see Ambrose responding to new stimuli. At some time in the mid-380s he will fall under the influence of a Neoplatonist philosopher and will discover a commentary on a book of the Bible, the Song of Songs, which will suggest a powerful way of interpreting this text, although this will not be entirely new even to Ambrose and will co-exist with rather than supplant one he had adopted earlier. Ambrose does not often give the sense of dominating his sources and using them for his own purposes, as Augustine does. Somewhat later the activities of Theodosius I will encourage him to consider how King David acted in similar circumstances, and the appearance of apparently unorthodox doctrine concerning the Virgin Mary will force him to think through issues concerning her more deeply. He will ruefully comment to a correspondent that one of his early works was written when he was not yet an experienced bishop (*ep.* 34(=45).1), and he certainly advanced in the technical expertise with which he approached the Bible. But the steady working out and making explicit of themes only present *in nuce* in earlier works, and the sense of intellectual positions being developed in response to changing circumstances, which give so much

---

6. Such a passage could be 'fortuitous' (*ep.* 77(=22).4).
7. Pizzolato (1978): 9.

INTRODUCTION

interest to the thinking of Augustine, are not features of Ambrose's mind.

We have not mentioned one other part of Ambrose's literary output, which might be thought likely to reveal something of its author. In addition to his formal works he wrote many letters, some of which he arranged for publication towards the end of his life in ten books, perhaps imitating the way the letters of Pliny were organized for publication.[8] Of these, the tenth book contains two letters addressed to his sister Marcellina, who lived in Rome, which offer versions of affairs in Milan in 386, while another four, addressed to various emperors, are important sources for the political history of the period and the role Ambrose played in it. A further group of seventeen letters, generally styled those 'outside the collection', was assembled after his death. It includes seven letters to emperors and one to his sister, in which he reproduced a sermon preached in the presence of Theodosius in 388. These letters show that from time to time Ambrose played an influential role in political life, which must sometimes have diverted his attention from his scholarly enterprises.[9] But caution is called for in their use. It would have been possible for Ambrose to have amended the texts of his letters when he prepared them for publication, and we have one sign that he was prepared to do this. A letter has come down to us in its original form as well as that in which it was published, and in the latter version it has been subjected to a number of small but sometimes significant alterations; we can only wonder whether such changes were made to other letters.[10] Moreover, most of the three letters to his sister are taken up with sermons Ambrose preached, and while stenographers may well have taken down the words of his sermons verbatim it is certainly possible that Ambrose amended the texts for transmission to Marcellina; indeed, a degree of brotherly boastfulness may have coloured Ambrose's recounting of his successes.

8. We know of letters he failed to include, such as those he seems to have sent to his brother Satyrus (*exc.fr.* 1.26).
9. Zelzer points out the alternation of periods of political influence and writing activity in the life of Ambrose, comparing him in this respect with Cicero (1987: 207f).
10. *Ep.* 1a(=40) is the original version of *ep.* 74(=40). The differences are listed at *SAEMO* 21:188f; see further below page 186.

The other nine books of the collected letters contain formal compositions which are generally devoid of personal interest. One of the important people in Ambrose's life was Simplicianus, who instructed him prior to his baptism and later succeeded him as bishop of Milan. We have four letters which Ambrose wrote to him. He represented them as having arisen from conversations he had enjoyed with Simplicianus concerning passages in the Bible, but while they imply warm relations between the two men they give little away. Letter 7(=37),[11] for example, which is concerned with the happy life (*vita beata*), is resolutely scriptural in its content, containing over a hundred biblical references. Much of it simply reproduces in translation, without acknowledgment, words written by Philo, a Jewish scholar who lived in Alexandria at the time of Christ. There is little here to interest a biographer of Ambrose. Indeed, an editor of his letters has suggested that some of them are no more than 'make-believe letters' to fictitious correspondents which were written as vehicles for the exposition of the Bible.[12] The practice was familiar in the period,[13] so it would not be surprising had Ambrose engaged in it. Many letters of late antiquity are impersonal rather than intimate, but even the requests to pass on greetings to common friends one finds in the correspondence of some authors, which enable us to gain an idea of networks of friendship and alliance, are not found in Ambrose. The

---

11. Ambrose's letters are numbered according to two different systems. Whenever I cite a letter, the first reference is according to that used in the *CSEL* and *SAEMO* editions, and the second that used in *PL*.
12. Ambrose wrote that Bishop Justus had admonished him to write '*epistulares fabulas . . . ad interpretationem . . . oraculi caelestis*' (*ep.* 1(=7).1), and Faller suggests that such compositions were not genuine letters (ed. *CSEL* 82/1: 1). This may be to understand '*fabulas*' too narrowly, for it need not mean 'made-up' as opposed to 'genuine'. Nevertheless, Ambrose's correspondence contains signs of artificiality: *ep.* 40(=32) begins by discussing a point raised at the end of the preceding letter, and the beginning of *ep.* 64(=74), a letter devoid of any personal touches, begins by reminding Irenaeus of a passage of the Apostle he had heard read out that day. Further, the utter obscurity of many of his correspondents could be held to suggest that some of them were fictive.
13. Marius Victorinus playfully exploited the convention when he addressed a reader as '*O amice candide*', which could mean 'O friend Candidus' or 'O candid friend'.

lack of personal warmth his letters reveal raises a question to which we shall return later.

A number of sources contain information of a more biographical nature. Our earliest is that by Rufinus, a scholar best known for his translations of Greek Christian texts into Latin, who returned to Italy in 397 after spending some decades in the East. He was a friend of Bishop Chromatius of Aquileia, a connection which takes us close to Ambrose, for Chromatius had been consecrated bishop by him, received a letter from him on the office of bishop not long afterwards,[14] and drew heavily on Ambrose's works in his own writings. In 402/3 Rufinus produced a translation of Eusebius' *Ecclesiastical History* which he dedicated to Chromatius, to which he added two books concerning events which had occurred in the period 324–395, the second of which touches on Ambrose. Its nearness in time to Ambrose and its author's relationship with Chromatius indicate that we should take seriously what he says about him.

More voluminous is a biography of Ambrose written somewhat later by Paulinus, who had been Ambrose's secretary (*notarius*) towards the end of the bishop's life. This suggests that his biography will have been well informed by written sources, although Paulinus may not have been close to the centre of Ambrose's entourage, for he was a much younger man who only attained the rank of deacon after he left Milan. Towards the beginning of his work, Paulinus mentions his sources. He states that he drew on the evidence of reliable people, in particular Ambrose's sister Marcellina, on things which he had seen himself or found out from people scattered far and wide who said that they had seen Ambrose after his death, and on what people wrote to him before they knew he was dead. This suggests a solid body of material. It was probably Paulinus who edited the letters outside the collection, a task for which his former position as Ambrose's secretary would have equipped him well.[15] His account is therefore a priceless source for the life of Ambrose. Nevertheless, there are reasons why we should approach it with care.

---

14. *Ep.* 28(=50), a commentary on part of the book of Numbers in which Ambrose partly follows Philo.
15. See in particular Klein (1970): 365–70.

One difficulty arises from the circumstances of its composition. Paulinus states that he wrote at the time when John, a former tribune and *notarius*, held the office of praetorian prefect (*VAmb.* 31.5). While we know of a person of this description, he was praetorian prefect twice, once in 412–413 and again in 422. There are arguments for dating Paulinus' work to either of these periods, but those for the latter date are stronger.[16] This would mean that Paulinus wrote some twenty-five years after the death of Ambrose. Furthermore, the incidents in Ambrose's life at which Paulinus was present only occur in the few years before the death of the bishop (*VAmb.* 32ff); only at that stage does Paulinus attempt chronological precision (*VAmb.* 32), and his *Life* is heavily weighted to the last few years of Ambrose's episcopate. It is therefore the work of one who was an eyewitness for only a few of the many years Ambrose was bishop, and his account of events in the distant, earlier years need not be reliable. Moreover, he represents himself as having written with the encouragement of Augustine, bishop of Hippo (*VAmb.* 1). This may seem a welcome indication of reliability, for Augustine had followed Ambrose's sermons closely when he lived in Milan, been baptized by him in 387, and regarded him as his spiritual father. But the verb Paulinus uses to describe the kind of encouragement Augustine gave him (*hortaris*) does not imply that he was closely involved. Augustine may have had no input into his book, and Paulinus' use of his name may have been a matter of convention.

Nevertheless, Paulinus seems to have written when Augustine was engaged in theological controversy with Pelagius and his followers. It was a time when Ambrose was becoming more important to Augustine. While there are no direct citations of Ambrose in any of his works prior to 418,[17] thereafter he often drew on Ambrose's writings to support his arguments. What would have been more useful to Augustine than the publication of a short book which would advance the reputation of Ambrose? Moreover, Paulinus is almost certainly to be identified with another person of this name who was involved in anti-Pelagian activities, which would

---

16. I agree with Pellegrino, in his edition, 5–7, and Fischer (1984), against Lamirande (1981).
17. Paredi (1963): 212; Brown (1967): 272.

make an alliance between him and Augustine all the more plausible.[18] A connection with contemporary polemic may lie behind Paulinus' portrayal of Ambrose as a commanding figure whose enemies persistently met with dire fates (e.g. *VAmb.* 11,12,16,17,18), an interpretation not entirely in keeping with reality, and the strong attack on unnamed detractors of Ambrose with which Paulinus chose to conclude his book (*VAmb.* 53–55).

No-one could accuse Paulinus of having minimized the worthiness of his subject. He states that Augustine encouraged him to write a work similar to Athanasius' *Life of Antony*, Jerome's *Life of Paul*, and the *Life of Martin*, bishop of Tours (*VAmb.* 1). We may now be inclined to place Paulinus' work with the three others in a general category of early Christian hagiography, to which Paulinus clearly intended it to belong.[19] But Ambrose is very different from the other subjects, all of them monks committed to lives of heroic self-denial who frequently worked miracles. Two lived for over a century, and the third, the only one to become a bishop, was a reluctant recruit to the episcopate. And if assimilating Ambrose into the category of distinguished holy men were not enough, Paulinus unblushingly applied to him words used of Jesus in the Bible.[20] It would be too much to expect realism from such an account. Sometimes we can see Paulinus working on his material. For example, he writes that Ambrose once went to the *magister militum* Macedonius to intercede for an accused person, but found the doors shut and could not enter. He spoke threatening words: 'You will come to church and the doors will be shut so you will not be able to enter.' After the Emperor Gratian died Macedonius fled to a church, looked for a door, but could not find a way in (*VAmb.* 37). It is a neat story, but perhaps its very neatness should make us suspicious of the prophecy attributed to Ambrose, and the threat that Macedonius would come to church but not find what he wanted is very similar to a threat Ambrose made to the Emperor Valentinian, contained

---

18. See Paredi (1963): 212, although the initiative may have come from Paulinus rather than Augustine.
19. Hence his use of the word for 'and so' (*igitur*) to begin its biographical part.
20. Luke 2:52 is used at *VAmb.* 16, Luke 9:29 at *VAmb.* 42.1.

in a letter which we know Paulinus read.[21] We may take it, then, that Paulinus drew on words written by Ambrose in another context so as to heighten the impact of the story of Macedonius.

Other narrative sources are of less value. Three eastern historians of the first half of the fifth century, Sozomen, Socrates and Theodoret, wrote church histories which contain material on Ambrose, particularly his dealings with emperors, but it is already developing in the direction of legend. More useful are the proceedings of a church council held at Aquileia in 381, at which Ambrose played a prominent part. These are exceptional among early conciliar documents in that they give what seems to be a verbatim account of the debate in addition to the decrees which were issued. The letters of a contemporary, the senator Symmachus, open up aspects of the political, intellectual and religious history of the period, as do two large bodies of material less closely connected with Ambrose. The works of other ecclesiastical writers of the time, especially Augustine and Jerome, provide a context for his thoughts and activities. While their works form a vast ocean of material which no-one can be confident of having mastered, the background they provide is often illuminating. In particular, Augustine's autobiographical *Confessions* preserve memories of Ambrose's preaching and some important events in Milan. The Theodosian Code, a compilation of legislation issued in the period beginning with the reign of Constantine which was published on the order of Theodosius II in 438, provides data of a different kind. Because of Ambrose's involvement with emperors, some of the laws it preserves touch directly on his life, and as the Code tells us when and where laws were promulgated we can sometimes link pieces of legislation with his activities.

This balance of sources has governed the approach taken in this book. It would be impossible to write a study of Ambrose which illuminated him in a psychologically plausible way; he will always remain less knowable than Augustine.[22] On the other hand, we can approach him as a thinker, and

---

21. Compare Paulinus '*et tu quidem venies ad ecclesiam*' with Ambrose '*licebit tibi ad ecclesiam convenire*' (*ep.* 72(=17).13). For Paulinus' use of this letter elsewhere, see Pellegrino's edition, 15.
22. Cf. the speculations of McLynn (1994): 35.

we shall be mainly concerned with him in this respect. Our account will be built around clusters of material, presented in a largely chronological sequence. After a chapter devoted to Ambrose's early life and becoming a bishop, we shall examine his attitude towards women, a subject which generated some of his earliest writings. Thereafter we shall consider the way in which he approached the Bible, before going on to look at how Ambrose dealt with relations between the church and the state, and more generally the church and the world, and the role of the church within the city. These two chapters will consider tensions between the theoretical constructs within which Ambrose operated and the practical realities with which he had to deal. We shall then use one of his most substantial books, the *De officiis*, as the basis for a discussion of how Ambrose attempted to synthesize the very different classical and biblical ways of thinking. The following chapter will discuss issues which arose towards the end of Ambrose's life, and we shall conclude with a brief survey of aspects of his influence in the medieval centuries. This will necessarily be highly selective, and will seek to do no more than suggest some of the main lines of the topic.

The most detailed modern study of Ambrose is that of Homes Dudden (1935), who also wrote long books about Pope Gregory the Great and Henry Fielding. I have read his work twice, the first time often in a spirit of exasperation at what now seems self-indulgent prose and a complaisant attitude towards his subject, but later with a growing respect for his success in mastering Ambrose's voluminous writings. Among other studies, that of Paredi (1960) in particular is marked by its respectful learning. Two recent works in English have prompted important revisions of generally accepted views. McLynn (1994) approaches Ambrose from a political point of view, regarding him as a figure whose position was less secure and successes less clear-cut than they have hitherto been seen. Here, Ambrose emerges as someone who created his own position and sometimes held it with difficulty. The triumphalist view of Paulinus, who felt that the Lord generally gave the church triumphs over its enemies and that he usually protected it (*VAmb.* 13,16,31), cannot survive McLynn's subtle study. Williams (1995) offers an informed account of Ambrose's dealings with those Christians usually termed 'Arians'. Again, his study tends to diminish the position of

Ambrose, for against much modern scholarship, which has assumed that they were an unimportant minority whose cause was already destined to futility when Ambrose became bishop, Williams brings out the continuing threat they posed. But the Ambrose these recent books describe is a man of affairs, and the portrayal of him in the following account may be found complementary. Whereas McLynn's Ambrose is approached in relation to people like the senator Symmachus rather than Augustine and Jerome (xix), my attempt at placing him works from the other direction, approaching him as a thinker, in particular a commentator on the Bible.

Behind the monographs on Ambrose stands the vast amount of writing published in journals and collections of papers, to which the bibliography at the end of this book provides no more than an introduction. The study of Ambrose in recent years has profited from the learned philological traditions of German scholarship, and exciting work has been done by Italian scholars. Much of the best writing continues to appear in French, sensitive to both the classical and Christian sides of late antiquity. Yet, despite all that has been written about him over the centuries, Ambrose remains hard to know. Towards the end of his life, he remarked: 'I have not lived among you as so to be ashamed of continuing to live, and I am not afraid to die, because we have a good Lord' (*VAmb.* 45). His words were quoted by Augustine, who took the 'good Lord' to be God the Father.[23] But Ambrose's use of this expression elsewhere makes it certain that he had Christ rather than the Father in mind.[24] It is a disturbing thought that a theologian of the acumen of Augustine, who had known Ambrose personally, should have misunderstood him, which imposes humility on any who seek to understand him now. But Ambrose is a big enough figure to make the effort worthwhile. I hope readers of this book will feel something of the excitement I have had as Ambrose so often took me by surprise, and join me in contemplating his contribution to the articulation of a body of teaching '*juvenescens et juvenescere faciens*'.[25]

---

23. Possidius *VAug.* 27.
24. Fischer (1988).
25. Irenaeus *Adversus omnes haereses* 3.28.1.

Chapter 1

BEGINNINGS

. . .

A NEW BISHOP

The choice of a bishop was not a matter taken lightly in late antiquity. The increasing power of the church in society and the high degree of authority bishops enjoyed within the churches they led had made the job increasingly important, and hence desirable. A story was told that Praetextatus, a pagan intellectual whose death in 387 prevented his becoming consul in the following year, used to tease a pope: 'Make me bishop of Rome and I shall become a Christian on the spot!'[1] According to the practice of the church the people of a town or city had the right to be involved in the choice of their bishop, which meant that elections generated widespread interest. The choice of a bishop was sometimes a catalyst for outbreaks of the civil unrest which were common in the cities of late antiquity.[2] The death of a bishop of Rome in 366 was followed by rioting and fighting between the supporters of two rivals for the office which culminated in a massacre, after which 137 bodies were found in the church now known as Sta Maria Maggiore.[3] When disagreement over the election of a bishop of Milan in 374 seemed likely

---

1. Jerome *Contra Ioannem Hierosolymitanum* 8 (*PL* 23:377). The term 'pagan' is problematic, it being pejorative and ascribing to different views a uniformity which largely existed in the imagination of Christians. Unfortunately, there is no easy alternative to it.
2. Ambrose was to ask an emperor how many houses belonging to prefects of Rome had been burned down without punishment being exacted (*ep.* 74(=40).13).
3. Ammianus Marcellinus 27.3.13.

to endanger the peace of the city, the authorities could not afford to stand by.

This was the year in which Bishop Auxentius died. He had become bishop in 355, when his predecessor, Dionysius, was among a number of bishops exiled by an emperor opposed to their theological convictions. Auxentius had been an unusual occupant of an Italian see, for he had been born in Cappadocia, halfway across modern Turkey, and knew little Latin. Under him the church of Milan took on a distinct oriental colouring.[4] He was also unusual in his adherence to a minority position in Christianity. The fourth century was a time of major debate within the church, which was complicated by the ties between the church and the empire which followed the conversion of Constantine. While there were various areas of contention, the central issue was the relationship between God the Father and the Son. Judeo-Christian theology has posited a sharp distinction between the Creator and the creation. Given that these two categories contain all things that exist, the Son of God whom Christians believe to have become incarnate as Jesus of Nazareth must belong in one or the other of them. According to a theologian of Alexandria who flourished in the early fourth century, Arius, the distinction between the Father and the Son was such as would place the latter in the realm of the creation. Against this understanding, the council of Nicaea (325), making use of an important concept in Greek philosophy, proclaimed that the Father and the Son were of 'the same substance' (Greek '*homoousios*'), and condemned the teaching of Arius. The canons of this council and the Nicene Creed, which was to be finalized later, failed to command universal assent, but the opponents of Nicaea could not agree on exactly how the Father and the Son were related. Those standing in the Nicene tradition were content to label their opponents 'Arians', for however diverse their teaching was it seemed to stand in some relation to that of Arius, and in this book we shall use this term when quoting from or paraphrasing authors who employ it, but in other contexts we shall use the

---

4. Little Latin: Athanasius, in *PG* 25:784. Oriental colouring was shown in such a small detail as the breaking of the Lenten fast on Saturdays as well as Sundays. This remained the practice in Ambrose's time (*Hel.* 10.34).

value-free terms 'Nicaeans' and 'anti-Nicaeans'. The former had been unhappy at the see of Milan being in the hands of Auxentius, but despite the efforts of Nicaean leaders such as Bishop Hilary of Poitiers, he remained in possession of his see.

Auxentius profited from the attitude of the Emperor Valentinian I (364–375). He was a no-nonsense military man, content to stand in the middle when it came to religious differences and issue laws which gave all people the freedom to worship as they thought best.[5] His policy of alternating between pagans and Christians in appointments to the office of prefect of the city of Rome[6] was in line with this attitude, as well as being politically shrewd, for in the face of widespread conversions to the new religion the leading families of Rome proved reluctant to abandon their old beliefs. Valentinian's easy-going stance meant that he was perfectly happy to receive communion from Auxentius when in Milan. He saw himself as being an ordinary member of the laity. This was a stance more modest than that adopted by Constantine, and an easy one for an emperor whose position was strong. But such humility could allow a bishop to treat the emperor as no more than one among the congregation, and as our study of the successor of Auxentius proceeds we shall see him overthrow the principles of Valentinian's policy, one by one.

The death of Auxentius was followed by wild scenes, for which our best source is a passage in the *Ecclesiastical History* by Rufinus. This author describes a tense situation which involved adherents of two factions, by which he doubtless means the Nicaeans and anti-Nicaeans. According to Rufinus, their serious disagreement and the dangerous dissension threatened speedy disaster for the city, whichever side won. The events in Rome which had followed the death of a pope scarcely a decade previously furnished a warning of what could occur in such circumstances, and there would have been few places in which it was more likely for it to take place than the cathedral. That in Milan was a large building, probably capable of holding nearly 3,000 people, and it had been built in the centre of the city, just a few minutes' walk

---

5. Standing in the middle: Ammianus Marcellinus 30.9.5. Laws: *cod.Theod.* 9.16.9.
6. Chastagnol (1960): 428f.

from the forum.⁷ We are told that the representative of imperial authority in Milan, the governor (*consularis*) Ambrose, seeing that the city was threatened by ruin, hastened to the church, planning to moderate the sedition of the people. When he had spoken for a long time urging quiet and tranquillity, suddenly a shout arose from the people, and there was just one voice yelling out 'Ambrose bishop!' The people cried out that he was to be baptized immediately and given to them as their bishop; there would not be one people and one faith unless Ambrose was given to them as bishop. He resisted, but the emperor ordered that the desire of the people was to be fulfilled with all speed, saying that it was the work of God that the discordant faith of the people and minds which had been at odds had been suddenly came to share the one opinion. So it was that Ambrose was baptized and made a bishop.⁸

There is no reason not to accept the outlines of the account provided by Rufinus, which formed the basis of a later telling of the story by Ambrose's biographer Paulinus.⁹ Aspects of Rufinus' account recur in Paulinus, in particular the great importance placed on the will of the people. But Paulinus, writing some fifty years after these events, was a man with a mission, and it may well be that some of what he says, which modern scholars have sometimes taken at face value to suggest the appropriateness or indeed inevitability of Ambrose's becoming bishop, was crafted precisely to create this impression. This may account for one important detail which Paulinus adds to Rufinus. Paulinus reports that, while Ambrose was speaking to the people, the voice of an infant was suddenly heard to utter the words 'Ambrose bishop!' At this all the people, both Arians and catholics, cried out 'Ambrose bishop!' While Rufinus and Paulinus have the same words, they place them in the mouths of different speakers. The latter has the more impressive story, for the word '*infans*' literally means 'not yet speaking', although Paulinus seems

---

7. On the cathedral, Krautheimer (1983): 76.
8. Rufinus *HE* 11.11. It is possible that Rufinus' telling of the story was influenced by the account of the election of Pope Fabian given in the history of Eusebius, which he had translated (*HE* 6.29.3f); so Thelamon (1981): 339.
9. For what follows the chief source is Paulinus *VAmb.* 6–9, whose dependence on Rufinus is brought out by Pellegrino, in his edition, 16f.

to use it in the general sense of 'child'. Paulinus may not have intended his story to be taken literally, for he qualifies it as 'something which is said to have happened', and it is oddly reminiscent of Augustine's narration of his conversion, a little over a decade later, in which he heard in a Milanese garden the voice of a child repeating the words 'Take and read' (*conf.* 8.12.29). Perhaps the young of the city at that time were given to portentous utterances. In any case, Paulinus' point is not that the utterance of the words was miraculous, but that the nomination of Ambrose came from someone who, being a child, was presumably not associated with one of the factions in the church at Milan.[10]

. . .

AMBROSE

Little is known about the life of Ambrose prior to his becoming bishop. A number of pious stories of his early life were known to Paulinus, but no less than the tale of the speaking child they suggest that the career of Ambrose was pre-ordained, and need not be taken seriously. According to one story, when he was a baby sleeping with his mouth open, bees swarmed over his face and mouth and kept on going in and out of his mouth. His father, who was strolling nearby with his wife and daughter, in a remarkable display of sang froid, forbade a servant girl to intervene, for he wished to see how such a strange incident would end. After a while the bees flew up into the air so high that they passed from sight, and the terrified father said 'If this little child lives he will be something great.' Paulinus placed this story in a biblical context, seeing in it evidence for the Lord being already at work while his servant was still an infant and the fulfilment of a biblical text, 'Good words are as a honeycomb' (Prov. 24:16; *VAmb.* 3). The story would have conveyed a different meaning to many of his readers, who would have deduced from it that Ambrose was to be compared to such

---

10. '*Infantes*' speak at *VAmb.* 48.1, although Ambrose predicates '*infantia*' in the sense of 'speechlessness' of adults at *virgb.* 3.3.9. While Augustine uses the word in its literal sense (e.g. *conf.* 1.6.10, 1.8.13) there is no need to take it in this way here. The story of the infant is unknown to Sozomen (*HE* 6.24) and Socrates (*HE* 4.30).

figures as Plato, who had an experience of this kind when an infant, and they would have taken it as a sign of the sweetness of the speech which would proceed from such a mouth.[11] According to another story told by Paulinus, as a young man Ambrose offered his hand to be kissed, saying that he was going to become a bishop (*VAmb*. 4), but it need not be taken at face value, for it was a literary convention for boys destined to become bishops to behave in an episcopal fashion.[12] Similarly, Paulinus tells how Probus, Ambrose's superior when he was *consularis*, had told him to act not as a judge but as a bishop (*VAmb*. 8.3).[13] Such data are of no value as background to the adult Ambrose. Deductions drawn from more general evidence take us further.

He had been born, probably in 339, at Trier, a town on the River Moselle less than a hundred kilometres from that frontier of the Roman empire which followed the lower reaches of the River Rhine. Ambrose was later to describe the Rhine as a noteworthy wall of the Roman empire against fierce peoples (*exa*. 2.3.12), but influences flowed across it in both directions, and the area around Trier was coming under the influence of Germanic tribes who were of increasing concern to the empire. Another indication of the marginal status of the region within the empire was the survival of Celtic speech, which could apparently still be heard there.[14] In some respects Trier was a typical large Roman city, which boasted a forum, an amphitheatre, a circus capable of seating 50,000 people, large baths and a cathedral. It was unusual in its enormous imperial reception hall, thirty metres high, constructed in the first decade of the fourth century. Around it stood villas, the country homes of the wealthy which were often built so as to command views of valleys. Yet the face this city presented to the world was a military one, for it was surrounded by six kilometres of walls, some three metres thick and six metres high, and it was described by a poet of the

---

11. Roman versions of the story of Plato occur in Cicero *De divinatione* 1.78 and Pliny *Naturalis historia* 11.18.55. See in general Opelt (1968).
12. Rufinus describes Athanasius playing at being a bishop (*HE* 1.14; *PL* 21:487).
13. There is no reason to believe that Probus orchestrated the election of Ambrose, as suggested by Corbellini (1975).
14. This is the implication of Jerome *Commentarium in epistolam ad Galatas* 2.3 (*PL* 26:382C).

time as feeding, clothing and arming the military strength of the empire.[15] Trier was the headquarters of one of the senior officials of the empire, the praetorian prefect of the Gauls, who was responsible for the financial and judicial administration of Gaul, Spain and Britain, and Ambrose was the son of the holder of this office.[16] He was therefore born into a family of significance in the administration of the empire, and furthermore a prosperous one, which owned estates in Africa. The images of Roman power among which he grew up may never have left Ambrose.

At some time his father died, and Ambrose lived in Rome with his mother and his elder sister Marcellina. The family was devout. It may have been Christian for generations,[17] and Marcellina made a profession of virginity in St Peter's basilica before Pope Liberius, one Christmas in the early 350s; years later, in one of his earliest books, Ambrose purported to reproduce the address the pope delivered on the occasion (*virgb.* 3.1.1–3.14). The involvement of the pope may be a sign of the social standing of the family, and if we accept Paulinus' assertion that bishops used to visit the family home (*VAmb.* 4.1) we have another sign of the family's standing in Christian circles in Rome. This is confirmed by one of the letters of Jerome, in which he included Marcellina among the noble women to whom he sent his greetings (Jerome *ep.* 45.7).

Ambrose's life, however, seemed pointed in a secular fashion, as he began to lay the foundations of a fine career. His biographer Paulinus speaks of his having been instructed in the liberal arts (*VAmb.* 5.1), which is doubtless true, although his writings suggest that his secular learning was limited. The greatest benefit Ambrose derived from his education was an excellent knowledge of Greek, far beyond that which

---

15. Ausonius *Ordo urbium nobilium* 6.4. On Trier see Heinen (1985).
16. Arguing from the name of Ambrose's brother, Uranius Satyrus, Mazzarino suggested that their father was the Uranius to whom a law of 339 (*cod.Theod.* 11.1.5) was addressed, and made the further suggestion that he was killed in 340 (1973: 1989). But the argument is weak. To suggest, for example, that the silence of Ambrose on his father implies a tragic end for the latter ignores the issue of how much one would have expected to learn in any case.
17. Ambrose saw Soteris, a virgin martyr, as an ancestor of his sister (*virgb.* 3.7.37f; *exh.virg.* 12.82), but his language is imprecise.

Augustine's provincial education allowed him to command. In 365, together with his brother Satyrus, he was appointed to the staff of Probus, the praetorian prefect of Illyricum whose headquarters were at Sirmium, in the Balkans. It would have been a worthwhile posting for an ambitious person, for Probus, who was to enjoy the office of consul in 371, was well placed to exercise patronage; a story was later told that in about 391 two Persians travelled to Italy so they could prove at first hand the wisdom of Ambrose and the power of Probus. Having done this they went home (*VAmb.* 25). Thereafter Ambrose was appointed *consularis* of the province of Liguria and Aemilia, and moved to Milan to take up the appointment he still held when he became a bishop.

. . .

TAKING OFFICE

Ambrose may have seemed an odd choice as bishop. He had a weak voice[18] which ill-suited him for a job which required him to preach in a large basilica where he had to compete with other voices, perhaps especially those of women, who were thought inclined to talk and be noisy.[19] Sometimes fights broke out when women lost their jewellery and suspected others of retrieving it.[20] More importantly, he had not been baptized. He was certainly a Christian by belief, but the ordination of unbaptized men was contrary to church law, and later in his episcopate Ambrose wrote in a letter that the ordination of neophytes, or newly baptized people, was prohibited (*ep.ex.coll.* 14(=63).65; cf. I Tim 3:6). But his case is not unique. In 381, following the resignation of Gregory of Nazianzus as bishop of Constantinople, Theodosius I was to select as his successor a layperson, Nectarius, who, despite being of advanced years, had not been baptized. A few years after he had been baptized as an adult, Ambrose would be recommending the practice of infant baptism (*Abr.* 2.11.81, 84). But the death of unbaptized believers, such as that of the

---

18. On his weak voice, *apol.alt.Dav.* 5.28 and *sacr.* 1.6.24; see also Augustine *conf.* 6.3.3.
19. *Sacr.* 6.3.15, 4.17; *virgb.* 3.3.11–14; cf. *ps.* 1.9 on the difficulty of obtaining silence when lessons were read.
20. *Abr.* 1.9.89 (on the interpretation of '*lites*', *SAEMO* 2:121 n. 17); *virgt.* 68.

Emperor Valentinian II in 392, did not cause him concern (*ob.Val.* 51), for the postponement of baptism was not as important then as it would be seen to be later, when its importance had been emphasized by a more precise understanding of original sin. Indeed, for much of the fourth century a deferral of baptism could be seen as a sign of moral seriousness. Together with Ambrose's having remained unmarried, his remaining unbaptized could have been thought to indicate a high degree of religious conviction. The divided state of the Milanese church may have made his status as an unbaptized person significant in another way, for it may have suggested that he was not strongly committed to either of the two factions. It was certainly true that his family was Nicaean by conviction, but on the other hand the Emperor Valentinian, whom he had represented in Milan, had practised an even-handed religious policy and speedily given his consent to the ordination of Ambrose. There would therefore have been good grounds to believe that Ambrose would be a broad-minded bishop. He would have been an ideal compromise candidate.

But his response to the cry of the crowd was not positive. 'How I resisted ordination!' he was to recall at the end of his life (*ep.ext.coll.* 14(=63).65). While such humility may seem impressive, there were precedents going back to the time of the Roman republic for good candidates resisting high office, which meant that, paradoxically, resistance could be seen as a sign of a valid vocation.[21] Hence, someone who really wanted to become a bishop could feign reluctance for tactical reasons. Paulinus tells of a number of ways by which Ambrose sought to evade the burden of office. On leaving the church where he had been acclaimed as bishop he had the raised platform on which he sat in his capacity as judge, the tribunal, prepared. Climbing onto it, he ordered that torture be applied to some individuals. Such an act would certainly not have made him popular, and it may have been an attempt to disqualify himself from episcopal office, for papal legislation of the time forbade the ordination of those who employed torture.[22] Nevertheless, the people cried out 'May your sin be upon us!' Then Ambrose went home,

21. Lizzi (1989): 98f.
22. 'Siricius' *ep.* 10.5 (usually attributed to Pope Damasus; *PL* 13:1190f).

expressing the wish to devote himself to philosophy, presumably on the understanding that the practice of philosophy was contrary to episcopal office.[23] When this device failed he made another attempt to dissuade the people by having prostitutes brought into his house, but the people cried out even more 'May your sin be upon us!' He then sought to flee by night to Pavia, but next morning was mysteriously found at the gate through which passed the road to Rome.[24] After this the people kept him under guard.[25] Approval for his consecration was sought from the Emperor Valentinian, who was then at Trier, and it was quickly forthcoming. In the meantime Ambrose had fled to an estate owned by a senator, Leontius, from which he only emerged when approval of the people's choice came from Valentinian. He was baptized on 30 December, by a catholic bishop according to Paulinus, and consecrated bishop on 7 December 374.[26]

The involvement of an emperor in these proceedings reflects the importance which Milan was coming to occupy within the empire, and the desire of the emperor that a reliable person be at the head of its church. More generally, it points to the power emperors had come to enjoy in church affairs. Auxentius had become bishop under unusual circumstances, and prudence may have dictated that imperial approval of his successor be sought. Perhaps Valentinian felt that Ambrose would prove complaisant to imperial authority. But such an expectation would have been sadly misplaced.

In his narrative of Ambrose's accession to office, Paulinus emphasizes that he was the people's choice. He uses the noun 'people' (*populus*) eight times, and his tenor is unmistakable: following the child's words Ambrose was acclaimed by 'all the people', and his ordination took place 'with great support and to the joy of all'. But this should be taken with a grain of salt. Paulinus may have wanted his readers to believe that

23. Early in the fifth century Synesios, another unbaptized person, would only become bishop of Ptolemais on the condition that he could still practise philosophy.
24. Even accepting the truth of this story, it is going too far to see Ambrose's re-entry into Milan as a variant of the *adventus* ceremony, as does McLynn (1994): 47.
25. '*Custodiretur*' (*VAmb.* 8.2), a word Augustine uses to describe what was done to those forced against their will to become bishops (*ep.* 173.2).
26. Paulinus *VAmb.* 9.3; I follow the interpretation of Fischer (1970).

Ambrose enjoyed overwhelming popular support from the beginning of his episcopate, and as he was not present at the time his account may constitute a projection of conditions later in Ambrose's tenure of office backwards, to a time of which he was personally ignorant. Years afterwards, preaching on the text 'Honour thy father and mother' on the anniversary of his consecration, Ambrose could address the people of Milan as his parents, for it was they who had given him the episcopate; while individually they were his children, taken together they were his parents (*Luc.* 8.73). But this is not to say that they all supported him in 374. Ambrose moved with caution during his early years as bishop, which suggests a desire to hold together rather than divide the Christian community over which he had unexpectedly come to preside. The new bishop was determined not to rock the boat.

. . .

BACKGROUND AND EXPERIENCE

At the very least, Ambrose's accession to the episcopate was an unexpected career move, and it therefore becomes important to establish what experiences and attitudes he brought to the office of bishop. He later described himself as having been 'snatched to the episcopate from the tribunals and the fillets of administration' (*off.* 1.1.4) and as

> that man not brought up in the lap of the church,
>   not tamed from childhood;
> but snatched from tribunals,
>   carried away from the vanities of this world.[27]

It will be worth our while teasing out some of the implications of this self-description.

It is clear that Ambrose was not brought up in the lap of the church. To be sure, he had been raised in a household which received bishops as visitors and which was pious enough to produce a consecrated virgin, but the world of his family may have been one he saw himself as leaving

---

27. *Paen.* 2.8.72; cf. his referring to his having been called to the episcopate 'from the din of civil quarrels and the dread inspired by public administration' (*paen.* 2.8.67).

behind when he became a bishop, for one of his last works contains a reflection which may be autobiographical: the true flight of a bishop is the renunciation of family and a kind of estrangement from one's loved ones, the one who acts so as to serve God denying himself when it comes to his own people (*fuga* 2.7). That he had not been baptized would have made him a stranger to much of the worship of the church, for its practice in his day was still to dismiss catechumens from the liturgy after the readings from the Bible and the sermon. It is a sobering thought that Ambrose may not have attended a full celebration of the eucharist until a week before he became a bishop. He was by no means the only bishop in the period to have been raised unexpectedly to the episcopate, but some of the others, such as Martin, who became bishop of Tours at almost exactly the same time, were at least men of monastic experience. We known little of the bishops who preceded Ambrose in Milan, but of the twelve popes who held office during the fourth century, nine were natives of Rome, in which church it was standard practice for promotion to episcopal office to be from within the ranks of the local clergy. We may therefore imagine a typical new bishop of the period as having been formed by long exposure to the values and experiences of a local clerical caste, or, failing this, having been prepared by ascetic practices. Ambrose had totally escaped either kind of formation. Seen against the background of the western bishops of his day, he emerges as an odd man out.

Ambrose also asserts that he was carried away from vanities. His career in civil life was later scornfully alluded to by Jerome:

> Yesterday a catechumen, today a bishop; yesterday in the amphitheatre, today in the church; in the evening at the circus, in the morning at the altar; formerly a fan of actors, now a consecrator of virgins![28]

One of his enemies would later utter vaguely worded accusations of an immoral life, while Ambrose himself was to

---

28. Jerome *ep.* 69.9. Ambrose is not named, but the fact that this passage comes after a reference to the blindness of people who held a position we know Ambrose adopted makes it certain that it refers to him.

imply that he had lived badly before becoming a bishop.[29] But the assertions of hostile authors writing invective on the one hand, and a rhetorical deployment of a topos of humility on the other, are scarcely compelling evidence. As to sexual experience, the lack of precise evidence to the contrary and the sense Ambrose persistently gives of being interested in things to do with women but not experienced in them, suggest that he had remained a virgin.[30]

Of more importance than any prior moral irregularity in determining the nature of his life as bishop was a habit of command into which he had entered. Such irregularity as there was in Ambrose's background lay here, for papal legislation forbad the ordination of magistrates.[31] Not only was Ambrose the son of a praetorian prefect, but the office of *consularis* he had held was one of weight, being two grades above the office of *praeses* which Augustine could only hope to obtain by marrying a wealthy woman.[32] This was a lofty background for a bishop of the fourth century, during which most bishops came from the class of citizens who were leaders in their towns, the curials.[33] Tribunals of the kind from which Ambrose had been snatched aroused fear in the community, and among Christians a tribunal could suggest the one which the Lord would sit at the Last Judgment (*ps.118* 20.14). When Paulinus came to describe the tactics Ambrose used to avoid being made bishop, he cast him in the light of Pilate sitting in judgment on Christ, and he interprets the words he twice attributes to the people, 'Your

---

29. *Paen.* 2.8.73; Jerome *ep.* 69.9 (*'lascivos sordidos annos'*); Palladius *frag.* 115 (*Scolies ariennes*, ed. Gryson).
30. Physical displays of affection among plants and animals are common in the *exa.* (e.g. 3.12.49), but Augustine was able to draw on more extended experience, for example in referring to the sense of touch (*conf.* 10.6.8). The *De officiis* suggests that Ambrose considered avarice more of a problem for the clergy than lust.
31. See above, n. 22.
32. *Conf.* 6.11.19. Metaphorically, Augustine associates the rank Ambrose held with the status St Paul held under God (*conf.* 8.4.9). The first known holder of the office of *consularis* of Aemelia and Liguria subsequent to Ambrose, Romulus, went on to become prefect of the city of Rome, while the first office held by Virius Nicomachus Flavianus, one of the most eminent men of his generation, was that of *consularis* in Sicily (*PLRE* 771f, 347–49).
33. Gilliard (1984).

sin be on us', in the light of the words of the Jews to Pilate, 'His blood be on us' (*VAmb.* 7, Matt. 27:25). For Paulinus, Ambrose in his elevated position suggested another agent of the power of the state, Pilate, just as the difficulty he experienced as an official representing it in controlling a difficult crowd may well have made him think of the position of Pilate when Christ was brought before him.

It could be argued that little changed after Ambrose was ordained. A portrayal of him in a mosaic of the early fifth century in the Basilica Ambrosiana at Milan shows him dressed as an aristocrat. When Paulinus came to write his biography he implied continuity in Ambrose's life before and after he became a bishop. Not merely is Ambrose said to have responded to being acclaimed bishop by having a tribunal prepared, ascending it and ordering that tortures be made ready, but on a trip Paulinus states he made to Sirmium he sat on a 'tribunal', which here seems to mean a bishop's throne, a significant verbal reminder of continuity (*VAmb.* 11.1). From the tribunal he warned an anti-Nicaean virgin to beware of the judgment of God; she died on the next day. Later, responding to the challenge of two Arians to preach on the incarnation, he ascended a tribunal, unaware that his enemies had already died. It was no surprise that, after Ambrose died, people coming up from the pool in which they had been baptized thought they saw Ambrose sitting in the tribunal in the cathedral (*VAmb.* 11,18,48). In one of his theological works Ambrose was able to describe an exchange between Christ and an anti-Nicaean on whom he was sitting in judgment in vivid terms; the taunting words with which the passage begins are those of Ambrose:

> Go on, speak; go on, speak, I say. 'Christ, I think that you are unlike the Father.' He will answer: 'Show clearly, if you can, show clearly, I say, how you think I am unlike him!' Say something else: 'I think you were created.' Christ will answer you: 'If the testimony of two people is true (John 8:17), ought you not at least believe me and the Father who called me "begotten"?' 'I deny that you are good.' And he will say: 'Let it happen to you in accordance with what you believe, so that I will not be good to you.' 'I don't think you are omnipotent.' He will answer: 'Then I can't forgive you your sins.' 'I call you a subordinate.' 'Why then do you seek freedom and forgiveness from one you think is subordinate and like a slave?' (*fid.* 2.13.108–112)

One can only hope that the blustering words Ambrose places in the mouth of Christ do not reflect his own conduct as a judge. Other passages in his works suggest that he never forgot his experiences as a judge, for they often suggest legal experience.[34] In an even more impressive display of continuity, Ambrose not only threatened people with torture to dissuade them from making him their bishop, but was believed to have retained his ability to punish after he died, for it was then that he tortured throngs of demons (*VAmb.* 48.2f) and that two people who spoke ill of him died after receiving severe wounds (*VAmb.* 53f). If Ambrose's writings lack the polish and skilful organization of material shown in those of Augustine, a former teacher of rhetoric, his dealings with others frequently displayed the power and force of a man used to the courtroom.

Ambrose thus emerges from Paulinus' account as a formidable person. Even the demons, immensely threatening figures in hagiographic texts such as the *Life of Antony*, which was being read in Italy during Ambrose's time, seem in Paulinus' account to be in constant fear of Ambrose (*VAmb.* 20.3, 21), to such an extent that an evil spirit overestimated Ambrose's power, falsely attributing his being tortured to the bishop (33.3f). After Ambrose died someone had a vision of him rejoicing in the company of Elijah, he and the prophet having been two men who never feared to speak before kings and other powerful figures (*VAmb.* 47.3). Ambrose's boldness could be exaggerated, for as we shall see he may have been a less imposing figure at some stages of his episcopate than Paulinus implied, and he was often plagued by enemies at court. But the connection between Elijah, the prophet who rebuked Ahab, and bishops acting as they ought was one Ambrose made himself: if kings had committed no serious sins they had no reason to fear being rebuked by the prophets of God or by bishops (*ps.* 37.43, written after 389). This was doubtless true, although the emperors with whom Ambrose had most to do were all younger than he, two of them

---

34. Ambrose discusses the testimony of unreliable witnesses (*para.* 12.56), the conduct of a judge in a doubtful case (*ps.118* 8.25), the benefits of pleading guilty and the principles of sentencing (*Cain* 2.9.27, 10.38), and the conduct of a good judge (*ps.118* 20.36–39); at *Tob.* 10.36 he speaks as a judge. He is aware of the possibility of his works containing flattery of a kind appropriate to the law courts (*ep.* 32(=48).3).

little more than boys. Others, too, were put in their place. When one of his deacons claimed to have received a vision, Ambrose ordered him to remain indoors for a year, but the cleric made his way to Constantinople, where he was appointed bishop of the important see of Nicomedia.[35] No-one could doubt that Ambrose projected strength; more difficult to assess is whether this crossed the line into bullying.

. . .

THE OFFICE OF BISHOP

Ambrose settled into the daily round of life as a bishop. Some of the functions he came to exercise were those bishops had been carrying out for centuries. Ambrose would have been the source of the sacraments among his people. Not only would he have officiated at the Easter baptisms, but Milan seems to have had a daily celebration of the eucharist by Ambrose's time, and it would be reasonable to think of the bishop as the usual celebrant.[36] It was also his responsibility to bind and loose sinners in penance, this power having been given to bishops alone (*paen.* 1.2.6f). To this was added the duty of teaching which was imposed on bishops, and Ambrose saw himself exercising this in the careful attention he devoted to the scriptures (*off.* 1.1.2f). One of the tasks reserved to the bishop was explaining the Creed to candidates for baptism, just as he would expound on the sacraments of baptism and eucharist and the text of the Lord's Prayer to the newly baptized, these being texts it was not proper to divulge to those outside the church (see below, page 147). Beyond this, there was a constant and demanding need to preach on biblical passages read out in church, which lay behind much of Ambrose's writing. A passage in which he recommends a proper style of speech allows us to deduce something of his own style as a preacher: one's voice should be plain and straightforward, its melodies coming from nature and not art. One should enunciate the words clearly, in a manner full of manly flavour. One should avoid a rough and uncouth sound, attempting a rhythm not appropriate to

---

35. Sozomen *HE* 8.6.
36. The evidence is not clear-cut, but see *patr.* 9.38 and *virgb.* 1.11.65, with Augustine *conf.* 5.9.17, 9.13.36.

the theatre but one serving the religious truth (*off.* 1.23.104). Early in his time as bishop he found himself in a situation common among teachers: his devotion to teaching was a means by which he could himself learn (*off.* 1.1.3f; cf. *ps. 118* 2.5 on those who speak before they have learned). A lot of learning lay ahead of Ambrose when he became bishop, and we can deduce that he began a programme of reading the Bible and commentaries on it, but there is a persistent scattering of errors on biblical matters in his writing over the years.[37] His priorities emerge in a letter he wrote to a newly ordained bishop, in which he develops an image of a bishop as the pilot of a ship making its way across turbulent seas before launching in an unexpected direction: the sea is Holy Scripture (*ep.* 36(=2).1–3).

We have one hint as to his own intellectual formation as a bishop. When Augustine was in Milan some years after Ambrose was ordained, he had an interview with Simplicianus, a 'servant of God' whom he described as the father of Ambrose in receiving grace and one who was truly loved as a father by him. It is not clear in what way Simplicianus was Ambrose's father in receiving grace, but Ambrose himself writes that he saw in Simplicianus 'the love of fatherly grace' (*ep.* 7(=37).2). Perhaps, there being no bishop in the city after the death of Auxentius, it fell to a person of lesser rank to baptize Ambrose, and Simplicianus carried out the task,[38] or perhaps Simplicianus merely gave him a crash course in preparation for the sacrament. Simplicianus seems to have specialized in bringing intellectuals to baptism, and given that he encouraged Augustine in his reading of Neoplatonist books it is not impossible that he encouraged Ambrose in this approach to Christianity.[39] But this is certainly not proven,

---

37. It is surprising to find a bishop state that Jesus was born in Nazareth (*Luc.* 4.47). Elsewhere Ambrose states that Deborah was a widow and Barak her son (*vid.* 8.43, 46), errors which the sly Jerome mentioned as having been committed by 'certain inept people' (*ep.* 54.17). Other mistakes are presumably careless slips: *Abr.* 2.3.11; *off.* 2.30.154. Ambrose was also capable of the odd mistake in secular learning: he thought the Euphrates and Tigris rivers flowed into the Red Sea (*ep.* 62(=19).2).
38. This would go in the face of Paulinus *VAmb.* 9.2, which implies that Ambrose received baptism from a bishop.
39. Augustine *conf.* 8.2.3f.

and little can be deduced about any intellectual influences which may have played on Ambrose.

To the traditional responsibilities of a bishop, new ones had been added, the job description having changed considerably in the decades immediately prior to Ambrose's ordination. The rapid increase in the power of the church in the fourth century had turned the bishop into a person who held considerable power in the community as well as the church. Ambrose professed to have a conservative view of the role of the bishop in society: he would restrain crowds and be zealous for peace, unless there occurred a wrong against God or contempt of the church (*ep.* 74(=40).6). There were constant demands on his time, such as would lead Ambrose to write a circular letter rather than letters to individual people (*ep.* 47(=87)). He found himself dispensing patronage, as evidenced by eight surviving letters the pagan senator Symmachus thought it worth his while writing to him on behalf of various people.[40] It was open to the public to appeal to a bishop in legal cases, in which he seems to have had power of jurisdiction, not merely arbitration,[41] although Ambrose sometimes preferred to bring matters to an end by getting the parties to agree rather than by pronouncing a verdict (*ep.* 24(=82).4). The frequent presence of the emperor in Milan meant that Ambrose found himself interceding at the highest level for those exiled, imprisoned and facing the death penalty (*ep.* 74(=40).25; *ep.ex.coll.* 11(=51).1). While we know of one fruitless attempt to intercede with a high official (Paulinus *VAmb.* 37), Ambrose mentions in one of his works a bishop interceding for a man being led to his death and an emperor thereupon being lenient (*ps.118.* 8.41), and this may well reflect personal experience. Moreover, the church had become a wealthy body. Personally, Ambrose was poor. On becoming a bishop he gave the gold and silver which he possessed to the church and the needy, and he gave the family estates to the church, reserving the profits for his sister, so that he was left with nothing (*VAmb.* 38.5). But the body over which he presided was wealthy. Some of its assets were in the form of expensive vessels used in the liturgy, which a bishop could sell to raise money for the

---

40. Symmachus *ep.* 3.30–37.
41. Vismara (1987).

redemption of those taken captive in battle, a growing concern in the period following the defeat of a Roman army by a force of Goths at the battle of Adrianople in August 378 (*off.* 2.15.70, 28.136–39). The wealth which a bishop had at his disposal is suggested by an accusation some of Ambrose's enemies were to make, that those to whom he distributed charity would be his supporters (*ep.* 75a(=21a).33). The ability of bishops to use wealth in such ways was another sign of a change in the balance of power in society, away from the state towards the church.

It followed from these tasks that a bishop would spend much of his life in public. Years after Ambrose became a bishop, when Augustine sought a private discussion with him, he found him surrounded by such crowds of people of affairs that he gave the appearance of never being at leisure (*conf.* 6.3.3, 6.11.18). This would have been in accordance with Ambrose's recommendation to his own clergy that they be easy of access (*off.* 2.12.61), but such accessibility came at a price. Ambrose saw a member of the clergy as someone who lived in public: he lived as if he was in a theatre where he would be looked at, unlike a monk who lived hidden away in secret, or he could be said to live in a racecourse, whereas a monk lived in a cave (*ep.ext.coll.* 14(=63).71f). He wished the clergy to act in a way which would win them public esteem (*off.* 1.50.247). They had to pay attention to how they appeared in public, for their bodily posture was a sign of their mental disposition, the movement of the body being like a voice of the soul (*off.* 1.18.71; see further below, page 161). Needless to say, a person living in this way was subject to the temptations of a public figure: generosity could be the fruit of exhibitionism rather than of a concern for justice (*off.* 2.16.76). In particular, a bishop must not behave in an evil way, because in him the life of all was formed (*ep.ext.coll.* 14(=63).46). Ambrose lived a busy life in public; for such a man the notions of the self-sufficiency of someone with a beautiful soul (for example, *Is.* 4.11) and an interior life lived by someone placed among the people (*sacr.* 6.3.12) were important.[42]

---

42. Significantly, a discussion of the virtue of silence immediately follows a passage on the bishop's role of preaching which opens the *De officiis*; see further on silence *ep.* 33(=49).

Near the beginning of the third book of the *De officiis*, Ambrose alludes to a saying of Scipio which Cicero quoted at the beginning of the third book of his own *De officiis*: he was not alone when he was alone, and he was never less at leisure than when he was at leisure (*off.* 3.1.2; cf. Cic. *off.* 3.1.1). Ambrose trumps Scipio, claiming that he was not the first to know this. He had been anticipated by Moses, who was aware of crying out even when he was silent. While at leisure Moses stood, fought and triumphed over enemies he had not touched; so much at leisure was he that others held up his hands! When he was silent, he spoke; when at leisure, he was active. This notion fascinated Ambrose. In a letter addressed to a Bishop Sabinus, Ambrose asserted of himself that he was never less alone than when he seemed to be alone, nor less at leisure than when at leisure, and went on to broaden the point: Mary was alone, and she spoke with an angel; she was alone, and busied herself with the salvation of the world (*ep.* 33(=49).1f, where Peter and Adam are also discussed). Elsewhere he writes of Mary as not seeming alone to herself when she was alone, in the presence of so many books, archangels and prophets.[43] The presence of the theme, across works of different genres written at different times, may be a hint that Ambrose found it relevant to himself.

The position of bishop was a demanding one, and Ambrose was not inclined to underestimate the dignity of the episcopate. 'Where will Christ be sought?' he once asked, going on to provide an unexpected answer: 'Why, in the breast of a prudent bishop!' (*virgt.* 9.50) 'Where is the church?' he enquires in another work. 'Why, where the rod and grace of a bishop are in flower!'[44] He boasted to his sister that Jews honoured the bishops of the church (*ep.ext.coll.* 1(=41).10), and breezily compared his technique as a writer of letters to that of St Paul, seeing the apostles as his ancestors in the art

---

43. *Virgb.* 2.2.10. Positive references to being alone also occur at *Iac.* 1.8.39; *Is.* 4.11.
44. *Is.* 8.64. The theme is persistent in Ambrose: when Christ told Mary Magdalene to go to his brothers, his words could be taken as referring to the elect and most observant bishops (*virgt.* 4.23); bishops are those in whom the beauty of the church resides (*ob.Val.* 7); if any gold or silver were to be found on Ambrose it was not through his own acts but the mercy and grace of Christ and the episcopal ministry (*ps.118.* 20.13).

of letter writing (*ep.* 37(=47).3, 6). In one of his letters, Ambrose carefully distinguishes between bishops and the people: bishops should have nothing of the common folk about them, nothing of the general people, and nothing in common with the pursuits, practices and customs of the rude masses. Sober gravity, serious living and a singular weight of dignity will be their characteristics (*ep.* 6(=28).2, written to a layman). He felt that bishops had nothing to fear from comparison with holders of secular office, for they had their own nobility which placed them ahead of prefects and consuls (*exh.virg.* 82). A reading 'my dignity' in a codex of the psalms suggested the dignity of the Christian, in the service of so great an emperor; dignities, honours and ranks could be seen as having been held by apostles, prophets and doctors (*ps.*118.22.15; cf. the expression 'honor ecclesiasticus' at *off.* 2.24.119). Such concerns will resonate throughout Ambrose's episcopate.

Our best witness as to how Ambrose appeared in public is Augustine, the fifth book of whose *Confessions* is artfully composed so as to play off two men with whom he had significant encounters. It begins by describing Augustine's dealings in Carthage with a leader of the Manichean sect, Faustus. Augustine depicts him as a man of sweet eloquence, in whose charm and well-chosen language he took delight. Indeed, there were many who delighted in Faustus and praised him, but when Augustine succeeded in obtaining a discussion with him in a small group he realized that Faustus was a man of little reading from whom he had nothing to learn, however agreeable and seductive his discourse was (*conf.* 5.3.3, 6.11–7.12). At the end of book five, Augustine describes how, having come to Milan as professor of rhetoric, he sought out Ambrose. The bishop received him kindly, indeed as a son, and Augustine began to attend his sermons, doubtless partly motivated by the professional interest of a rhetorician. In language strikingly similar to that he used of Faustus, Augustine states that he was delighted by the sweetness of Ambrose's language. But it was more learned, if less cheerful and soothing, than that of the Manichean. And so, although Augustine had started to go to church to find out not what Ambrose said but how he said it, nevertheless, little by little something of the subject matter came into his mind along with the words he liked so much, as Ambrose showed that the old Scriptures need not be taken literally, as the Manicheans had taught him, but as if they were riddles (*conf.* 5.13.23–14.24). Just as he had with Faustus, Augustine sought a private discussion with Ambrose, but he found him surrounded by people, only infrequently eating and reading in silence (*conf.* 6.3.3). He rejoiced to hear Ambrose repeating to the people in his preaching 'the letter kills but the Spirit gives life' (II Cor 3:6), for he opened up according to the Spirit those texts which seemed to teach perversity when taken according to the letter by taking away that which had veiled them in a mystery (*conf.* 6.4.6). We shall have occasion to turn to this passage of Augustine again later (below, page 172 n. 28). But for the time being we may observe that Ambrose is contrasted with Faustus with respect to the difficulty of obtaining a private interview as well as the content of his teaching. Augustine gives the impression that Ambrose was remarkably busy, whatever his interior life may have been.

. . .

DEATH OF A BROTHER

Before Ambrose had been bishop for long there was a death in the family, that of a brother whose existence is hinted at in no source we have hitherto discussed.[45] Only from two orations delivered on his dead brother do we learn that, in addition to his elder sister Marcellina, there was a middle sibling, Satyrus; the narrow base of evidence reminds us of the sheer elusiveness of large parts of Ambrose's life. Had Satyrus died before Ambrose became bishop we would not have known of his existence, and the fact that our knowledge of him comes almost entirely from funeral orations does not augur well for its balance. Like his younger brother, Satyrus had remained unmarried while enjoying a successful career, but when Ambrose became bishop he moved to Milan and lived with him, devoting himself to administration. Satyrus

45. The dating of the death of Satyrus hinges on the identification of the barbarians whose activities are referred to at *exc.fr.* 1.1, 30–32. If they were the Quadi and Sarmati, Satyrus died in 374 or 375 (so *PLRE* 809), but arguments for 378 are concisely given by *SAEMO* 18:10f, and other evidence confirms that Satyrus was buried in the spring of 378 (Picard (1988):604ff). Unless otherwise stated, all information in the following three paragraphs comes from the *De excessu fratris*.

was also similar to Ambrose in deferring baptism well into his adult life. It took a dramatic incident to bring him to the font. On one occasion, threatened with shipwreck, he leaped overboard with a eucharistic Host wrapped in a handkerchief tied around his neck, and swam to safety. Only after this did he seek baptism, which Ambrose asserts he would only receive from a catholic bishop in agreement with the church of Rome.

At some later time Satyrus set to sea again, to settle a dispute concerning property in Africa. Having resolved the matter he sailed homewards, only to experience what Ambrose refers to, in vague language, as a shipwreck. In Rome he received disturbing news. Ambrose describes him being told by a relative, the noble Symmachus, that Italy was burning with war, and that if he continued northwards to Milan he would run into danger. Symmachus was a leading pagan intellectual and substantial property holder with estates in Africa as well as Italy, a circumstance which may explain why Satyrus sought him out. Despite the ravages of barbarians, which Ambrose describes in a remarkable purple passage, Satyrus pressed on to Milan, where he became ill and died in the arms of his brother. He was buried at the shrine of the martyr Victor, outside the walls of the city. Ambrose commemorated him in two discourses, one delivered on the day of his death and the second a week later. Almost all we know of Satyrus is contained in these addresses,[46] which tell us more about Ambrose than their subject.

The first is drenched in tears. Ambrose rhetorically wondered why he was weeping so much (*exc.fr.* 1.4,6), but made no effort to hide his tears (*exc.fr.* 1.10,15,21,28, etc.). The shedding of abundant tears at the death of a loved one is a familiar topos which doubtless reflects a familiar reality, although Ambrose's exuberant development of it stands in contrast to Augustine's initial inability to cry when his mother died.[47] He makes overtures to pagan opinion, or at least acknowledges it, and his heavy use of classical authors suggests something of his education and a preparedness, despite his being a bishop, not to turn his back on non-Christian

---

46. Symmachus *ep.* 1.63 is the only other literary source to refer to him; the family connection is known from *exc.fr.* 1.32.
47. *Conf.* 9.12.31–33; see further below, p. 142f.

writings. Indeed, when he wrote this oration Ambrose was the first theologian in the West to compose a *consolatio*, a non-Christian genre.[48] In the second and longer oration Ambrose seeks to show that death is not an evil, a theme to which he will later devote an entire book, and the confidence which is to be gained from the resurrection. What the second oration loses in personal interest it gains as Ambrose uses his sources to develop interesting arguments. Not unexpected is his heavy reliance on the Bible and his use of St Paul's teaching on the resurrection; more typically Ambrosian is his use of examples from Genesis and texts from the Song of Songs which are not explicitly connected with the resurrection. Allusions to non-Christian authors again come thick and fast. In the first oration Ambrose draws especially on two Latin authors writing in the Stoic tradition, Cicero and Seneca, as well as Ovid and a little-known Greek author of the third century, Menander Rhetor, while in the second he uses two works of Cicero, the Cato maior and Tusculan orations, and Athenagoras, a Christian author of the second century who wrote in Greek. Ambrose represents himself as persistently taking points up with people he identifies as pagans or philosophers (*exc.fr.* 2.50,58,86,128ff). One attempt to bring together biblical and pagan is particularly revealing. Ambrose states that Solomon was of the opinion that 'Not to be born is best by far', and that on this point he was followed by those who seemed to excel in philosophy (*exc.fr.* 2.30); (see Ecclesiastes 4:2f, thought to have been written by Solomon.) The phrase he attributes to the Old Testament author seems rather to belong to a lost work of Cicero,[49] so his hypothesis that Solomon was followed by pagan philosophers thus falls to the ground, but the notion that the insights of classical philosophy were purloined from the biblical authors will be important for Ambrose.

Taken together, the two orations raise important issues. They make it clear that Ambrose had a relationship with earlier authors, biblical, Christian and secular, but raise difficult questions: was Ambrose, in the midst of his borrowings,

---

48. Fenger (1982).
49. Cf. *SAEMO* 10:245 n. 5. It can be identified as Ciceronian because it is quoted by the Christian author Lactantius, who refers to it as 'a very vain saying', a different evaluation from that of Ambrose.

an original writer? Was he able to synthesize the diverse materials with which he worked, or did they co-exist uneasily in his work? These matters will claim our attention later. The orations also raise the question of celibacy. Not only did Satyrus never marry, but Ambrose represented him as blushing in the presence of females, even relatives. Such was his love of chastity and his closeness to his siblings that he did not seek a wife; he shared in the chastity of his sister, a virgin, and the holiness of his brother, a bishop (*exc.fr.* 1.52–54). As it happened, the topic of virginity is one to which Ambrose was devoting a good deal of thought at just this time. It will be appropriate to consider it in the following chapter.

Chapter 2

WOMEN

Women and their relations with men were a complicated and important issue for Ambrose, who devoted some of his earliest writings to them.[1] In 377, less than three years after he had become a bishop, he wrote his *De virginibus* (Concerning virgins). Like other authors, Ambrose approached his first book with some trepidation. While portions of it are probably based on sermons (see e.g. 1.2.5), the work is a polished piece of formal writing, designed to impress. It opens with a complicated sentence over a hundred words long and proceeds to a display of the topos of humility, in which Ambrose recalled the teaching of Jesus that people would have to give account for every idle word they spoke. He returned to the topic in the *De virginitate* (Concerning virginity), probably written in the late 380s[2] as a response to critics of the first book. Meanwhile, not long after finishing the *De virginibus*, he had written both the *De viduis* (Concerning widows), and a work dealing with the time Adam and Eve spent in paradise, the *De paradiso* (Concerning paradise). Late in his life Ambrose returned to these themes. The *De institutione virginis* (Concerning the education of a virgin, written in about 393) contains a sermon he delivered on the consecration of a virgin,

---

1. I take this to be a sign of his interest in the topic, whereas McLynn sees it as a bid for support (1994): 53ff. If it was this it failed. See on the themes of this chapter Brown (1988) and the careful discussion of Lamirande (1979).
2. Some scholars date this work to the period immediately after the *De virginibus*, but the commentary on part of the Song of Songs it includes invites comparison with the commentaries contained in the *De Isaac* and *Expositio psalmi CXVIII*, both works of the late 380s (see *SAEMO* 14/1:69).

while the *Exhortatio virginitatis* (Exhortation to virginity) was based on a sermon given at the dedication of a church built by a wealthy widow in Florence in 394.

Ambrose's thinking on women is structured, coherent and nuanced, but never given systematic expression. Rather, it emerges across a body of writings. In this chapter we shall therefore seek to draw out themes from Ambrose's works rather than summarize them one by one, using evidence from various works as the discussion proceeds. As we shall see, while Ambrose tended to believe that women were inferior to men, his view of them was differentiated. He thought that there were three kinds of women, virgins, widows and wives, and that while marriage imposed slavery on a woman, virginity brought her freedom. In this respect, his teaching was strongly opposed to traditional Roman values. Encouraging women to commit themselves to lives of virginity, Ambrose used the erotic language of the Song of Songs. This was a risky strategy, for the use to which he puts this text seems to fly in the face of its content, and themes he draws from it appear to be opposed to those which he developed in other works. His attitude towards women will therefore be worth careful consideration.

. . .

THE TWO SEXES

Ambrose sends out mixed signals on his attitude towards women. He read the Bible with sufficient care to be puzzled by what seemed to be the occasional sexism of its language. Why was it that psalm 1 begins 'blessed is the man who walketh not in the counsel of the ungodly' (*ps.* 1.14)?[3] Why did Paul wish 'that men pray everywhere' (*sacr.* 6.4.17, on I Tim 2:8)? It was not clear to Ambrose why the Greek texts he followed used the gender-specific rather than the inclusive noun for 'man' in these passages. He saw the genders as complementary, not only in reproductive functions but also in the qualities they displayed: Rebekah was swayed towards one of her sons by a feeling of love (*affectus*), while Isaac was

---

3. Ambrose was far more interested in this question than Basil, whose commentary he had in front of him (*PG* 29:216D–217A).

inclined towards the other by his judgment (*iudicium*).[4] But discussing an incident when Christ touched a deaf man, Ambrose took it for granted that it would not have been fitting for him to have touched a woman (*myst* 1.4), and he assumed that a reference to the procreation of men was to be taken as including that of women, because the more important includes the less important.[5] His commentary on Luke treats the women mentioned in that gospel slightingly. Of three parables concerning them, he offers extremely short discussions of the woman who had leaven (*Luc.* 7.187) and the woman who lost a coin (7.211), while the widow who beseeched the unrighteous judge is given the briefest possible mention, out of sequence (5.114).

Despite this, Ambrose felt able to distinguish the genders precisely: if there was an intrinsic unity between man and woman, there was a functional subordination of the feminine to the masculine.[6] Although they share one nature, the first in creation is the first in importance (*ps.* 1.14). Discussing the apparent redundancy within the phrase 'forty days and forty nights' the Bible used to indicate the period when rain fell during Noah's flood, he noted the possibility that it indicated the violent deaths of both men and women, 'day' referring to man, he being pure and like the light, and 'night', a concept with negative connotations for Ambrose, to woman.[7] Discussing the phenomenon of cross-dressing, Ambrose accepted that the Greek women who practised it were seeking to imitate the nature of the better sex, but could not understand why men would want to give a false impression of being the inferior sex (*ep.* 15(=69).4; cf. *exc.fr.* 2.7). That Zacharias prophesied at greater length than his

---

4. *Iac.* 2.2.7, on Gen. 25:28. A similar apposition at *Luc.* 7.200: heresy, like Eve, tempts the rigour of faith with womanly affection (perhaps alluding to the Empress Justina); cf. *ps.118* 15.18: the woman caused her husband to change by her affection. Nevertheless, the two states of mind existed together in Joseph: overcome by a feeling of love, he was restrained by counsel as his reason contended with love (*Ios.* 10.57). See too on the genders *Cain* 1.10.47.
5. But on procreation, see *exa.* 1.10.37.
6. Pizzolato (1976): 188, with reference to *fid.* 4.28.
7. Night is also associated with women at *Noe* 13.43; on night, cf. e.g. *Cain* 2.4.16; *exa.* 1.10.36 (the pre-eminence Ambrose attributes to the day may have masculine overtones, cf. 1.10.37 and below, p. 45); *Luc.* 7.49; *Nab.* 8.38; *ob.Theod.* 39.

wife Elizabeth was fitting, for it belongs to a woman to learn divine things rather than teach them (*Luc.* 2.35).

Yet women came in various categories. Ambrose pictured himself as a worker in the countryside who wished to see the field of the church which had been entrusted to him in a fertile condition: it would bloom with the flower of integrity, be strong in the dignity of widowhood, and overflow with the fruits of marriage (*vid.* 14.83). Within the field one could see buds verdant with the flower of virginity, widowhood powerful in dignity like forests in the open countryside, and grain fields which filled the barns of the world with the rich produce of marriage (*virgt.* 6.34). Biblical exemplars of the three states were to hand, for they were represented respectively by Mary, Anna and Elizabeth, women important in the birth and infancy of Jesus: after a married woman and a virgin prophesied, it was necessary that a widow do the same (*Luc.* 2.62). Each group had its own characteristic: at a time when women were victims of barbarian impurity, Ambrose thought of virgins as being sacred, widows as dignified and married women as modest.[8] The order in which Ambrose mentions the three classes of women is fixed, and clearly represents his preference.[9] As widows occupied an intermediate position, we shall chiefly concern ourselves with the other categories, beginning with the one Ambrose esteemed least.

. . .

THE WIFE

Ambrose supported marriage. Against those who condemned it (*Luc.* 4.10, referring to Manicheans), he insisted that fertility was a gift of God to parents and that God had given his approval to marriage at the beginning of Genesis (*Luc.* 1.30). As the first woman was created for the purpose of procreation, Ambrose believed that the purpose of marriage was

---

8. *Off.* 3.13.84. See elsewhere on the *gravitas* of widows *bon.mort.* 6.25 (where *suavitas* is attributed to virgins), *Cain* 2.3.12; *Luc.* 5.89, *vid.* 14.83; the modesty of married women is exemplified by Sarah (*Abr.* 1.5.37, 42).
9. The categories occur in the reverse order at *vid.* 4.23, but Ambrose goes on to reveal where his sympathies lie. Elsewhere he observes that virginity has its rewards, widowhood its merits, and conjugal modesty its place (*ep.ext.coll.* 14(=63).40).

having children. Ambrose could infer that Elisabeth and Zacharias had ceased to have marital relations prior to the conception, in their old age, of John the Baptist, having children being the only reason for getting married (*Luc.* 1.45). Yet within marriage, the husband and wife would play very different roles.

Ambrose thought that a good example of a married couple acting in their proper roles was provided by Abraham and Sarah: while Abraham stood outside the tabernacle and offered hospitality to passing strangers, Sarah guarded her womanly modesty, carrying out the tasks of a wife with a sense of shame. When one of a group of visitors asked Abraham where his wife was, his purpose was to teach the degree of shame and modesty which was appropriate to women. Ambrose considered that this story taught what was fitting behaviour in a wife (*Abr.* 1.5.37, 42, on Gen. 18). He reads this biblical narrative in a very Roman way, for the qualities of shame and modesty he applies to Sarah are not present in the story told in Genesis, but virtues the Romans praised.[10] Admiring these qualities as he did, Ambrose was scandalized by the behaviour of women who, rather than being within the secluded parts of the home where they would be neither heard nor seen by strangers, appeared drunk in public. Whereas the apostle orders them to keep quiet in church and ask their husbands questions at home (1 Cor. 14:34f), such women dance in the streets under the gaze of intemperate youths, tossing their hair, dragging their tunics behind them, their clothing torn and their arms naked, clapping with their hands, leaping with their feet, shouting loudly, making young men lust for them, with a gait like that of actors, come-on eyes and an elegant playfulness (*Hel.* 18.66). One wonders how many women of this kind were to be encountered in the streets of Milan, but there is no doubting the centrality of the home to Ambrose's attitude to married women. He sees significance in the Lord's having 'built' the rib he took from Adam into a woman, for it is in a man and a woman together that the full perfection of a home can be seen. But it turns out that the home is a female domain: a man without a wife can be thought of as being without a home, for

---

10. Roman women of the republican period practised a cult of *Pudicitia* (cf. Livy 10.23.3–10); the virtue of *verecundia* was similar to it.

just as a man was fit for public offices, a wife was fit for domestic services in the home.[11] Elsewhere, Ambrose sees the creation of the woman while the man was asleep as having been important. This indicated that the man, the one who would seize the initiative in human reproduction, came first. He would be the one to take a shining role in public activity, while the woman, darker and shut in by the walls of the home, would resemble the night. Indeed, having been created from the man's rib, she owed her very existence to him. The man would shine in public activity; the woman's activity would be less visible, she being enclosed within the walls of the house (*Noe* 13.43).

The primeval human couple was Adam and Eve, and from the time of St Paul, Eve has carried a heavy burden in Christian thought. Ambrose's attitude towards her is complicated. Discussing the creation narratives in Genesis, he pointed out that, although Adam was created outside paradise and Eve inside it, the man in an inferior and the woman in a superior place, it was nevertheless the woman, the first to be deceived and the one who deceived her husband, who was found inferior. This, he felt, was why the apostle Peter speaks of women being subject to their husbands and obeying them as lords.[12] But Ambrose turns the argument in an unexpected direction. Given that Adam fell because of Eve, no-one should trust in the virtue of another without having first tested it, but neither should he claim for himself someone he had received as a helper. If he is found to be the stronger, the grace is to be shared and men are to hold their wives in honour (*par.* 4.24). To be sure, the fact that God found it necessary to create Eve demonstrated that women were necessary for men. Ambrose interpreted God's statement 'It

---

11. *Par.* 11.50, following Philo *Quaestiones in Genesin* 1.26. There is an important apposition between public and domestic, the second adjective preserving the word for home (*domus*), and '*officia*' (public duties, the title of a book Ambrose addressed to his clergy in which he proposed an etymology which derived the word from the verb 'to do things' (*efficio*) (*off.* 1.8.26); elsewhere he applies the word to the clergy (*ep.ext.coll.* 14(=63).71)) and '*ministeria*', a word usually applied to tasks carried out by inferior persons.
12. But whereas I Pet. 3:1 has wives being in subjection to their husbands, Ambrose adds the notion of wives obeying husbands as lords from Gen. 3:16. 1 Pet. 3:1 is similarly misquoted at *par.* 4.24.

is not good that the man should be alone' (Gen. 2:18) in the light of the failure of the preceding narrative to add the phrase 'God saw that it was good' after the creation of the first man, despite its occurrence after the creation of other things. On the other hand, the creation of male and female (Gen. 1:27) was followed by the statement 'And God saw all the things which he had made, and behold they were very good' (Gen. 1.31). But how could this be reconciled with Eve's having been the agent of sin? Eve had been created for the purpose of procreation, for God preferred that there be many he might save through the forgiveness of their sins rather than a solitary Adam free from guilt. Hence, when the Bible spoke of Eve as having been created as a 'helper' for the man, it referred to the help she provided in procreation. Her role would be similar to that played by the earth when it receives the seeds of plants. After all, Ambrose remarks, it often happens that important people receive help from those of lesser merit. It was not an encouraging view, but Ambrose insists that the woman was necessary to the man. One reason for the animals being brought before Adam (Gen. 2:19) was to enable him to see the universality of the male and female genders; from this he would learn his need for the partnership of a woman (11.49).

The creation, then, involved a gradation and a reciprocity between the genders. But as the text of Genesis proceeded it became clear that it was because of the woman that the man fell. The Devil, overcome by envy of the newly created humans, tempted Eve, and Ambrose expressed this in terms which will be crucial to his thought. The Devil's tools, he thought, were enjoyment and delight.[13] He approached the woman because the man had received directly from God the command not to eat the fruit of one of the trees in the garden. Eve responded to the Devil by repeating the command God had given Adam not to eat the fruit of the tree in the midst of the garden, concluding with the words 'You shall not eat of it, neither shall you touch it, lest you die' (Gen. 3:2f). But Ambrose, a precise reader of the Bible, pointed out that this constituted an expansion of God's words

---

13. *Voluptas* and *delectatio*, two words which Cicero had already brought together in referring to the delight of the eyes and the enjoyment one derives from the stomach: *Pis.* 66.

to Adam, for the initial command had been against eating the fruit, without any mention of touching it. He found this expansion reprehensible, and disagreed with those who held that Adam had passed on the commandment to Eve in an altered form. Why, then, did God rebuke Adam first when he spoke to the errant couple? This was because the weaker sex begins with deviation from duty, while shame belongs to the stronger. Error originated with the female, and sense of shame with the man.

In some ways, Ambrose's view of Eve was positive. She behaved well in acknowledging her guilt before God, and so received a mild sentence which would benefit her. Yet the profit entailed subordination: she would be turned towards her husband and serve him. This was so that she would not easily delight in sinning; being placed under her husband, she would not disgrace him, but be ruled by his counsel. Ambrose saw the relationship between Adam and Eve after the Fall as foreshadowing that between Christ and the church. The latter would be turned towards Christ and be in a situation of slavery, subjected to the Word of God, this being much better than the freedom of this world (14.72).

Much of Ambrose's view of women is concentrated in his understanding of the Fall: the service a wife renders her husband and the association of women with enjoyment and delight, and of men with counsel. Doubtless Eve's defence, 'The serpent beguiled me', was plausible, and her conduct seemed pardonable to God because of the deceptive nature of the serpent. But, just as the woman does, the serpent stands for enjoyment, as Ambrose will observe elsewhere, going beyond anything to be found in Genesis (*ep.ext.coll.* 14(=63).14). The serpent stood for enjoyment and Adam was deceived by his appetite for it. In an important statement, Ambrose observes that the serpent represents bodily delight, the woman our senses and the man our mind. Delight takes the senses captive, as they do the mind. It moves the sensibility, which in turn influences the mind. That sin originates in delight explains why the serpent, the woman and the man were condemned in that order, for delight generally captivates the sensibility as well as the mind (*para.* 15.73; cf. *Abr.* 2.1.1).

So it is that Ambrose's picture of Eve is nuanced. In a backhanded way he sees her as emerging more creditably than Adam from the Fall: the woman was deceived by the serpent, the wisest of all creatures and, indeed, an angel; the man merely by the woman, his inferior (*inst.virg.* 4.25). Nevertheless, Ambrose sees her as the one responsible for the coming of sin into human life, perhaps placing more weight on her than does St Paul, whose epistles refer five times to Adam but only twice to Eve. Negative references to Eve abound in his works. Yet it is noteworthy how often negative comments about Eve are balanced by positive references to other women: just as sin began from women, so good things take their beginning from women (*Luc.* 2.28). Ambrose was not surprised that the first appearance of Christ after his resurrection was to Mary Magdalene: as it had been a woman who first tasted death in the person of Eve, it was appropriate for a woman to be the first to see the resurrection, for she who had passed on guilt to the man now passed on grace (*Luc.* 10.156). In another discussion of Christ's appearance to Mary Magdalene, Ambrose points out that when she did not believe, Christ called her 'woman', the noun generally applied to Eve, but when she began to be converted she was called Mary, so taking the name of the one who bore Christ (*virgt.* 4.20 on John 20:15), and he will often link Eve with the highly positive figure of Mary: if foolishness came through a woman, wisdom came through a virgin.[14] But this is to anticipate a theme we shall consider later.

Whatever subordination to Adam Eve may have experienced before the Fall was much less than that which followed it. The lot of a wife, as described in the *De virginibus*, is not a happy one. While a fertile wife may boast of her offspring, Ambrose believes that her children bring as much trouble as comfort: 'She marries and she wails . . . She conceives and she becomes heavy . . . She gives birth and she is sick.'[15] He enunciates a theme which will be crucial in his thought:

> Need I remind you of the burdensome condition of slavery to which women are subjected and the servile obligations they render to men? God ordered them to act as slaves even before there were slaves (*virgb.* 1.6.27).

---

14. *Luc.* 4.7; cf. *inst.virg.* 5.33; *Luc.* 4.39; *para.* 10.47 (although here Mary is *mulier*); *Spir.S.* 3.11.74. More detail in *SAEMO* 14/2:219 n. 49.
15. *Virgb.* 1.6.25. Elsewhere Ambrose lists a mother's sufferings: the insult to her modesty, the loss of her virginity, the danger encountered in giving birth, and her protracted discomforts and troubles (*Luc.* 2.66).

The idea is powerful, and loses nothing by the language in which it is expressed. Ambrose depicts the standing of the wife in the technical vocabulary applied to slavery in ancient times[16] and emphasizes the point by forceful repetition (*servitia . . . servire . . . servos*). He also alludes, in a verbally precise way, to a portion of the biblical narrative passed over in his commentary on paradise, for the reference to a time 'before there were slaves' refers to the period before Adam was granted lordship over Eve following the Fall.[17] These thoughts are followed by a powerful passage which no less an authority than Augustine would later quote as an example of an exalted style of writing, in which Ambrose argues that the vice of make-up was born of women's dread of displeasing their husbands. From a counterfeiting (*adulteratio*) of the face, women go on to think of the counterfeiting (*adulteratio*) of chastity. Madly, they change the appearance nature has given them, fear of their husbands' judgment making them suppress their own. A woman who seeks to please another is already displeased with herself; the husband loves another when a woman seeks to please by looking like another.[18] Here, Ambrose continues, expensive necklaces hang down; there is a gilded dress with a train. Enticing perfumes, ears burdened with gems, eyes whose colour has been changed: what remains the same, where so many things are altered? Does a woman who loses her senses believe that she is still alive? (1.6.29; the word 'senses' is ambiguous; we shall later be concerned with Ambrose's attitude to the

16. He elsewhere applies the word '*famulatus*' to the relationship between an animal and its master (*Cain* 2.1.3); the Vulgate translation of the Bible uses it for the 'service' the Israelites were obliged to render in Egypt (Ex. 1:14). See too *cod.Theod.* 4.8.7. An *addictus* was a person who had been enslaved as a punishment.
17. Gen. 3:16, a text not discussed in the *para*. The notion of lordship is entailed by the first component of the verb used in LXX, '*kurieusei*', as it is in the Vulgate's '*dominabitur*'.
18. *Virgb.* 1.6.28; see Augustine *De doctrina christiana* 4.21.50, who also quotes a passage of Cyprian on the same subject. Note in a similar vein *exa.* 6.8.47: 'you do not please the one you desire to please, who realizes that what pleases is not yours but something else, and you displease your Creator'. This passage also contains a significant use of the charged verb 'adulterate' to describe the activity of women who use make-up. But even those who professed a zeal for chastity used such devices: *exh.virg.* 12.81.

five senses). Virgins do not know of such things, which are torments rather than ornaments.[19] There is no difference between a golden necklace and an iron chain around the foot (1.9.55). Elsewhere, Ambrose observes that women take delight in shackles for their feet, as long as they are bound by gold; they do not think of them as burdens if they are expensive, or as chains if treasure sparkles in them. Indeed, when gold is placed in their ears and weights hang down from them, they delight in being wounded (*Nab.* 5.26). In such ways, Ambrose is persistently negative about the status of the wife in marriage.[20] Indeed, the 'enjoyment' which Ambrose associated with women was experienced by men rather than themselves; he writes of men but not women enjoying sex. Such a man was Theotimus, who suffered from poor eyesight and loved his wife. The doctor told him to give up sex, but lust overcame him: 'Farewell, kindly light!' he cried out in the ardour of his passion.[21] But Ambrose's negative view of the standing of women is concerned with those who are married, and for those seeking freedom there was a simple solution. They could dispense with husbands.

19. '*Tormenta potius quam ornamenta*' 1.6.30. Such play on words by Ambrose is frequent on this topic: jewellery makes women '*onerare aures, curvare cervices*' (*paen.* 2.9.88); cf. '*aurum auribus inseratur*' (*Nab.* 5.26, quoted below). Note too alliteration: '*Noli . . . accipere cincinnos corporalium capillorum*' (*virgt.* 12.71).
20. Elsewhere Ambrose comments that a wife should be subject to her husband as the church is to Christ (*ep.* 16(=76).14, with reference to Eph. 5:24), and that wives owe their husbands obedience (*ep.* 35(=83).3). The position can be made more gently: a wife defers to her husband but does not serve him; a man directs his wife as one who governs her, but nevertheless honours her (*ep.ext.coll.* 14(=63).107). Men should see themselves as husbands, not lords: God wished them to be governors of the inferior sex (*exa.* 5.7.19). Further, conjugal slavery is experienced by men as well as women (*vid.* 11.69), and the chains of marriage bind both partners. Commenting on Paul's question 'Are you free from a wife?' (I Cor. 7:27), Ambrose observes that a man who marries binds himself with chains for his mind and flesh (*ps.118* 3.32).
21. *Luc.* 4.64; sexual passion is metaphorically linked with blindness (cf. *ps.118* 15.18). The word Ambrose here uses for love, '*amare*', refers to an irrational love, capable of bending the mind (*Luc.* 4.63) and to reason (*Ios.* 10.57); one could love (*amare*) one's wife too much. Ambrose's other words for love, '*caritas*' and '*dilectio*', have more elevated meanings: Otten (1963).

THE VIRGIN

Ambrose expressed his thinking on this point by words he attributes to the widow Juliana, in a work written in 394. The discourse directed to her children which Ambrose puts in her mouth encourages the practice of virginity, while recognizing that this cannot be commanded; among its benefits is that virgins, not being fastened by the tie of marriage, do not know slavery (*exh.virg.* 4.19). Turning specifically to her daughters, Juliana restates a familiar Ambrosian theme: marriage is a chain by which a wife is bound to her husband and made subject to him, and while it is true that neither a man nor a woman has power over their own body (cf. I Cor. 7:12), the man's greater strength means that the woman enjoys even less power than he does. The fact that slavery is common to the married partners (cf. *vid.* 11.69) does not make the woman free, but binds her the more severely. Juliana encourages her daughters to imitate Paul, whose flight from the chain of marriage allowed him to be so great an apostle. Her daughters were people

> to whom virginity alone can give freedom, since she who marries is sold into slavery by her own money. Slavery is a better state than wedlock, for slaves are bought at a price, while wives pay to become slaves! A bride who is up for sale is burdened with gold, she is valued in accordance with her gold. I know from experience, children, the toils of intercourse, the indignities of marriage, and this was under a good husband. But even under a good husband I was not free: I served a man and laboured to please him.

But, as she saw it, the Lord had mercy on her, for her husband joined the clergy and no longer counted as a married man.[22]

The continuities with Ambrose's thought in the early works we have already examined are evident. There is the same brutal insistence on the slavery which marriage entailed for women; words derived from the Latin word for slave (*servus*) occur four times in the passage quoted above. Again we find the notion of the wife seeking to please her husband. But

---

22. *Exh.virg.* 3.17ff; the passage quoted is at 4.23f. See as well Faust (1983): 123ff.

here, women are offered the prospect of freedom. Elsewhere, in a letter to a pope which Ambrose edited on behalf of a group of bishops, we find juxtaposed a wife, bound by the chains of marriage, and a virgin free of chains, categories which he assimilates into the stages of salvation history: the former was under the law, the latter under grace (*ep.ext.coll.* 15(=42).3).

The state of consecrated virginity had existed for some time within Christianity when Ambrose became a bishop. Virgins were a matter of family pride, for his sister Marcellina was a consecrated virgin in Rome, while another virgin, the martyr Soteris, was a remote ancestor, so that Ambrose could allude to his sister's 'hereditary chastity' (*virgb.* 3.37; cf. *exh.virg.* 12.82). The ostensible occasion for the *De virginibus* was the celebration of the feast-day of another virgin, St Agnes, who was twelve years old at the time of her martyrdom, when she displayed devotion beyond her years and strength beyond nature (*virgb.* 1.5).[23] In this work Ambrose, who was always fascinated by martyrdom, gives an enthusiastic account of the death of Agnes (1.2.7–9) before turning to the general theme of virginity. He provides a quotation from the Song of Songs: 'Your name is ointment poured forth. So the young girls love you and attract you' (Song 1:3, quoted at 1.3.11). He imagines virgins arriving in heaven to the joyful applause of the angels, and Miriam with her tambourine urging on choirs of virgins singing to the Lord (2.2.17).[24] In the Old Testament Elijah and Miriam were virgins, but with the coming of Christ this 'way of heavenly living in human bodies' spread throughout the world. It was something specifically Christian, being infrequently encountered among pagans. Hence, Ambrose placed virginity above marriage, while maintaining that he did not advise people against marriage. The latter was a remedy for weakness, but virginity was the glory of chastity; marriage is not censured, but virginity is praised (*virgb.* 1.6.24).

23. In common with other authors, Ambrose stresses that virginity is something beyond nature (cf. 1.2.8, 3.11). Indeed, 'in virgins we see on earth the life of the angels which we lost in paradise' (*inst.virg.* 17.104; cf. *virgb.* 1.3.11, 1.8.48–51, with *exh.virg.* 4.19).
24. Significantly, whereas the Bible describes Miriam leading women (Ex. 15:20), Ambrose has her leading virgins, as he has at *virgb.* 1.3.12. Exodus is silent as to her virginity.

Ambrose backed up his points by discussing a part of a book of the Bible which was to remain among his favourites, the Song of Songs, also known as the Song of Solomon. It is a book of largely amorous content, which initially made its place within the Jewish canon of scripture insecure. Over the centuries, Jewish and Christian exegetes had interpreted it as an allegory, and at various stages Ambrose was attracted to more than one interpretation. In the *De virginibus* he introduced into the Latin world an interpretation derived from the writing of Athanasius, which saw the leading female character in the Song, referred to in the text as the bride (*sponsa*), as a virgin.

The passage Ambrose considers begins with words one would have thought inappropriate to the topic of virginity: 'You are utterly beautiful, my love, and without fault. Come hither from Lebanon, my bride!' (*virgb.* 1.38, quoting Song 4:7f). With these words Ambrose plunges into the world of the most sensuous book of the Bible. Similar themes occur in one of his later works, the *De virginitate*, much of which is taken up with a commentary on another part of the Song of Songs. In the latter book Ambrose jumps into the text by quoting verses describing a garden of sweet smells in which pleasant fruits were eaten (10.54, on Song 4:16f). He describes Christ, his hands dripping with myrrh, as knocking at the door of the soul, a female personage who has taken off her tunic and washed her feet. The soul which begins to open to him exudes the fragrance of the myrrh and aloes which were used at the burial of Christ, whose very name is as an ointment poured out of its container; he it is, Ambrose assures his audience, who poured himself out so that he might breathe on you. After mentioning biblical passages which seemed to refer to this ointment, Ambrose addresses female members of his audience: 'Pick up your vessel, virgin, and draw near so that you can be filled with this ointment!' The woman who has this ointment receives Christ, just as the soul does.

> Move your hand to your nose and investigate the odour of your deeds with the tireless and ever alert keenness of your mind. The odour of your right hand will caress you and your limbs exude the fragrance of the resurrection. Your fingers are moist with myrrh – that is, spiritual deeds are fragrant with the grace

of the true faith. So take enjoyment, virgin, from your body
within. You are so sweet to yourself, so pleasant to yourself, and
you do not begin to be displeased with yourself, as often happens
to sinners. Naked simplicity will make you more happy when
you have taken off the clothing of bodily illusion. Christ longed
for you, like this; Christ chose you, like this. And so he comes in
by the door which has been opened, and he cannot let you down,
he who promised that he would come in. And so embrace him
whom you have sought . . . hold him, ask him not to leave in a
hurry, beg him not to recede. (*virgt.* 12.73f)

This is a strong passage, almost certainly part of a sermon
Ambrose delivered before a congregation. Jerome felt that
the Song was the last book of the Bible a young woman
should come to (*ep.* 107.12), and the words spoken by the
woman in the Song at the point Ambrose is concerned with
(Song 5:5f) are charged, but their impact is heightened in
the expanded version he provides, which is couched, as some
of his most beguiling passages are, in the intimacy of the
second person singular. It will be worth our while considering it in detail.

. . .

THE SENSES

Ambrose encourages a virgin to enjoy her senses of smell
and touch. He was a person to whom the senses were important. One of the ways in which he organized his thinking was
in accordance with the five bodily senses, and he generally
gave sight and hearing the primacy above smell, taste and
touch.[25] He saw the five senses as being all too easily captured by bodily and worldly enticements, as was suggested
by a reference in the Bible to four kings rebelling against

---

25. Towards the end of the list the order varies; see e.g. *bon.mort.* 9.41; *Cain* 1.10.41; *ep.* 2(=65).5, 73(=18).31; *exa.* 6.9.61; *fuga* 1.3, 4.20; *Noe* 6.14; compare St Paul's sequence 'eye . . . hearing . . . smelling' (I Cor. 12:17). A confused order occurs at *Abr.* 2.7.41, and something like the reverse order at *Luc.* 7.113, 140. This is hard to explain, but in the tenth book of the *Confessions* Augustine frequently gives the sequence sight, hearing, smell, taste and touch (6.8, 8.13, 9.16f, 12.19, 21.30, 35.54f; a minor variant occurs at 27.38), yet in the most important working through of the senses they are listed in precisely the opposite order (30.41ff).

five, for the four were the elements out of which human flesh and the world were made, while the five were the five senses, all too easily swayed by bodily and worldly delights (*Abr.* 2.7.41, on Gen. 14). All five were dangerous: the eye gazes and overturns the sentiments of the mind, the ear hears and distracts one's intention, smell gets in the way of thought, the mouth is at fault when it nibbles, while touch produces fire (*fuga.* 1.3). But the senses were not equally susceptible. While sight and hearing were dangerous (*Noe* 10.34), they could be distinguished from the others. Hence, Christ's statement that five in one house would be divided, three against two and two against three (Luke 12:52), distinguished things we hear or read from the superfluous delights of the body which come from the other three senses.[26] Significantly, Ambrose observes that belief is based on sight and hearing (*Luc.* 4.71); whereas sight and hearing aid the mind, smell and taste are as foods for the body (*Abr.* 2.8.57; we shall later consider the apposition of mind and body); ointments, in particular, occasion seductive impulses (*Hel.* 10.36). And the sense of smell, which relished ointments, was associated with women. Appropriately, at baptism the bishop touched men on the mouth and women on the nose, for this allowed the latter to receive the good odour of eternal piety. They could say in the words of the apostle, 'We are the good odour of Christ to God', and they would have the complete fragrance of faith and devotion (*sacr.* 1.3).

The hierarchy of the senses with which Ambrose usually operates is utterly at odds with the world of the Song of Songs, which is overwhelmingly one of the 'superfluous delights',[27] and despite his reservations about smell, taste and touch, Ambrose luxuriates in its language. In one of his last books, he returns to the theme: virgins are to let the ointment of heavenly grace flow into the depths of their hearts and the secret places of their inmost parts (*inst.virg.* 13.83), they are represented as wearing perfumed clothes (16.100), and Ambrose mentions the filling of a house with the odour of

---

26. *Luc.* 7.140f; according to *exa.* 6.9.64, touch provides the greatest enjoyment.
27. Note the opinion of Robert Alter, in Bloch and Bloch (1995): 122f: 'Sight and sound have their place, but it is definitely a secondary place... Again and again... it is taste and smell that predominate, almost always implying or associated with the pleasures of touching.'

ointment when Mary, the sister of Lazarus, washed the feet of Christ (13.84, 17.108; John 12:3 is often quoted). He finishes his consideration of the Song in the *De virginitate* by describing the Word of God coming into a garden to collect faith, taking hold of its odours, finding heavenly food, feasting on sweet honey, and uttering the words which follow those he first quoted at the beginning of the passage: 'I have gathered my myrrh with my spice, I have eaten my bread with my honey' (16.98, quoting Song 5:1). Such expressions represent an extraordinary triumph of the senses which Ambrose elsewhere described as dangerous. Perhaps we should see here the expression of an underlying hostility towards women, with Ambrose using language he found distasteful to encourage them. But it may be more plausible to see these emphases as being in part strategic, representing an attempt to play on female susceptibilities. Ambrose would have been engaged in the practice, unexpected in a bishop, of using sensuous language to encourage young women to commit themselves to lives of virginity.

. . .

THE BODY

In the passage from the *De virginitate* quoted above, Ambrose goes on to urge a woman to take enjoyment from her body. Here again he seems to be thinking in terms antithetical to his own values, for as he understood Genesis, enjoyment had been involved in the fall of Eve, surely a poor role-model for virgins. And his emphasis on the body is puzzling, for no-one could accuse Ambrose of having been well disposed to the human body.

One area in which the thought of late antiquity is most unlike that of the modern world is the hostility many of its thinkers, especially those influenced by Neoplatonism, displayed towards the body. For Ambrose, the body is a prison enclosing the soul.[28] He writes of the soul as observing itself in the wretched dwelling of the body but not losing its

---

28. See for example *Cain* 2.10.36; *exa.* 6.9.55; *exc.fr.* 1.73, 2.20; *Luc.* 2.59, 8.48; *para.* 12.54; *ps.118* 4.6. Further references in *SAEMO* 14/2: 53 n. 107; discussion in Courcelle (1965). On the general theme, Seibel (1958).

nature because of its association with this earthly home. It groans, weighed down by being joined to the body, because the corruptible body is a burden to the soul and its earthly dwelling bends the mind with many thoughts. Knowing that it walks by faith and not according to appearances, it wishes to leave the body and be present with the Lord.[29] Elsewhere, Ambrose offers what might be thought an implausible reading of the words of the bride in the Song of Songs, whom he here takes to be the soul, 'I washed my feet; how shall I defile them?':

> This is, I washed my feet when I went forth and lifted myself up from my association with the body, from that relationship and the familiarity of fleshly embrace. How shall I make them dirty by going back to the enclosure of the body and that dark prison of its passions? (*Is.* 6.52, on Song 5:3)

The structures of Ambrose's thought emerge in his early book *De paradiso*, which binds together a number of issues. In a passage which begins and ends by referring to the opinions of Philo, whom he does not name, Ambrose asserts:

> The one before us relates that sin was committed through enjoyment and the transgression of the senses, taking the figure of delight under the form of the serpent and seeing in the figure of the woman the sensibility of the feelings and mind, which the Greeks call 'aisthesis'. When she had been deceived, according to the history the mind [*mens*], which the Greeks call 'nous', fell into sin. Rightly therefore in Greek 'nous' stands for man and 'aisthesis' for woman. And so certain people have understood 'Adam' as meaning earthly 'nous'. (*par.* 2.11; cf. *Luc.* 7.143)

Similar is a passage in Ambrose's book on Abraham, in which he again follows Philo. Offering a moral interpretation of an incident when the patriarch was told to take a heifer, a nanny-goat and a ram, among other animals (Gen. 15:9), Ambrose suggests that humans are made up of flesh, sense and word. Our flesh (*caro*) is a heifer, for both are worn out by their countless labours. Our senses are like the nanny-goat, which suggests the exciting things which assail a

---

29. Ep. 21(=34).4, with references to Wisd. 9:15 and II Cor. 5:7f. Ambrose closely follows Origen (*PG* 14:1111).

leaping soul. The sight of a beautiful woman, a sweet smell, or hearing and touch can bend the firmness of the soul and, as it were, set it against its own nature. It is fitting, Ambrose continues, that the nanny-goat is female, for our senses are as well, the Greek word *'aisthesis'* being feminine. They are like animals which lose strength in the act of giving birth, as they pour forth the product of their generation and their delight, but when their longings are excited again, fresh impulses develop (*Abr.* 2.8.51).

Ambrose's position is therefore more coherent than one may have thought: woman is to the body and delight as man to the soul, or mind, and reason. It is based on disparate sources, his reading of the Fall following Philo and his thought on the body and the soul being indebted to Neoplatonic thought. We shall consider Ambrose's use of Neoplatonic material later (below, page 169ff), but for the time being it will be enough to note how he managed to integrate it with biblical material. The command given to Abraham to leave his country and kindred meant flight from the attractions and bodily delights which the soul must suffer with the body for as long as it remains bound to it (*Abr.* 1.2.4). And the attractions and delights which were associated with the body were, Ambrose felt, linked with women. Just as the body and the soul could be distinguished, so could the flesh and the mind: the flesh, made soft by feminine lightness, casts the mind down from its position (*Luc.* 4.63).

In a passage towards the beginning of his *De Isaac*, written when he was strongly under the influence of the Neoplatonist Plotinus, Ambrose brings together some of these concepts, again interpreting the quality connected with woman as a threat to that connected with man:

> The woman is delight, an enticement to the body. And so beware lest the strength of your mind be bent and softened by an intercourse involving bodily enjoyment . . . For when strength of mind is undone, utterly pernicious ideas of bodily delight pour forth . . . Had the lively mind remained under careful guard, it would have held these in check. (*Is.* 1.2)

In another work, Ambrose speaks of how it is

> when the soul does not connive at the enticements of the body and is not bound by delight in the enjoyments of the flesh, but

the mind, pure and freed from the slavery of this world, attaches and attracts to itself the senses of the body for its own pleasures, so that by the use of hearing and reading it may feast upon growing virtue and, henceforth not to know hunger, may take its full of the nourishing spiritual foods within. For reason is the food of the mind and nourishment excelling in sweetness.[30]

. . .

SWEETNESS TEMPTING MEN

Ambrose goes on, in the passage quoted above, to describe the virgin as being sweet and pleasant to herself. The terms may seem anodyne, and Ambrose often applied such language to the pleasures of music.[31] Yet music could be evil. Ambrose was aware of an argument that the music generated by the heavenly spheres could not be heard on earth lest people were made captive by its pleasantness and sweetness, which could lead to their going out of their minds (*exa.* 2.2.7). It was therefore fitting that when he needed an image of the threat women posed men he thought of the Sirens, described by Homer as female creatures whose sweet and alluring singing enticed sailors towards the shore, whereupon they were shipwrecked in a rocky place. As it happened, mistranslations in the Greek versions of the Old Testament mentioned the Sirens on several occasions, which opened the way for Ambrose to discuss the danger they posed.[32] Cicero, discussing the Sirens in terms very similar to those used by Ambrose (*de finibus* 5.49) interprets them in a positive light, but the latter's understanding of them is quite different. The Sirens, Ambrose holds, lead people astray, 'by the appearance of enjoyment and the sweetness of melodious charm' (*Tob.* 5.16; the same ideas are also discussed with relation to the Sirens at *fid.* 3.1.4f). The sweetness of their singing enticed the sailors who heard them, bringing about their shipwreck; similarly, the enjoyment of this world can delight us and

---

30. *Luc.* 7.142. We shall return to the positive evaluation placed on hearing and reading and the brief reference to virtue.
31. As at *Luc.* 7.237; *off.* 1.12.114; *ps.* 1.10; *ps.118* prol. 1. See further on music below, pp. 140ff.
32. Kaiser (1964): 112.

deceive us (*ps.* 43.75, cf. 80). What do those young women stand for if not the attraction of unmanly delight, which captures a firm mind and makes it womanish (*Luc.* 4.3)? There is no danger so hidden as worldly pleasure which, as it soothes the intellect, destroys one's life and dashes the mind to pieces on the rocks of the body. When the Maccabees died one would have heard triumphal music leading people to sacrificial victory; the seductive songs of the Sirens did not attract the hearer in this way, but to shipwreck (*Iac.* 2.12.56). Ambrose sees women, whether prostitutes, Sirens or indeed wives, as tempting men; only rarely are women thought of as being tempted by men.[33] One has a sense of manly restraint constantly under attack by temptresses, and in times of political controversy Ambrose will never forget the ability of women to lead men astray.

. . .

MASCULINITY

Ambrose's strong images therefore point to a world of masculinity threatened by women. Ideally, a strong mind which had in itself the chief virtues would command the senses of the body not obey them (*Abr.* 2.5.19). Yet women and the things which Ambrose regarded as being associated with them posed a dire threat. One has to be on guard lest the woman, that is passion, make man, that is mind (*nous*), effeminate, for it was she who was deceived by delight of the senses (*ep.* 34(=45).17). The possibility of manly virtues becoming womanish worries Ambrose. Understandably, the theme is prominent in a work addressed to a male audience, the *De officiis*, in which he affirms that desire for power makes the manly character of justice womanish (*off.* 1.28.138), that

33. Sarah did not greet visitors lest their eyes be drawn to her (*inflectant*, a key verb) (*Abr.* 1.5.42); the male sex can easily be taken captive by female beauty (*ep.* 28(=50).13); wives tempt their husbands (*inst.virg.* 4.30f). Yet Potiphar's wife was tempted by Joseph's looks (*ep.* 36(=2).20; *Ios.* 5.22–26; *ps.118* 12.31; that LXX describes her husband as a eunuch (Gen. 37:36) may make one sympathetic to her), and a young woman can lift her eyes to the countenance of a youth, while a woman's veil keeps others and herself from harm (*paen.* 1.14.68f).

avarice makes manliness womanish (1.39.193), and that fear of suffering is unmanly (2.3.9). The story of Samson and Delilah was an alarming example of a man's undoing. When Samson's hair was cut off above the bent knees of a woman he lost the ornament of his manliness; money poured into the lap of a woman and grace departed from the man (2.26.131). Luxury so softened the warrior Holophernes that the temperance of Judith had the paradoxical effect of making her the stronger (*ep.ext.coll.* 14(=63).29). Another example of an unmanly man was Herod, who made his promise to Salome's daughter when amid troops of dancers. He is implicitly contrasted with Jephthah, who was willing to sacrifice his daughter in fulfilment of a vow: 'I cannot accuse a real man', comments Ambrose (*off.* 3.12.77f). A man must struggle against hostile spiritual powers with the strength, or manliness of his mind (*animi virtute*) (*Luc.* 4.37), rather than being unmanned by pleasure (*exa.* 3.7.30). The notion of 'manliness' was important to Ambrose, and it will be worth our while exploring it in more detail.

In an early work, Ambrose asserts that those who give themselves over to the passions of the body and indulge in delights, things which he persistently sees as connected with women, stray from the teacher of virtue (*virtus*) (*Cain* 1.6.24). Elsewhere, in an unusual move, he interprets the soul as receiving thoughts and giving birth. Some of the qualities associated with the soul (*anima*) are evil and feminine, such as malice, petulance, indulgence, intemperance and shamelessness, and weaken the manliness (*virilitas*) of our mind (*animus*). On the other hand, good qualities which are masculine, among them chastity, patience, prudence, temperance, fortitude and justice, make it easier for our mind (*mens*) and flesh to fulfil the tasks of virtue (*virtus*).[34] The qualities Ambrose sees as masculine all involve restraint, while the feminine ones suggest its overthrow. Men, in Ambrose's view, have to struggle to remain upright.

The association of masculine qualities with the exercise of virtue is particularly interesting because the Latin nouns for 'manliness' and 'virtue' both originate from the word for 'man' (*vir*), and the etymologically plausible association of

---

34. *Cain* 1.10.47. Further, the spiritual offspring of the apostle Paul were masculine (*Cain* 2.1.2).

virtue with the male gender is one Ambrose did not hesitate to make.[35] He argues that our faculty of sensory experience is partly tamed and governed by the mind, and partly untamed, in which case it rushes forward to the irrational delights of the body. Those aspects of our nature which are kept under control are masculine and perfect; those which are leaderless turn the state of the body and manly vigour into something womanish, by a kind of loss of strength (*dissolutio*). Among these is that law of the flesh which, attacking the law of the mind of which St Paul speaks, makes it a captive of the law of sin. And so, in order to be freed from that body of death, Paul placed his hope not in his own virtue but in the grace of Christ (*Cain* 2.1.4; cf. Rom. 7:23–5). When the Pauline allusions are read in the context in which Ambrose places them, the word '*virtus*', here translated 'virtue', which Ambrose adds to the biblical text, could also mean 'manliness'. Ambrose holds that a mind victorious over worldly cares and bodily enticement will be able to shut out the blandishments of enjoyment. He is under no illusions as to the difficulty of this enterprise, but he advises his readers to recognize what is masculine and what is feminine.[36]

. . .

WOMEN PLEASING THEMSELVES

One more point may be briefly made before we leave the virgin whom Ambrose addressed in the language of the Song of Songs. When he spoke of a virgin not being displeased with herself, he was implicitly contrasting her with the married women who wore make-up for fear of displeasing their husbands, and with Juliana in her married state, when she had laboured to please her husband. By excluding men from their lives, virgins were free to please themselves. Indeed, Ambrose represents the widow Juliana as telling her children that her own widowhood and the chastity which she commended to them were, so to speak, indications of female dominion (*exh.virg.* 8.54).

---

35. Hence the family group of a tested man (*vir*) is the lineage of virtues (*virtutum*): *Noe* 4.10. Note too the association of '*vir*' with '*virtus*' at *off.* 2.26.131. See already Cicero *Tusc.* 2.18.43.
36. *Cain* 2.2.8.

VIRGINITY AND SOCIETY

It is easy to imagine young women enthralled by Ambrose's advocacy of virginity and weighing their options. Others, however, would not have been impressed. A Roman inscription which has been preserved in more than one copy reflects a view opposite to that of Ambrose:

> May whoever loves flourish, and may whoever does not love die! May whoever forbids love die twice over![37]

The author of these sentiments would certainly have wished Ambrose a speedy end. The verb he or she used for 'love' (*amare*), is that which Ambrose applied to the unfortunate Theotimus, whose ardour led to blindness (above, page 50). A contemporary of Ambrose, the Gallic author Ausonius, wrote a poem on a wedding composed of phrases which he took from Vergil and rearranged; so sexually explicit is it that the edition of this text in the Loeb Classical Library refrains from offering a translation of the final passage, which describes what happened after the couple entered the bedroom. Ausonius may have written his work in connection with the marriage of Gratian in 374; just a few years later the same Gratian would receive theological works from Ambrose. There must have been those in circles not far distant who saw him as a life-denying kill-joy.

Ambrose's teaching was not merely opposed to the inclinations of most people. While some, such as the Manicheans, held views more radical than his, Ambrose's position was contrary to the values of Roman society. Whereas the figure of Sarah could be assimilated into a Roman thought-world, that of the virgin could not be. The Christian cult of virginity stood against Roman tradition, which approved of large families. The Emperor Augustus had legislated against celibacy, and hostile attitudes towards it lingered. Ambrose professed himself scandalized that people who venerated the adulteries of their gods imposed penalties on celibacy and widowhood (*vid.* 14.84). Constantine had abolished financial penalties for celibacy and childlessness, but as recently as

---

37. *CIL* 4:1173, 4091.

363 the pagan Emperor Julian, a few days before leaving Antioch on his last campaign, enacted legislation according to which a father of thirteen children was to be free from serving as a decurion.[38] The *De virginitate* indicates that Ambrose's enthusiasm for virginity had encountered strong opposition. No-one stopped Abraham when he intended to sacrifice his son Isaac, he comments, but when the sacrifice of chastity is offered someone comes forward to stop it (*virgt.* 3.10). He defended himself against charges of having prohibited the marriage of girls who had been initiated into the sacred mysteries and consecrated to virginity, pointing out that virgins lived the life of the angels, who neither marry nor are given in marriage (*virgt.* 5.24ff). Some alarmists claimed that the overthrow of marriage would cause the world to perish and the human race to fail, an argument he sought to turn on its head by claiming that the lands where virginity was practised most widely had the largest populations.[39] The fate of Ambrose's own family could have served as evidence for his critics. His elder sister was a consecrated virgin and his brother had not married by the time he died, having apparently come to a private decision to remain single, so the family line would end with Ambrose's generation. We have no reason to think that any of the siblings was disquieted by this prospect.

The family of Ambrose may not have been typical, but it could be compared to that of another person of whose conduct Ambrose strongly approved, the senator and ex-*consularis* Paulinus who, together with his wife, adopted an ascetic life. Their only child had died in infancy, so the line of this family would end, just as surely as that of Ambrose. In one of his letters Ambrose purports to quote those who scorned Paulinus: 'From that family, that stock, that talent, so great an eloquence has departed from the senate . . . This cannot be borne!' But his response was sharp: things which might seem shameful from a bodily aspect could be worthy of reverence from the standpoint of religion (*ep.* 27(=58)). Class considerations made the issue seem more important.

38. *Cod.Theod.* 8.16.1 (Constantine), 12.1.55 (Julian).
39. The average woman needed to bear five children for the population to remain stationary: Brown (1988): 6. Ambrose's defence: *virgt.* 7.35f; cf. *exc.fr.* 2.65.

Milan was famous for its large number of elegant homes, the inhabitants of which Ambrose would have targeted when advocating virginity.[40] What would happen to the fortunes of families whose young women devoted themselves to religion rather than produce offspring? The future of wealthy families and their fortunes was at stake.

It is therefore not surprising that parents led the opposition to the new teaching. Ambrose, who on one occasion observed that God could provide the parents of dead children with better ones (*ps.118* 9.18), can be suspected of having little sympathy for parental feeling, and the thought that their sins would be remitted by the merits of their progeny was clearly not enough to console those whose daughters sought to remain virgins. They made their wants clear: 'Daughter, you owe us grandchildren!' (*exh.virg.* 7.45). Ambrose encouraged a virgin not to worry if her parents denied her a dowry, for the husband she would gain, by whom he means Christ, would be a wealthy one, and thanks to his treasure she would not need to seek an income from what her father left. It was doubtless true that a woman's desire for physical integrity would stand in the way of family succession, but Ambrose told girls that when their parents raised this objection they were hoping to be defeated. Virgins were to overcome kindly feeling towards their parents; if they overcame at home, they would overcome the world (*virgb.* 1.11.62f).[41]

The first book of the *De virginibus* ends powerfully, describing the resolution of tensions generated within a family by the decision of a young woman to become a consecrated virgin. Ambrose describes her standing at the altar, surrounded by her family. They urge her to marry, doubtless to a man they had chosen for her who may not have been suitable in the eyes of a bishop,[42] but she spurns them:

40. Ausonius *Ordo* 7.2. See recently Lawrence (1997).
41. Goody argues (1983) that the clergy encouraged asceticism to gain control over property or donations, and the widow Juliana's paying for a church in Florence could support this interpretation. Yet Ambrose's works contain no direct evidence for this strategy. Indeed, he said that no-one lamented a law which denied the clergy the right to inherit private property (*ep.* 73(=18).13, referring to *cod.Theod.* 16.2.20).
42. The spouse parents had in mind may not have been a Christian: see on mixed marriages *Abr.* 1.19.84f (cf. *Luc.* 8.3); *ps.118* 20.48 and *ep.* 62(=19).

Would the veil of marriage really cover me better than the altar, which sanctifies these very veils? More fitting is the altar cloth on which Christ, the head of all, is consecrated each day. What are you doing, relatives? Why are you still seeking to tempt my soul to marriage? I've seen this coming for some time. You offer me a husband? I've found a better one! Exaggerate this person's wealth as much as you like, boast of his nobility, praise his power: no-one can be compared to the one who is mine. He is rich in the world, powerful in command, noble in heaven. If you have such a person I do not refuse the choice; if you have not, don't you make provision for me, my family, but look on me with envy! (*virgb.* 1.11.65)

The young woman's speech is noteworthy. She speaks in short, jerky sentences of simple grammatical structure, and frequently poses rhetorical questions. In these respects her speech is similar to others which Ambrose purports to quote in his writings,[43] and we can imagine readers as well as hearers of Ambrose being struck at the immediacy of the words placed in her mouth. Silence followed her outburst, which was broken by a person who blurted out 'What if your father were still alive? Would he have allowed you to remain without a husband?' But the young woman, in whom religion was stronger than family feeling (*pietas*), answered: 'Perhaps he died so that he could not get in the way of this.' The person who asked the question died shortly afterwards. The others became afraid, and those who had opposed her began to support her. 'Here you have, girls, the reward of devotion. Parents, beware of committing an offence of this kind!' (11.66). The story is obviously crafted to appeal to young women. The brave girl offered a remarkably strong role-model, and it is hard to imagine a piece which would more effectively play on the feelings of young women.

So it is that Ambrose exalts religion over family feeling: 'first, girl, defeat family feeling [*pietas*]; if you defeat the home you also defeat the world!' (*virgb.* 1.11.63). The sentiment is

---

43. See for example words put in the mouth of Helena (*ob.Theod.* 43, where the first six units of speech which can be taken as sentences, two of them lacking verbs, are made up of only 45 words); the Jews (*ob.Theod.* 49); the deacon Laurence and Pope Sixtus (*off.* 1.41.205f), and the synagogue (*ps.118* 2.9). As far as we can tell from writings which closely follow material delivered orally, Ambrose's style of speaking in public was similar (cf. below, p. 146).

not unexpected in a bishop, but it is striking. The Latin word *'pietas'* has a range of meanings which can involve no more than a general sense of proper behaviour, and Ambrose frequently uses it in this way. Nevertheless, it can bear the more precise meaning of loyalty towards the members of one's family, in particular one's parents and children. Exemplary in this regard was Vergil's hero *pius* Aeneas, who saved his father and son from the blazing ruin of Troy, but was prepared to abandon his wife to die in the flames of the city and his lover Dido to commit suicide in the flames of a funeral pyre. Vergil's way of editing women out of his story may seem clumsy, but suggests the connection between *pietas* and blood relationship, and it is noteworthy how often Ambrose uses the word in this restricted sense.[44] He neatly makes the point in a discussion of the crucifixion: Jesus displayed *pietas* towards his mother while on the cross, but after he told Mary and John to look on each other as mother and son, the two divided the duties of *pietas* between them.[45]

Normally Ambrose took a positive view of family feeling. He was puzzled by the opposition to it implied by Christ's injunction to hate the members of one's family (*ps.118* 15.15–17, on Luke 14:26), and encouraged reverence towards parents (*patr.* 1.1). Indeed, he was happy to encourage a virgin to display *pietas* towards her relatives (*inst.virg.* 17.112). But, overall, religion was superior to the duties of *pietas* (*Luc.* 7.146), and the message of the story Ambrose told concerning the young woman is clear. It reversed what he thought of as the usual situation of women. Whereas wives customarily feared their husbands, a virgin could arouse fear in her family. For a woman facing a lifetime of slavery as she sought to please a husband, virginity offered superior prospects. Enticingly,

---

44. *Ep.ext.coll.* 14(=63).109. Further biblical examples of *pietas*: *apol.alt.Dav.* 3.18 (Lot and his daughters), *apol. Dav.* 1.16 (Jephtha's daughter); *ep.* 7(=37).7 (Jacob and his sons), 38(=55).3 (Japheth and Noah); *virgb.* 2.2.12 (Mary and Elisabeth). Among animals, Ambrose mentions the *pietas* of storks towards their elderly parents (*exa.* 5.16.55; the behaviour echoes that of Vergil's hero *'pius* Aeneas' towards his elderly father), and among emperors the *pietas* of Valentinian towards his sisters and theirs towards him (*ob.Val.* 37f) and Gratian and his brother (71), and that of Honorius towards Theodosius (*ob.Theod.* 3).
45. *Ep.ext.coll.* 14(=63).109); *Luc.* 10.129f (cf. *ep.* 71(=56a).6.

Ambrose describes a virgin who has been given a kingdom, gold and beauty. She bears an unconquered mind which is not held captive by the allurements of enjoyments; rather, she is a lord, just like a queen (*virgb.* 1.7.37). Concepts of this kind, which Ambrose elsewhere applies to men, must have been very attractive to young women.

. . .

WOMEN IN PRIVATE AND PUBLIC

In the second book of the *De virginibus*, Ambrose gives examples of women leading lives of virginity. The list begins with Mary: 'When did she offend her relatives by so much as a glance, when did she dissent from her kinsfolk?' he asks (*virgb.* 2.2.7), apparently forgetful of the disobedient virgin whose words he had admiringly quoted at the end of the first book. But his words soften the message of his source at this point, a letter to virgins attributed to Athanasius,[46] and we may deduce that filial obedience was not important to him. He represents Mary as only leaving home to go to church, and then in the company of her parents or kinsfolk. When Gabriel visited her he found her without a companion in the inner parts of the home, she being indeed a virgin in the home. How did she pass her time? Among her virtues was reading, an occupation she followed so keenly that when Gabriel came upon her he found her by no means alone but in the company of books, archangels and prophets.[47] Later, purporting to reproduce words spoken by Pope Liberius when his sister Marcellina was consecrated,[48] Ambrose emphasizes the quietness of the life which lay in store for her: she would avoid crowded banquets and flee from greetings. She would

---

46. Lettre aux vierges, in S. Athanase, *Lettres festales et pastorales* trans. L.-Th. Lefort, Louvain 1955 (=*Corpus Scriptorum Christianorum Orientalium* 151, Scriptores Coptici 20), pp. 61.26–29. Ambrose's use of this text is discussed by Aubineau (1955).
47. Charmingly, Ambrose takes it for granted that when Gabriel visited Mary she had already read a prophecy concerning herself in Isaiah (*Luc.* 2.15.18).
48. Suspicions as to the authenticity of Liberius' address are increased by the discourse attributed to Bishop Alexander of Alexandria contained in the letter on virgins attributed to Athanasius: Rosso (1983): 448–50.

avoid speech, silence being better than talking too much. In church and elsewhere, Ambrose believes that a virgin should keep her mouth shut.[49] He assumes that she will be reading a book when someone asks her to take food and that her life will be one of reading, work and prayer (*virgb.* 3.4.15f; cf. *ep.ext.coll.* 14(=63).82). Such a lifestyle, we may note in passing, would have been beyond the reach of many. We know that there was a servant in the home in which Ambrose's sister Marcellina lived (*VAmb.* 4.1), and the regimen he suggests for virgins is another pointer to the level of society from which he envisaged such women being recruited. But in general terms, the life he envisages for them is remarkably domestic. Doubtless there could be excitement in the life of a virgin. As the third book of the *De virginibus* moves towards its end, Ambrose describes with relish and, perhaps, a degree of masculine interest, the martyrdom which St Pelagia and her companions underwent when their chastity was threatened.[50] The days of persecution had passed by the time of Ambrose. But he could still hold up models of virginal independence such as Pelagia and Mary, who was subject to no man but God alone (*inst.virg.* 12.79), and although he seems to have been the first author in the West to call Mary 'Mother of God' (*exa.* 5.20.65, *virgb.* 2.2.7), it was as a virgin rather than a mother that Ambrose chiefly thought of her.

Yet there is a paradox in Ambrose's position. While generous in the dignity he offers virgins, he holds back from genuine empowerment. His commentary on Luke omits all but one of the nine verses of the Magnificat, which has spoken to many of the strength of Mary; in his opinion, she was a gentle and humble person whose description of herself as the handmaid of the Lord was fitting (*Luc.* 2.16). He

49. *Virgb.* 3.3.11–3.14. Whereas women were notorious for being noisy, virgins, like Mary, were characterized by silence; see for example the advice given a virgin to open her ears and close her mouth (*inst.virg.* 10.66, with other references supplied in the footnote ad loc. in the *SAEMO* edition). There are interesting reflections in Pellegrino (1979).
50. *Virgb.* 3.7.33–36. Augustine was uncertain whether such conduct was proper (*civ.dei* 1.26, a view which may have been influenced by the persistence of suicide among the Donatists with whom he had to deal), and Ambrose himself is uncomfortable with the death, effectively by suicide, of the mother of the Maccabees (*Iac.* 2.11.53, on II Macc. 7:41).

repeatedly affirms that Mary lived within the home,[51] and similarly expected Christian virgins to be in the secluded parts of a house (*ep.* 56(=5).16, cf. 22). They would presumably be unlike the vestal virgins, women of similar social origin whose lives were nevertheless more public; a person who is exposed to the daily importuning of the eyes of the intemperate cannot be modest (*virgb.* 1.4.15). One is left with the paradox that, if the status of virginity freed women from the slavery of marriage, Mary and other virgins were confined to the home just as much as the married woman Sarah had been.

Ambrose's thinking on women is hard to summarize, being rich, nuanced, and both giving and withholding. In some ways his attitudes were those of the Roman world, while in others he stands defiantly opposed to the practices of his society. The mental processes which underlie his thought are also interesting: elements of powerful consistency rub shoulders with areas of sloppy and loose thought. He shows a tendency to operate with sharply defined, often binary categories which provided a framework into which he could slot the data of Scripture. As we shall see, Ambrose frequently proceeds in this way: he blocks out opposing categories, in the light of which he interprets the contents of the Bible. But this raises the question of how Ambrose interpreted the Bible, a topic to which we shall turn in the next chapter.

---

51. The theme is made insistently in *virgb.*, esp. 2.2.9f (Mary alone in the innermost parts of the house), 15 (a virgin within the home). See also *ep.* 56(=5).16; *exh.virg.* 10.71; *Luc.* 2.8. Virgins seem to have lived in the family home at Milan (*virgb.* 1.7.32) as well as at Rome; practice at Bologna was different (1.10.60).

Chapter 3

THE BIBLE

Ambrose's most important intellectual work was devoted to interpreting the Bible. Even his books on non-biblical topics often contain extended commentaries on relevant passages of Scripture. Hence, while Ambrose devoted no work specifically to the Song of Songs, he systematically worked through portions of it in various books. This concentration on the Bible arose naturally from his exercise of one of the chief functions of a bishop in late antiquity. Just as a teacher would sit in a raised seat, his cathedra, expounding the contents of a book to his students, so a bishop would expound the Bible to the people within the building later called, in recognition of this task, a cathedral. Many of Ambrose's works on the Bible contain references to scriptural passages 'which you have heard today', revealing their origin as sermons preached on passages read out in public worship, which were taken down by stenographers and later written up.[1] Short interrogative sentences and snappy one-liners reflecting oral delivery can give his commentaries a pleasing air of informality and apparent spontaneity: 'What is it to see God? Don't ask me!' (*Luc.* 1.7).

---

1. Such references also indicate carelessness in the preparation of the sermons for publication, as do the abrupt endings of some books. Nicaean polemic at the end of the second book of *Luc.* builds to a remarkably effective conclusion, as does the first book of *virgb*. But such works as *Hel.*, *apol.alt.Dav.*, and *Nab.* peter out in discussion of minor points, and the final book of *virgb.* comes to a very unsatisfying end. Those listening to an address on the Emperor Theodosius may have pricked up their ears at the welcome words 'To conclude' (*ob.Theod.* 33), but the oration continued until 56; a reference to a trumpet signals the end of an address (*exc.fr.* 2.105) which goes on until 135.

'You don't believe me? Well believe Paul!' (*Luc.* 2.88).
Ambrose usually operates as a preacher rather than a scholar.

. . .

AMBROSE'S WRITING ON THE BIBLE

His works of exegesis fall into various categories. A series of books on the opening chapters of Genesis are among his earliest pieces of writing, apart from an exposition of Genesis 1, the *Exameron* ('Six days'), which began as a series of sermons preached in Holy Week, apparently towards the end of the 380s.[2] It contains discussions of the characteristics of plants, fish, birds and earth-bound animals which have brought pleasure to almost all who have read them. These works follow the biblical narrative as far as Abraham; towards the end of his life Ambrose wrote on the later patriarchs as well. The outcome was a series of commentaries which covered, in varying degrees of detail and from different points of view, almost all of the first book of the Bible.[3] Most of these are unusual in the Ambrosian corpus in that they are formal compositions which did not originate as sermons. They allow us to see Ambrose steadily maturing as a scholar. His works written in the 370s lean heavily on previous exegetes. Long passages in the *De paradiso* and Cain and Abel are little more than paraphrases of the commentaries of Philo. Ambrose acknowledges few debts to his predecessors,[4] and sometimes seems concerned to cover his tracks. But when he wrote on the six days of the creation his debts to

---

2. *Ep.* 34(=45).1 implies this when read carefully, as does a reference to his old age when he prepared the book (*exa.* 4.5.20). A late date also sits better with his use of Basil's commentary on the six days of creation, dated by modern scholarship to about 378. The editing of this work for publication was not thorough, for a note which must have been written by the stenographer who transcribed one sermon survives (*exa.* 5.12.36).
3. Ambrose ignores chapters of genealogy (Gen. 5, 10f, 36), and chapter 38, which did not lend itself to his method of organizing the material around the lives of leading figures. His near silence on chapter 50 is harder to explain; perhaps he died before dealing with it.
4. Philo is mentioned once only, and then to be criticized (*par.* 4.25); Origen three times (*Abr.* 2.8.54, where he is queried, *ps.118* 4.16, and *ep.* 65(=75).1). For the relationship between Ambrose and Philo, Savon: (1977(a)).

Philo were far fewer, and while he often borrows from the commentary of Basil of Caesaraea on this topic, the borrowings are short. When Jerome, who often criticized Ambrose for lack of originality, claimed that the *Exameron* simply followed the opinions of Hippolytus and Basil,[5] he was unfair, for when this work is compared with his earlier commentaries it is clear that by the time be wrote it Ambrose had found his own voice. In particular, he turns away from the comparatively literal interpretation of the text offered by Basil.

Ambrose also wrote a series of short works which use parts of the Bible for didactic purposes. His work on Elijah dealt with drunkenness, that on Naboth with avarice, and that on Tobias with usury. A book on complaints made by Job and David, the *Interpellatione Iob et David*, is devoted to issues raised in the book of Job and the psalms, in particular psalms 42, 43, 73 and 74. In one of his last works, the *De fuga saeculi*, Ambrose turned to the cities of refuge described in the book of Numbers (Num. 35:11–14). His discussion is again heavily indebted to Philo, but does not follow him slavishly; rather, the interpretations of Philo are reworked so as to take on a different significance.[6] Other late works reveal the stature Ambrose had acquired as an independent commentator.

These works, written in the last decade of Ambrose's life, are long and ambitious in their aims, as the titles under which they have been transmitted suggest. The *Explanation of twelve psalms* deals with psalms 1, 36–41, 44, 46, 48–9 and 62; the fact that most of the psalms on which he commentated fall within a narrow range among the 150 contained in the Bible may indicate an unfinished project, similar to that we may conjecture he undertook with Genesis, to work through a defined portion of the sacred text.[7] Again, there are debts

---

5. *Ep.* 84.7. Elsewhere, Jerome wrote that he would rather be the translator of someone else's work than, as certain people were, an ugly crow adorning himself with the colours of others (*PL* 23:108, referring to Ambrose's *Spir.S*), and wrote of a croaking crow who rejoiced in the colours of all the birds, although he himself was dark (*PL* 26:229f). The subject of this ridicule was Ambrose; Hagendahl (1958): 115–17. We shall encounter other examples of Jerome's hostility towards Ambrose, the source of which has never been decisively established.
6. The issues are laid out in *SAEMO* 4:11f; more detail in Savon (1977a).
7. A suspicion strengthened by the existence of what amount to commentaries on psalms 42 and 43 in *interpell.* 2 and on psalm 51 in *apol.Dav*; gaps were being methodically filled in.

to earlier commentators, in particular Origen and, for the first half of the commentary on psalm 1, Basil, but, as is the case with the *Exameron*, the sustained close dependence on earlier writers of his first works has vanished. Longer and more meditative are the *Exposition of psalm 118* (psalm 119 in most modern Bibles), and the *Exposition of the Gospel according to Luke*, the latter being unusual among Ambrose's commentaries for its failure to consider every verse. In considering Luke, Ambrose draws on Origen for the first two books in particular, Eusebius for the third, and for the remaining seven a commentary Hilary of Poitiers had written on Matthew, which Ambrose puts to greater use than any other source written in Latin. Sometimes he still followed his predecessors very closely, to the extent that a passage in his exposition of Luke has been used to fill two lacunae in a papyrus, discovered near Cairo in 1941, containing his source, a work of Origen.[8] But again, these long works are relatively independent, and Ambrose's borrowings largely verbal. Rather than paraphrasing or translating passages he found in earlier commentators, Ambrose increasingly came to use them as stimuli to his own thought. This growing independence may have been connected with the circumstances in which the different works had their origins, for the sermons on which many of the later works were based would not have lent themselves to sustained borrowings. The two expositions are the most substantial of Ambrose's books, and all three are products of his maturity, in which the workings of his own mind are seen most clearly. They will form the basis for our consideration of Ambrose's handling of the Bible.

The topic is not an easy one, for the genre of commentary is one which resists summary. Nor is Ambrose particularly reflective on the task of exegesis; he has nothing to say as thought-provoking as the crisp observation of his near-contemporary Hilary that the matter is not subject to the words but the words to the matter.[9] Our method must therefore be different from that adopted in the preceding chapter. We shall begin by examining what Ambrose tells us of his approach to the Bible, go on to locate his practice against

---

8. Puech and Hadot (1959).
9. *'Non sermoni res sed rei est sermo subiectus'*: *De trinitate* 4.14 (*CCSL* 62:116).

that current in his time, and consider his attitudes to the Bible and the ways in which he thought of parts of it.

AMBROSE'S APPROACH TO THE BIBLE

In a letter addressed to one Irenaeus, the figure to whom more of Ambrose's letters are addressed than anyone else but who is unknown outside his correspondence, Ambrose writes:

> While I was resting my mind for a little while in the midst of reading, having put aside my night-time study, I began to turn over that line which we had used that evening at Vespers, 'Thou art more beautiful than the children of men, how beautiful are the feet of those who bring good tidings of him.' And truly, there is nothing more fair than that highest good, even the preaching of which is fair.[10]

This passage contains a number of pointers to Ambrose's approach to the Bible. Although he writes in Latin, he quotes from the text he had begun to think about in Greek. This had been the language of early western as well as eastern Christianity. But as time passed it had been increasingly supplanted by Latin, and the church of Milan in the time of Ambrose would have conducted Vespers in Latin. Despite this, the language in which the sacred text presented itself to Ambrose as he reflected on the passages which had been read out was Greek.

The passage which Ambrose quotes comprises pieces from two parts of the Bible. The first portion reproduces the Septuagint text of Ps. 45:2 exactly, but the status of the second, which is connected to the first by the repetition of the word 'beautiful', is more complicated. It is clearly meant to reproduce some words of St Paul (Rom. 10:15), but Paul has people bringing good tidings 'of good things' rather than 'of him', and the form of Ambrose's 'bring good tidings' has more in common with the Greek form of an Old

---

10. *Ep.* 11 (=29).1. Ambrose's '*inter legendum cum paululum requievissem animo*' recalls Augustine's description of him: '*reficiebat... lectione animum*' (*conf.* 6.33). On the notion of the highest good (*summum bonum*), see below p. 172.

Testament text which Paul was quoting (Is. 52:7) than that which the apostle gave it. Perhaps Ambrose conflated the texts as he turned the words over in his mind, for it is generally true that we have to reckon not with different Latin texts used by Ambrose but citations from memory, supported by a Latin text, such as that proclaimed in the liturgy, and his personal familiarity with the Greek text.[11] For him, possessing a written text was quite different from appropriating its contents. Explaining a prohibition on writing down the Creed, he observed that when you write something down, you are confident of being able to read it again, and certainly do not think about it and meditate on it daily (*expl.symb.* 9). While Ambrose was certainly devoted to books, when he responded to Scripture he was, in part, responding to something he apprehended aurally. Similarity or identity of words, such as 'beautiful' in the example we have been considering, allowed one part of the Bible to suggest another. Ambrose was happy to jump from word to word.

The fact that Ambrose's night-time reading led him to turn over in his mind a biblical text from the liturgy suggests that he approached the contents of the Bible in a meditative way. He was not the kind of reader who would take notes on a passage to summarize its main points; rather, in common with many Christian readers, he saw a close connection between reading and meditation.[12] He felt that even when readers did not have a book in their hands they could imitate those animals which were regarded as clean in the law of the Old Testament. These animals usually ruminate when not eating; 'in the same way we bring forth from the treasury of our memory and our inner parts spiritual food on which we ruminate' (*ps.118* 7.25). The words of the Bible were pastures on which its readers fed each day and by which they were renewed and restored as they tasted them or chewed them over, and which would fatten up the flock of the Lord (*ps.118* 14.2). Such a process went beyond the operations of the intellect; indeed, Mary used to turn over what she had been reading in her sleep (*virgb.* 2.2.8).

Yet, despite the importance of the aural in Ambrose's apprehension of the Bible, he read in silence. Augustine

---

11. I follow the important reflections in Poirier (1979): 254.
12. A patristic truism; e.g. *ps.118* 12.28, 33.

describes him in the act of reading: his eyes moved across the pages and his heart sought the meaning, but his voice and tongue were quiet (*conf.* 6.3.3). The practice of silent reading was unusual in antiquity, but not unique to Ambrose; Augustine goes on at a crucial point of the *Confessions* to describe himself reading in silence (8.12.29). Perhaps Ambrose would have seen himself as reading in the way that Hannah prayed, crying out in silence without her lips moving (*ps.118* 17.9, on I Sam 1:13). Silence was important for Ambrose: he is interested in the silence of Susannah before her accusers, which he seems to have been the first commentator to connect with the silence of Christ when he was accused.[13] Silence comes before speech, he informed his clergy at the beginning of a long discussion of this virtue in the *De officiis* (*off.* 1.2.5–6.21).

This, then, was the practice which lay behind Ambrose's work on the Bible: the meditation on a text, at least sometimes in Greek, possibly suggested by the liturgy and hence apprehended aurally, and feeding on texts in silence. From such meditation and reading Ambrose moved to the writing of commentaries, producing works which reflect the ways in which texts were approached in his time. We may distinguish two broad ways.

. . .

LITERAL INTERPRETATION

Some commentators in late antiquity sought to elucidate the meanings intended by the authors of texts. The immensely long commentary on Vergil's *Aeneid* written early in the fifth century by Servius, for example, discusses the precise meaning of words and grammatical and rhetorical forms, while providing background historical and mythological information. Among Christians, much of the exegetical work of Jerome takes the form of brief notes explaining the meaning of the biblical text. Such an approach could leave the exegete of texts which had already attracted commentators with little new to say. Jerome told how his own teacher Donatus, on coming to the words of Terence 'there is nothing spoken which has not been spoken before', exclaimed 'Death to those who spoke before us!' (*CCSL* 72:257, on *eun.* prol.41).

---

13. Piredda (1991). See in general the excellent study of Pellegrino (1979).

Ambrose was perfectly at home with this method of approaching a text. While he has little to say on matters of grammar, he was alive to factual difficulties presented by the Bible. He discussed at length the apparently incompatible genealogies of Jesus supplied by Matthew and Luke (*Luc.* 3), and was aware of apparent contradictions in the accounts of the resurrection in the different gospels; he felt these represented similar events which occurred at different times, rather than different versions of the same events (*Luc.* 10.147ff, 171ff, 182ff). Discussing Peter's denial of Christ, Ambrose synthesizes the apparently divergent accounts of the evangelists. Usually he places little weight on Mark's gospel, but on this occasion he evaluates his narrative with care, for he believed that Mark was a follower of Peter and would therefore have learned the truth of the matter from him (*Luc.* 10.78; *Luc.* 6.12 deals with another case of apparent discord between the gospels). He felt that the statement of Christ that he would be three days and three nights in the heart of the earth, an apparent prediction of the interval between the crucifixion and the resurrection which was impossible to square with these events occurring on a Friday and Sunday respectively, could be explained by taking the darkness which covered the earth at the time of the crucifixion as a night (*interpell.* 1.5.14). Ambrose was alert to diverse meanings which could arise from precise readings of a text (e.g. *ob. Val.* 11). He saw the Bible as a collection of written texts which could be collated and compared.

While he usually takes for granted the meaning of the words contained in the text, he is concerned to establish what the precise words are. He read the New Testament in its original Greek, as well as translations into Latin. Like most Christians of his time, Ambrose was content to read the Old Testament in translations, having little interest in the original Hebrew text.[14] The chief translation was the Septuagint, a fairly free Greek version made in the Hellenistic period, perhaps at Alexandria, which meant that Ambrose sometimes reflects understandings of the Bible current in

---

14. Occasionally he tries to get towards the Hebrew (*exa.* 1.8.29), but in general believed that the LXX translation was an improvement on the original (*exa.* 3.5.20). He also read the Old Testament in Latin (*ep.* 34(=45).5).

some Jewish circles of that period.[15] But he became increasingly interested in checking the Septuagint by comparing it with three translations into Greek undertaken in the Christian period, those of Aquila, who produced a very literal translation, Symmachus, and, to a lesser extent, Theodotion. While this concern is apparent early in Ambrose's exegetical career (*para.* 5.27), it becomes increasingly overt as the long commentary on Psalm 119 advances, both in explicit references to various translations and in expressions in his Latin which seem to reflect translations into Greek other than the Septuagint; at one point he suggests a copyist's mistake in the Septuagint text (*ps.118* 22.27). His last work, an unfinished commentary on psalm 43, reveals a confident independence of judgment when it persistently compares differences in the four translations into Greek (esp. *ps.* 43 34–39).[16] Ambrose was also aware of the inability of Latin to express the force of such Greek words as '*telos*' (*ps.118* 12.45), and was not clear which Latin word was the better term for 'manger' (*Luc.* 2.42). His approach to Scripture could therefore involve a close reading of the text, and increasingly displayed what would now be regarded as sound scholarly instincts.

. . .

ALLEGORICAL INTERPRETATION

But people in Ambrose's time often approached texts in another way. In his own words, 'Allegory occurs when one thing is said and another meant.'[17] According to this principle, a text ostensibly dealing with one subject could be understood as really being about another. The Greeks had long been proposing allegorical interpretations of the text of Homer, and their approach had become established among Jewish

---

15. For example, he reads 'foreigners' rather than 'Philistines' at Gen. 26:18 (*ob.Theod.* 44).
16. Various translations are also compared at *off.* 1.4.15.
17. '*Allegoria est cum aliud geritur et aliud figuratur*' (*Abr.* 1.4.28; cf. *inc.* 7.66 on parables). Compare Augustine: in allegory, 'something is understood from something else' (*de trinitate* 15.9.15, *CCSL* A:481). Quintillian defined allegory as saying one thing when meaning something else: '*aliud verbis aliud sensu*' (*Institutio oratoria* 8.6.44, where examples are given, including Horace's famous use of the word 'ship' to mean 'state'); '*aliud dicere aliud intellegi*' (*ins.* 9.2.92).

exegetes of the Bible. Philo wrote heavily allegorizing commentaries on parts of it, especially the books of Genesis and Exodus. The New Testament contains a mild form of allegory, in a form scholars term typology, which allowed incidents in the Old Testament to be interpreted in the light of the superior revelation of the New. Some statements of Jesus could be taken to have been uttered with typological intent, for his observation that the Son of Man must be lifted up just as Moses had lifted up a serpent in the wilderness (John 3:14) could be thought to imply that what Moses did contained a hidden reference to the crucifixion. The technique was frequently employed by St Matthew, as for example in his apparently incongruous comment that the return of the holy family from Egypt fulfilled the statement of the prophet, 'Out of Egypt have I called my son' (Matt. 2:15), which referred in the first instance to the exodus of the chosen people from Egypt (Hos. 11:1). It was also used by the author of the epistle to the Hebrews, according to whom the law was 'a shadow of good things to come' (Heb. 10:1), and the author of the first letter attributed to St Peter (I Pet. 3:20f).

But St Paul uses this method most often. He states that the story of Abraham's two sons was uttered 'in an allegorical fashion', for it referred to the two covenants (Gal. 4:22–24, the only occurrence of a word based on 'allegory' in Paul). He saw Adam as having been a type (*typos*) of Christ (Rom. 5:14), and incidents in the history of the chosen people as having similarly been types (I Cor. 10:6, 11). When Paul's Greek was translated into Latin in the Vulgate Bible, the word '*typos*' was rendered as '*forma*' at Rom. 5:14, but at I Cor. it was translated by '*figura*', and it is clear that Christians familiar with both languages regarded the words as equivalent.[18] Christian commentators who practised typology therefore thought that they were doing no more than applying to the Bible a tool it had already applied to itself, and often quoted Paul's words 'The letter kills but the Spirit gives life' (II Cor. 3:6). The practice attracted hostile comment from Plotinus, a figure somewhat unusual in late antiquity in his coolness towards it:

---

18. See for example Junilius 2.16 (*PL* 68:33).

'Enigmas' is the pretentious name given by the Christians to the perfectly plain statements of Moses, thus glorifying them as oracles filled with hidden mysteries and beguiling the critical faculty by their extravagant nonsense.[19]

A typological approach therefore came naturally to a reader of the Bible in late antiquity. Just as the art of the period, by moving away from the naturalistic, was coming to place a greater burden of interpretation on its viewers, so it was felt necessary to decode teaching taken to be concealed in the Old Testament. Indeed, Augustine felt that all or nearly all the actions contained in it were to be taken not only literally but also figuratively (*doct. chr.* 3.22.32). Ambrose often describes something in the Old Testament as a '*figura*', a '*mysterium*', or a '*sacramentum*'. While technically a *sacramentum* could be seen as a sign, and a *mysterium* as what it signified, the Greek '*mysterion*' was translated by the Latin '*sacramentum*' in the Vulgate at Gal. 5:32, and for Ambrose the words mean much the same thing. Hence two of his works which are largely different versions of the same book are called one by each title, *De mysteriis* and *De sacramentis*, and employ the two terms interchangeably.

Ambrose's feeling for allegory has not been widely shared for some centuries, but the similarity of his thought world to that of some of the biblical authors may sometimes have taken him close to their intention. Touching on Luke's having written his gospel for the most excellent Theophilus (1:3), Ambrose observes, referring to the meaning of his name in Greek, that 'The gospel was written for Theophilus, that is to one who loves God. If you love God it is written for you. It is written for you, receive the gift of the evangelist!' (*Luc.* 1.12). Whereas some modern commentators on Luke solemnly discuss Theophilus' rank and possible identity, whether he was a Christian, and his relationship with Luke, Ambrose immediately seizes upon the name and makes an obvious point. It may be the very point Luke wanted his readers to make, in which case Ambrose stands closer to him than do many modern commentators on his gospel.

---

19. Porphyry *Against the Christians*, trans. in Peters (1990): 123.

THE CASE OF DAVID

Yet Ambrose cannot usually be read with a view to understanding what passages in the Bible meant to their authors. A portion of a defence he wrote of King David allows us to see the typological method being employed in a self-aware manner to lead away from anything an author could have intended. Ambrose felt that people would be astonished at the adultery and murder committed by David if they did not pay attention to the power of the Scriptures and the hidden nature of the mysteries they contained (*apol.Dav.* 1.1). His development of this point must have stunned his readers. Bathsheba, the woman taking a bath on whom David, strolling around his house, looked and with whom he went on to commit adultery, signified the church of the nations who would receive the washing of baptism from the true David, that is Christ. On the other hand Uriah, her husband, whose death David was to arrange, bore a name which meant 'my light', a clear pointer to his signifying the Devil, who turns himself into an angel of light. The exegesis is doubtless questionable morally, but Ambrose is brazen: 'We have analysed powerful pieces of evidence, it seems to me, and we have proved that this narrative occurred as a figure' (*apol.Dav.* 3.14f). One has a sense of Ambrose delighting to display his virtuosity in developing an implausible argument,[20] just as he seems to show off in another work in which Jesus is described as a goat, a hart and a snake in an extraordinary passage which ends by offering a spirited defence of wolves (*ps.118* 6.12–17).

Another discussion of David's activities provides additional depth. Here, Ambrose identifies the house in which he walked with that of which Christ spoke when he said 'with my Father there are many mansions' (John 14:2). The woman he looked upon was naked because, having been stripped of virtues, she lacked the girdle of immortality and was despoiled of the garb of innocence. So Christ loved his church, despite her nakedness. She was washing herself because she was dark (cf. Song 1:5f). Having seen her naked, Christ

---

20. Compare 'The adultery, I say, occurred as a figure of salvation, for not every case of adultery is to be condemned' (*apol.alt.Dav.* 2.10.50).

loved her ardently; he saw his beloved naked and, being himself the son of love, he loved her ardently. This is not shameful adultery, but the mysteries of charity! Moreover, her nakedness allowed her to be contrasted with the synagogue, a woman who was veiled, and indeed a veil still lies over the heart of the Jews (*apol.alt.Dav.* 8.40–9.45; cf. II Cor. 3:13–16). In the second discussion the unfortunate Uriah is no longer the Devil, but has become the law, the observance of which was terminated when Christ came (9.48). We will consider some of these themes later; for the time being it will be enough to note Ambrose's ability to impose a typological reading, indeed readings, on a narrative passage.

Ambrose's pleasure in constructing such readings was linked to his enthusiasm for the Old Testament. Of the twelve volumes devoted to his exegetical works in a recent edition, those on the Old Testament occupy ten, the exposition of Luke being his only entire work on the New Testament.[21] When Augustine was preparing for baptism he asked Ambrose for advice on what he should read. Ambrose told him to read the prophet Isaiah, but the new convert was baffled by the first passage he read and put the book aside. Later he believed that Ambrose had suggested he read Isaiah because this author announced the gospel and the calling of the gentiles in advance more clearly than others had (*conf.* 9.5.13). But why, one might ask, did Ambrose not recommend the reading of the New Testament, in which the gospel and the calling of the gentiles were not announced in advance but explicitly described?[22] Ambrose, who saw the Old Testament as a deep and dark well, and the New Testament as a flowing stream, found the well more interesting than the stream.[23]

---

21. The balance is slightly redressed by discussions of Paul's letters in various places: he wrote to Irenaeus on parts of Ephesians (*ep.* 16(=76)), while portions of Romans are discussed at *ep.* 63(=73) and *Iac.* 1.3.9–6.26).
22. While Riggi's suggestion (1975): 33 that Ambrose's choice of Isaiah showed psychological insight is not persuasive, one can respect the tradition of learned, almost in-house scholarship from which it comes. *Ps.118* 20.3 suggests the kind of reading of Isaiah which Ambrose may have had in mind.
23. *Ep.ext.coll.* 14(=63).78. Intriguingly, Ambrose felt that Origen's exposition of the New Testament was far inferior to that he gave the Old: *ep.* 65(=75).1.

THE BIBLE

One way of looking at the Bible was to see it as the one, mighty book. Using the language of Genesis, Ambrose described it as a paradise or garden in which God strolled (*ep.* 33(=49).3; cf. Gen. 3:8). He has recurrent images for it: the Bible can be seen as food or a banquet, and as water coming from heaven, whether in the form of rain, dew or snow.[24] Nevertheless, it was not homogeneous, being a sea into which many rivers flowed (*ep.* 36(=2).3). Its parts could be classified as natural, mystical, or moral. Genesis, which described the creation, was natural; Leviticus, which dealt with the mystery of the priesthood, was mystical; while Deuteronomy, which was concerned with organizing human life around the teaching of the law, was moral. In the same way, of the three books which Ambrose believed Solomon had written, Ecclesiastes was about natural things, the Song of Songs mystical things, and Proverbs moral things (*ps.* 36.1). Commenting on four wells dug by the patriarch Isaac, Ambrose suggested that the wells of injustice and hatred stood for moral doctrine, the well of breadth natural things, and the well of the oath mystical things (*Is.* 4.22f, on Gen. 26; the categories are again applied to the books of Solomon). The gospels could be distinguished along the same lines, each evangelist excelling in a different area. John, whose surpassing wisdom found the Word in the beginning and saw the Word with God, dealt in particular with natural wisdom; Matthew, who provided precepts for living, was concerned with morals, and what could be more in accord with reason than the contents of Mark's gospel? Luke's gospel, however, embraced all areas (*Luc.* prol.3f; Ambrose stresses the excellence of the gospel of which he wrote a long exposition). Ambrose returns to the complementary nature of the four gospels when, referring to the soldiers who divided Christ's garments, he observed that, when the pieces of clothing were divided, each evangelist took something: a scarlet cloak could be found in Matthew (27:28); John mentions a purple robe (19:2); Mark simply mentions purple (15:17), while Luke has white clothing (cf. 23:11; Ambrose's discussion (*Luc.* 10.117) is free in its use of texts).

24. Pizzolato (1978) is the best general study; on this point, 27–39.

But it was not merely the case that different books of the Bible had different characteristics. All three areas were found in the Psalms (*ps.* 36.1f), the long psalm 119 tending to be moral rather than mystical (*ps.118* prol.1). Individual texts could be interpreted in more than one way. One of Ambrose's first works, the commentary on Noah, repeatedly contrasts a simple or literal interpretation of texts with a deeper one (e.g. *Noe* 10.33f, 11.37f, 14.49, 15.50), while the first book of his commentary on Abraham provides a moral interpretation and the second covers much of the same ground from a 'deeper' perspective. Verses of Luke could be taken both morally and mystically (e.g. *Luc.* 4.28–35, 50; 5.36,85f), while different parts of one verse could be taken in various ways (*Is.* 4.14). And for Ambrose it is the deeper interpretation, or more precisely the moral and mystical meanings as opposed to the natural, which are of greater interest. The church has two eyes, moral and mystical; while the latter is the more keen, the former is sweeter (*ps.118* 11.7; cf. 13.23). Even here there is a hierarchy, the mystic reality being superior to the moral, as shown by Christ's statement that Mary rather than Martha had chosen the better part (*ps.* 1.42, on Luke 10:41f).

For Ambrose, the Bible was full of signifiers in need of decoding. Everywhere there were 'figures', such as the story of David and Bathsheba, or the appearance of a vision to Peter three times, which was a figure of the mystery of the Trinity (*Spir.S.* 2.105). Outward appearances in the Bible were a reliable guide to reality in the same way as they were in the eucharist, for the canon of the mass which Ambrose used understood the eucharistic offering to be the 'figure' of the body and blood of Jesus Christ.[25] The principle operated from the very beginning of the Bible. The mystery of baptism was so old that it was prefigured (literally 'given a figure in advance') at the origin of the world itself, for at the very beginning, when God created heaven and earth, 'the Spirit was borne over the waters' (Gen. 1:2). Ambrose comments in wonder: 'How old is the mystery!' (*myst.* 9; the role of the Spirit in the creation is treated in more detail at *exa.* 1.8.29). That the Christian sacraments and mysteries

---

25. *Sacr.* 4.5.21; on the consecration as effecting a kind of 'transfiguring' cf. *fid.* 4.10.124; *inc.* 4.23. See further Wilmart (1911).

were older than those of the Jews is an insistent theme (*sacr.* 1.6.23, 4.3.10f; cf. *myst.* 8.44–6). Hence, the Old Testament was significant in that it pointed beyond itself. Of what good is the law, Ambrose enquires, if you do not know the end of the law, if you are not aware of the mystery, if you do not know the *sacramentum* (*ps.118* 13.6)?

. . .

CHRIST IN THE BIBLE

Ambrose has much to say on the importance of Christ's coming. Before him there is winter, but after him flowers (*Is.* 4.35; cf. Song 2:11f). If Moses led the Jewish people through the wilderness, Christ leads through the grain-fields and the lilies, because his passion has made the wilderness flower like the lily (*Is.* 6.56; cf. Deut. 29:5, Matt. 12:1, Song 2:16). Yet he is to be found throughout the Bible. Each testament is a cup from which Christ can be drunk (*ps.* 1.33), while the three measures of meal in which a woman placed yeast signify Christ, hidden in the law, covered over in the prophets, and fulfilled in the preachings of the gospel (*Luc.* 7.188, on Matt. 13:33). Grace and law are so closely linked that they can be seen as one wheel turning inside another (*Iac.* 2.11.49 and *Spir.S.* 3.21.162 on Ez. 1:16). A passage in Job which seems to express power really reveals the mysteries of redemption (*interpell.* 1.4.11); the remission of sins was announced in type through a lamb and completed in truth through Christ (*ep.* 68(=26).6). Perhaps God only rested on the seventh day after the creation of the human being because this was a creature whose sins would be forgiven, or because of the passion of Christ, concerning which he himself said 'I slept, was quiet and rose again' (*exa.* 6.10.76, on Ps. 3:6, placed in the mouth of Christ). The eighth day and circumcision in the Old Testament were given as a sign, 'an indication of something greater, of a future truth' (*ep.* 69(=72).25).

Such an understanding had an important consequence. The Old Testament had become the property of the Christians: the people which had come together out of the nations claimed the law of the Lord and the oracles of the prophets, as well as the New Testament of the Lord, as its own (*ps.* 36.6). The Bible could be divided into two parts, that which announced that Christ would come and that which showed that he had come (*virgb.* 3.3.11), for even today, Moses and Elijah teach the mysteries of the death of Christ (*Luc.* 7.11). In the psalms Christ is born, suffers the passion, rests, rises, ascends into heaven and is seated at the right hand of the Father (*ps.* 1.8); the prophet Zechariah as well as the New Testament reveals the omnipotence of Christ (*inc.* 10.114). Just as the Hebrews of the exodus despoiled the Egyptians when they took away their vessels, the Christian people now have the spoils of the Jews, which means everything which they did not realize they had (*ps.118* 21.12). Even Philo had to confine himself to a moral interpretation of the Bible, being unaware of a spiritual one (*para.* 4.25). Perhaps, Ambrose suggests, the word of God appears as a lamp in the law, and a great light in the gospel. But for the Jews, the lamp was hidden under a bushel. The light of the law was not seen, while for the people arisen from the nations, that is the church, there is light, a light having arisen for the people who sat in the region of the shadow of death (*ps.118* 14.9, cf. Matt. 5:15, Is. 9:2, Luke 2:32). Ambrose takes Christ's advice to beware of the leaven of the Pharisees and Sadducees (Matt. 16:11) to refer to their teaching. But the church has hidden this teaching in its flour, softening the harsh letter of the law with spiritual interpretation and breaking it down as if it were a mill, revealing the secrets of the mysteries within from the husks of the literal text (*paen.* 1.15.82). Ambrose's approach denied the Jews the right understanding of their own scriptures.[26]

So it is that for Ambrose, as already for the writers of the New Testament, the Old Testament was saturated with Christ. When Christ said 'We sang for you and you did not dance, we mourned and you did not weep', he was alluding to his voice as it could be heard in the books of Psalms and Lamentations (*Luc.* 6.5, on Luke 7:32). The words of the psalmist, 'If I ascend into heaven, thou art there, if I descend into hell, thou art there' (Ps. 139:8) showed that Christ was always present with the Father (*Luc.* 2.94), while the verse 'You,

---

26. As has been well said concerning Augustine, the Jews are a 'hermeneutical device to define a premature closure of biblical discourse, short of the new realm of meaning it would enter in the light of the Incarnation' (Markus(1996): 42f).

Lord, have mercy on me and raise me up, and I will requite them' (Ps. 41:11) obviously referred to the resurrection of Christ (*ps.* 40.32). Ambrose reads the Old Testament in a resolutely Christocentric way. Christ's words that the Son of Man would be seen coming in the clouds (Luke 21:27) referred not only to his coming when his presence would fill the whole world, but also to the clouds which veiled the brightness of the mystery, clouds which included Moses, Joshua, Isaiah, Ezekiel and the Song of Songs, for Christ comes in them as well.[27] Ambrose saw the Old Testament as having been stripped of its autonomous coherence by the New.[28] The principle is made clear:

> There is a good deal of obscurity in the writings of the prophets. But if you knock on the door of the scriptures with the hand of your mind and examine carefully those things which are obscure, you will gradually begin to understand the reason for what is said and it will be opened to you by none other than the Word of God. You have read of him in the Apocalypse, that the lamb opened the sealed book which no-one hitherto had been able to open, because the Lord Jesus alone has removed the veil of the riddles of the prophets and the mysteries of the law by means of his gospel; alone, he handed over the key of knowledge and gave it to us so that we may open. (*ps.118* 8.59)

Hence, thinking of Scripture as water, Ambrose can assert that the Jew drinks and is thirsty, while a Christian who drinks cannot feel thirsty; the former is in a shadow, the latter in the truth (*myst.* 8.48).

. . .

TWO MIRACLES

But it was not merely a case of the Old Testament needing to be interpreted in the light of the New, for the New itself contained mysteries which cried out for explanation. Everything in John's gospel was a mystery! (*sacr.* 3.2.11). It will be worth our while examining in some detail Ambrose's treatment of the accounts in the gospels, disquietingly similar in the eyes

---

27. *Luc.* 10.39–42. The metaphor of veiling had particular resonance in Ambrose's time, when emperors were approached through veils: cf. *ep.* 76(=20).4.
28. The helpful formulation of Mazza (1989): 39.

of modern readers, of Christ's feeding 5,000 people and his feeding 4,000 people (*Luc.* 6.69–92). The narratives were not straightforward: why was the larger group fed by five loaves, and the smaller by seven? Ambrose deals with this problem in a roundabout way. He takes the 5,000 as standing for the five senses of the body; as these people were still involved in bodily things, they appropriately received food in the form of five loaves. The 4,000, on the other hand, although still in the body and involved with the world, there being four elements which make up the earth, nevertheless received what Ambrose calls the food of repose. This took the form of seven loaves, for the seventh day had been a day of rest for God after the world had been created in six days. This suggested to Ambrose the seventh beatitude, 'Blessed are the peacemakers, for they shall be called children of God' (Matt. 5:9; similar connections at *Luc.* 5.51). It was therefore not surprising that the 4,000 left behind fragments which filled seven baskets.

Typically, Ambrose does not let matters rest there: if you eat the five loaves in a material way, and then the seven, you will go on to eat eight loaves above the earth, eight being the number of the resurrection. Those who partook of the seven loaves stayed where they were for three days, perhaps having faith in the resurrection on the third day: 'We shall walk for three days so that we may feast with the Lord our God' (Ex. 5:3). According to John, the five loaves were made of barley, a food suitable for carnal people not equal to Elijah, who ate a meal cake made from wheaten flour (I Kings 17:12f). The two groups of people could also be distinguished with respect to their posture, the 5,000 lying on hay and the 4,000 reclining on the ground. Yet again, the comparison is to the disadvantage of the larger group: those who press on the ground are superior to those who lie on grass, Ambrose comments in language which recalls aspects of his thinking on women, for the latter are those whose bodily senses delight in soft things, and indeed 'all flesh is as grass' (Is. 40:6), while those upon the earth, which Ambrose, with a Mediterranean perspective, sees as producing wheat, wine and the olive tree, obtain the food of grace. Further, those who recline enjoy better rest than those who lie. If this were not enough, the former had two fishes and the latter an indefinite number, suggesting that the first group possessed not only the grace of the seven-fold Spirit in the loaves, but also, figuratively, the two testaments. The 4,000 had something else in common with the church, for both could be seen as having been gathered from the four parts of the world.

How are we to understand this exegesis? Correspondences of numbers are made much of, in a way which can appear forced and mechanical. Elsewhere, Ambrose comments that it was fitting for the widow Anna to have given thanks when the baby Jesus was brought into the Temple, for prophecies concerning Christ had already been uttered by Simeon, by a married woman and by a virgin, and there was now a need for a widow, so that neither sex nor status would be excluded. The classification is typically Ambrosian, with the categories of marriage, virginity and widowhood applying to women but not, apparently, to men. But, he continues, it is significant that Anna had been a widow for 84 years, because both seven twelves and two forties seem to indicate a sacred number (*Luc.* 2.62). If this is obscure as symbolism, the mathematics are even harder to understand.[29] His fascination with numbers points towards another characteristic of Ambrose's mind, a taste for synthesis rather than analysis. Faced with an apparent contradiction between the account of Christ healing one blind man in one gospel (Matt. 20:30) and two blind men in another (Luke 18:35), he breezily comments that there is no difference: the one is a type of the gentile people, and the gentiles were descended from Noah's two sons Ham and Japheth (*Luc.* 8.80). Similarly, while an account of Christ healing a man possessed by demons seemed to be discordant with a report that he had healed two men, the accounts were nevertheless concordant with respect to the mystery (*Luc.* 6.44, on Luke 8:27ff and Matt. 8:28ff). At Psalm 60:8, different manuscripts described Moab as the 'hall of hope' or 'pot of my hope', but both terms were applicable to Mary, who was a royal hall in that

---

29. Compare this with a passage in which Ambrose observes that the seventh day indicates the law and the eighth the resurrection. Hence, Hosea's taking a prostitute for 15 denarii (Hos. 3:1) suggested the coinage of the Old and New Testaments. From this it was an easy move to the 15 gradual psalms of David, the 15 degrees the sun climbed when King Hezekiah received an extension to his life (Ambrose's recollection of Is. 38:5, 8 is confused) and the 15 days Paul spent with Peter (Gal. 1:18; *ep.* 68(=26).8, 10).

she was subject to no man but God alone and whose womb was a pot (*inst.virg.* 12.79). The tendency is persistent in Ambrose. Confronted with divergent interpretations of the name Levi, he combines them and seeks to show that they recall each other.[30] He was never nonplussed when his sources attributed different meanings to letters of the Hebrew alphabet. The fourth letter, deleth, could mean either 'fear' or 'birth', but the meanings were in agreement, for birth refers to the things generated in this world, by which we understand bodily and material things which are destined to perish, and so not far removed from fear, indeed giving birth to it (*ps.118* 4.1). Similarly the twelfth letter, labd, could mean 'heart' or 'I keep', but one who has a heart keeps the commands of God, just as Mary kept all the sayings of the Lord in her heart.[31]

So it was that Ambrose often worked at a verbal level.[32] Even such unpromising issues as the precise meaning of the word 'was' in Genesis or 'there' in a psalm will be dealt with by examining usage in other scriptural texts (*exa.* 1.7.25; *ps.* 35.28). The Greek word '*oikumene*' means 'inhabited world'. But as Christ inhabits his followers (II Cor. 6.16), the inhabited world is the church (*ps.* 48.3). The occurrence of the rare Greek word '*pisticos*' at John 12:3 triggers a chain of thought concerning the virtue of faith, a similar word in Greek (*pistis: paen.* 2.7.63). Discussing the text 'You have tried me by fire and iniquity was not found in me' (Ps. 17:3), Ambrose examines the themes of finding and not finding in Scripture. Adam was found when he hid, but the tomb of Moses was not found; Ahab was found, but Elijah was not found, and the wisdom of God says 'The wicked will seek me and not find me' (Prov. 1:28). Hence Jesus was sought and not found, whereas Elijah found that he had done evil in the sight of the Lord. When Saul sought David he could not find him, but David found Saul whom he had not sought (*Nab.* 12.51). What could be more clear?[33]

---

30. Gryson (1966): 218.
31. See *ps.118* 12.1 on Luke 2:51; cf. 5.1 on the letter he and 10.1 on the letter Ioth. Ambrose's interpretations usually differ from those of Jerome (*ep.* 30.5).
32. More than did Augustine: for one example, Moorhead (1997).
33. Commenting on symbolism in the church fathers, Blaise notes: 'The quotations follow one another, not called up by logical necessity, but

COMING DOWN AND GOING UP

Let us consider how Ambrose approaches a recurrent theme in Scripture, that of downwards and upwards motion. The prototype was Christ, whose earthly life is framed in the Creed by the words 'he came down from heaven ... he ascended into heaven'. He thought of Christ as having undertaken a series of leaps: having leaped into the world he went down into the Jordan, ascended the cross, went down into the grave, rose again from the grave, and sat at the right hand of the Father (*Is.* 4.31; cf. *ps.118* 6.6). Ambrose used this understanding as a tool to interpret obscure passages. Hence, 'He shall come down like rain' refers to the Word of God coming down from heaven (*ps.118* 13.24, on Ps. 72:6). While Christ's coming down referred in the first place to his incarnation, it could be applied more broadly, for in his humility Christ went down to the cross and to hell (*ps.118* 20.3). So central was the image of Christ's descent that Ambrose expands scriptural references to incorporate it: it was Christ our peace, descending from heaven, who made both one (*Luc.* 7.141, on Eph. 2:14). Sometimes the descent is implicit: Ambrose goes beyond a parable in assuming that when the good shepherd sought a lost sheep he left ninety-nine other sheep up in the mountains (*Luc.* 7.210). He happily uses the image as a vehicle for the expression of familiar concerns, such as the relationship between Judaism and Christianity: Christ went up from the lower to the higher, that is from the synagogue to the church (*Luc.* 6.52). Further, when Jacob saw in his sleep angels going up and coming down a ladder (Gen. 28:12), he was foreseeing Christ, upon whom hosts of angels descended and ascended (*Iac.* 2.4.16, on John 1:51, although Ambrose reverses the order of the verbs).

But the image does not merely apply to Christ, for it can also be applied to humans. Just as Adam was wounded by robbers as he went down from Jerusalem, people go down with their sins and go up with their merits (*ps.118* 21.5; we

---

by the pure association of words' (c.1994: 17). This is fair comment, but his complaints of 'decadent rhetoric ... the disappearance of classical taste, of moderation, of appropriateness, or simply of good sense' point to lack of sympathy.

shall shortly consider the notion of Adam wounded by robbers). Christ, the one, came down, so that all might go up (*Luc.* 2.91); he came down from heaven to pluck us up from the lake and slime of this world and its muddy swamp (*ps.* 39.2). After Christ had retired to a mountain with his disciples to pray he came down to the throngs, where he found the sick, for every person has to be healed before being able, little by little, to go up the mountain as their strength increases (*Luc.* 5.46, cf. Matt. 8:1f). When the Spirit came down on Christ in the form of a dove, he gave us wings so that we would learn to fly away from land (*ps.118* 14.38). Just as Christ went down, the humble publican went down from the temple (*ps.118* 20.4; cf. Luke 18:14; Ambrose is aware of the elevated position of the temple within Jerusalem). Salim, the name of a place near which John the Baptist baptized, means 'the person going up'. Ambrose takes this to refer to Christ, the one who came down from heaven being the one who also went up into heaven. But a person who lays aside earthly things and is buried with Christ also goes up into heaven, rising with Christ from the death of sin to newness of life (*ps.* 37.3). Reflecting on Job's escape to a mountain, Ambrose observes that going up requires an effort, but coming down is dangerous.[34]

The image could easily be assimilated to baptism. Apposite here was Paul's statement that in baptism we were buried with Christ, and so as he was raised up we should walk in newness of life (Rom. 6:4), and Ambrose implicitly applies the notion of being raised up to believers when he mentions youth being renewed like the eagle's (*paen.* 2.2.8; cf. Ps. 103:5). To be baptized in Christ is to come down in his death and go up in his resurrection (*ps.* 37.10). Elijah's opening of the heavens is a 'type' of baptism, this being a case not of rain coming down but grace going up, and no-one goes up into the kingdom of heaven except through water and spirit (*Hel.* 22.84; cf. John 3:5). Such imagery was given powerful expression in the baptismal liturgy of Ambrose's time, in which the candidate went down into a large font and then came up. Ambrose's *De sacramentis*, largely concerned with baptism, is thus replete with language of going down and coming up:

---

34. *Ep.* 11(=29).22. The expression 'ascendenti ... labor' recalls Vergil *Aeneid* 6.129, which refers to the '*labor*' of a famous ascent.

the going down of the leper Naaman and, later, that of Christ into the River Jordan, the coming down of the Holy Spirit upon the latter, the coming down of the angel into the pool at Bethesda, the fire which came down from heaven at the invocation of Elijah, the iron axe which came up from the waters when Elisha called upon the name of the Lord, and the coming down of the Spirit signified by the tongues of fire at Pentecost all pointed to the mystery of baptism, when the candidates went down into the deep font and came up again. When the newly baptized came to the altar clad in white, the angels looked on and said 'Who is this who comes up from the wilderness all in white?' (cf. Song 8:5, a text also applied to baptism at *ps.118* 16.21). The church, rejoicing in her redemption, says 'My brother has come down into his garden and taken the fruit of his trees' (Song 4:16). Ambrose's theology of the eucharist was such as to steer him away from interpreting it in similar terms: rather than seeing the invocation of the Holy Spirit as effecting the consecration of the elements, he saw this as being achieved by the repetition of words used by Christ at the Last Supper. But here as well, he took note of Christ's being the living bread which came down from heaven (*sacr.* 6.1.4, on John 6:58).

. . .

A PARABLE

Our discussion of language found throughout the Bible can be complemented by analysis of one passage, a parable told by Jesus. According to Ambrose, parables are figures which need to be solved (*ps.* 43.56). Perhaps he was stating the view of Jesus, who did not expect all people to understand the parables he told (e.g. Mark 4:11–13). More than the other gospels, that of Luke contains a rich store of parables. Ambrose was selective in those he chose to discuss in his commentary on Luke, ignoring some of those best-known, such as those of the man who built his house on a rock, the sower who went out to sow, and the rich fool. Others are the subject of careful and detailed commentary.

As an example we may take Ambrose's exegesis of the parable of the Good Samaritan (*Luc.* 7.69–84, on Luke 10:30–35). The man who came down from Jerusalem on the road to Jericho is identified with Adam, who was cast out from paradise into this world. The robbers who attacked him were the angels of night and darkness. Who was the Samaritan, also going down, who healed his wounds? Ambrose believed that the word Samaritan means 'guard'. Hence, the Samaritan can be seen as the Lord, who guarded the little children, and as the Son of Man, who came down from heaven and went up into heaven. The Samaritan bound up the wounds of the man who had been attacked, poured oil and wine on them, and placed him on his beast. But the Lord himself bore our sins (Is. 53:5), and the shepherd placed the weary sheep on his shoulders (Luke 15:5). Perhaps this was a little awkward, but Ambrose points out that humankind has become like a beast (Ps. 49:12), and hence he placed us upon his beast lest we be like the horse or mule (Ps. 32:9), so that he who assumed our body might abolish the infirmities of our flesh. Hence, when the Samaritan brought the wounded man into the stable, it was we who were the beasts. Having cared for him, the Samaritan was not free to remain. On the next day, 'the day which the Lord has made' (Ps. 118:24), he gave the stable hand two denarii, the two testaments which, like coins, have stamped on them the image of the eternal king, before returning to the place from which he had come down (Eph. 4:9f). The reference to a stable hand led Ambrose to think of St Paul, who described himself as counting all things as dung (Phil. 3:8). But the apostle also said 'Christ sent me to evangelize' (Cor. 1:17), and so stable hands are those to whom it is said 'Go into all the world and evangelize every creature, and one who believes and is baptized will be saved' (Mark 16:15f), saved from death and the wound inflicted by the robbers. That stable hand who can cure the wounds of others is blessed; that person is blessed to whom Jesus says 'whatsoever thou spendest more, when I come again, I will repay thee'. A good steward will indeed spend more, and Paul is a good steward, whose words and letters overflow with what he had received, he being a good stable hand in the stable in which 'the ass has known the crib of his lord' (Is. 1:3) and which encloses flocks of lambs so as to keep away rapacious wolves howling at the enclosures. The day on which the Samaritan would repay the stable hand for any extra expenses was the Day of Judgment. From this rambling discussion, Ambrose draws a conclusion: since no-one is more our neighbour than he who heals our wounds, let us love the Samaritan as both our Lord and our neighbour. Let us also love the person who imitates Christ and who has compassion on the want of another in the unity of the body. It is not family relationship which makes a neighbour, asserts Ambrose, but mercy, since mercy arises from nature: nothing arises from nature so much as helping one who shares the same nature. Ambrose's exegesis displays a lack of interest in what many readers have considered the obvious moral point of the parable. For him, its significance was not moral but mystical, and his reading exemplifies his tendency to elevate the mystical interpretation above the moral. So fixed is this interpretation in his mind that he amplifies the text to have the Samaritan coming down. The parable does not indicate whether the Samaritan was going down from Jerusalem or coming up to it, but Ambrose's equating of this figure with Christ led him to apply the familiar image of descent to him. Further, given that Ambrose saw heaven as the celestial Jerusalem, it made excellent sense to understand the incarnation of Christ in terms of his coming down from that city. He loved to play on verbal similarities between different parts of the Bible, and sees a Christological significance in the neighbour. Indeed, just before delivering this parable Christ had taught 'Thou shalt love the Lord thy God' and 'Thou shalt love thy neighbour as thyself', words Ambrose took to refer to the Father and the Son and the incarnation of the latter (*Luc.* 7.69f).

. . .

AMBROSE'S PIETY

Ambrose's treatment of the Bible may not be to everyone's taste. His manoeuvres may too often seem to resemble games of intellectual football, the points he makes random and breathtakingly naive. It has been suggested that Ambrose's allegorical exegesis 'could, and did, make anything mean anything'.[35] But this is to exaggerate. The meanings he drew from texts were invariably connected with Christ. In that he interpreted the Old Testament in the light of the New he did not go beyond the practice of the New Testament itself, and interpreting part of the New in the light of other parts

---

35. Homes Dudden (1935): 459.

of the New, as he did with the parables, was simply an extension of this principle.

Ambrose's exegesis may seem abstract and bloodless. Yet he was a person of personal piety which became stronger as he grew older. Increasingly, Christ was not only the principle which allowed the disparate data of the Bible to be pulled together, but also the object of intense personal devotion. Ambrose often uses the expression 'Lord Jesus', whom he frequently invokes; only rarely does he invert the words to speak, more formally, of 'Jesus the Lord'. His religion is Christocentric: 'Come Lord Jesus, teach us!' (*Luc.* 5.52; cf. *ps.118* 12.4). This emphasis emerges with great clarity in the section of the commentary on Luke dealing with the crucifixion, which almost turns into a preaching of the passion. Apart from a few borrowings from Hilary, as far as we can tell it is completely original. A heavy use of the historic present in preference to the past tense, a strong visual sense[36] and abundant short sentences give the exposition a powerful air of immediacy:

> But now the victor picks up his trophy . . . Now we see the trophy, the victor climbs into his chariot . . . We should consider what kind of thing he climbs into . . . I see him naked . . . And an inscription is written . . . A remarkable inscription! . . . Now look at the garments of Christ, divided . . . The Lord quickly pardons someone, because he is quickly converted to him . . . And the Jews offered vinegar . . . 'And having said this he gave up the ghost.' (*Luc.* 10.107–127)

Ambrose employs the intimacy of the second person singular to invite his readers to accompany him to Christ's tomb: 'You come too' ('*Veni et tu*', *Luc.* 10.138), and a long devotional passage, in which the language of coming down and going up is prominent, is addressed to the Lord Jesus (*Luc.* 10.158–60). In another work, Ambrose observes: 'Christ is all things for you: a stone for you, so that you may be built, and a mountain for you, so that you may go up' (*interpell.* 4.4.17), and signs of the personal nature of his faith are frequent throughout his works.[37] Discussing the expression

---

36. Compare Helena's inability to believe herself redeemed unless she saw the cross (*ob.Theod.* 43).
37. See for example *Luc.* 5.27, 52, and the words attributed to Christ at the end of *bon.mort.*

'I am yours' used in Ps. 119:94 ('*tuus sum*'), he observes how hard it is to say these words. Various vices claim us, saying 'You are mine', and psychological conditions say 'He's mine', but Ambrose can say with truth 'I am yours', and hear from the Lord Jesus the words 'You are mine' (*ps.118* 12.37–42).

. . .

STRUCTURAL COHERENCE: THE CASE OF SHECHEM

Moreover, for all the apparent randomness of Ambrose's approach and the sense he often gives of playing fast and loose with the Bible, his approach is informed by structures, and subtle connections run throughout his work. The point may be illustrated by his discussions of a place-name often referred to in the Bible, Shechem. He seems to have taken as his starting point the interpretation given it by Philo, who took it to mean 'shoulder' or 'shouldering', seeing in it a symbol of toil.[38] Discussing a reference to Shechem at Gen. 12:6, Ambrose broadens Philo's interpretation, observing that it means 'shoulder' or 'neck', and hence the completion of a task which has been set, an interpretation he neatly supports by quoting an apposite reference to a shoulder at Gen. 49:15 (*Abr.* 1.2.5; also 2.3.8). But when Shechem is mentioned at Gen. 37:14, Ambrose takes it to mean 'shoulders' or 'back', which enables him to apply it to those not converted to the Lord who flee from his face and avert themselves (*Ios.* 3.9, the verb '*convertere*' being used so as to recall its literal sense of 'turn towards'). When Shechem is mentioned as having been given by Jacob to his youngest son Joseph in the Septuagint text of Gen. 48:22, Ambrose takes it to mean 'shoulders', and hence 'works', which leads him to remark that Jacob chose the holy Joseph as the heir of good works before his other sons, since his brothers were unable to equal his works (*patr.* 3.11; see further *ep.* 4(=27).16).

Doubtless there is some straining in the ways the original meaning is extended, although it is easy to see how the meanings of 'back' and 'works' could be taken to follow from the primary meaning of 'shoulder'. More interestingly,

---

38. Shoulder: *De mutatione nominum* 193; *Quod deterius potiori insidiari soleat* 9. Shouldering: *De migratione Abrahami* 221, *Legum allegoria* 3.25. In all cases but the last the meaning of 'toil' is supplied.

Ambrose extends the meaning of the word to 'one who goes up', and in this sense applies it to the church. His discussion of the phrase 'I will divide Shechem' (Ps. 60:6) includes the following passage:

> Shechem is the church, for Solomon chose her, she whose growing affection he could discern. Shechem is Mary, whose soul was pierced and divided by the sword of God. Shechem is, according to its meaning, one who goes up. As to who it is who goes up, listen to what is said concerning the church: 'Who is this, who comes up all white, leaning on her brother?' (*interpell.* 4.4.16, quoting Song 8:5)

Ambrose immediately identifies Shechem with the church. The move may seem gratuitous, but he goes on to allude to his grounds for making it. Behind the reference to Solomon stands a well-known incident in which that king proposed to divide in two a baby claimed as a son by two women, so as to establish who the true mother was,[39] and the verbal correspondence between the dividing of the baby and the dividing of Shechem mentioned in the psalm is precisely the kind of connection Ambrose loved to make between different parts of the Bible. That the judgment of Solomon involved two women may also be relevant, for as we shall see Ambrose frequently took women mentioned in the Bible to represent the church, just as, when two people occur in one story, as in the case of the two women who appeared before Solomon, he sometimes sees the better one as the church and the worse as the synagogue (below, pages 106ff, 183). Hence, Ambrose's interpretative strategies allowed him to work from the story of Solomon, to which he merely alludes, to the church. The case of Mary was straightforward, for a reference in the Bible to her soul being pierced by a sword (Luke 2:35) made the notion of being divided appropriate to her, and as it happened Ambrose thought that Mary represented the church (below, page 107f). When he goes on to connect Shechem with going up he resumes one of his favourite themes, and as we have seen he frequently sees biblical references to going down and coming up as applying to baptism; indeed, we have already encountered him

---

39. 1 Kings 3:16–28; the word 'divide' occurs at v.25. Ambrose explicitly discusses the judgment of Solomon at *off.* 2.8.44–7.

interpreting the verse of the Song quoted here in this light (above, page 94), just as we have seen him applying a reference to a woman bathing to the church receiving the washing of baptism (above, page 94). Ambrose's brief comments on Shechem therefore turn out to be by no means as disjointed as they may appear at first sight. They are informed by structuring themes and metaphors which allowed him to impose on the texts ready-made frameworks of interpretation.

. . .

ALLEGORY ACROSS THE CENTURIES

Ambrose's approach to the Bible is not exceptional. Many readers across the centuries, not all of them in the classical or Judeo-Christian traditions, have interpreted texts allegorically,[40] and such an approach was to predominate in the middle ages. In recent centuries many commentators on the Bible, especially those influenced by the Reformation and Enlightenment, have turned away from it. But fashions change, and Ambrose's approach to the Bible appears more cogent now, for modern literary theory encourages us to think of texts as being the property of their readers rather than their authors. This change in the balance of power between writer and reader was partially anticipated by Ambrose, when he remarked that, while the Bible nourishes us, we in turn can nourish one of the prophets when we give him our faith, the degree of progress we have made, our minds, our feelings, and the support of our hearts, which we have placed in the light of the gospel (*ep.ext.coll.* 14(=63).80), and has made it respectable for different readers, or the same reader, to see more than one meaning in a text. Hence, when Ambrose interprets the Song of Songs or the parable of the Good Samaritan in two ways it does not follow that one, at least, of them is 'wrong', for there may be an indefinite number of valid readings. Doubtless Ambrose would have parted company with modern

40. A Muslim theologian, the Baghdad scholar Ghazali, ob. 1111 (in his *Revivifaction of the sciences of religion*), observed that 'according to the opinion of some scholars, every verse [in the Qur'an] can be understood in sixty thousand ways, and that what still remains unexhausted (of its meaning) is still more numerous' (quoted in Peters (1990): 148).

literary critics in that he believed in an objective, supernatural reality to which the Bible gave access; for him, the lack of an authoritative reading was connected with its very authority.[41] But modern practice open to multiple readings has revivified a tradition of which Ambrose was one of the leading exponents.

---

41. Acute comments in Markus (1996): 9.

Chapter 4

CHURCH, STATE, HERETICS AND PAGANS

Starting from lowly beginnings, the Christian church seemed to carry all before it. Catholic authors of antiquity often give the impression that the success of their cause was inevitable, and their self-confidence was certainly one of the reasons for its success. But some of the apparent optimism of Ambrose and others was an exercise in putting on a brave face, for many chose to remain outside the church. In a parable told by Jesus, three people refused to come to the banquet prepared by God, and Ambrose knew just who they were: the pagans, Jews and heretics, who were excluded from the kingdom of heaven.[1] Throughout his episcopate, Ambrose devoted much energy to the groups who rudely turned down their invitations. Dealings with them had been complicated by the adoption of Christianity as the official religion of the empire, which necessarily implicated the state in the church's relations with those outside it, and Ambrose found that those in a position to exercise power could not always be relied upon to act as he would have hoped. In this chapter we shall examine important dealings Ambrose had with heretics and pagans in the 380s, and the dealings with the state which these brought in their wake.

. . .

THE SUCCESS OF THE CHURCH

Never has the standing of the Christian church within society changed so rapidly as it did in the fourth century. It opened with the last great persecution of the church (303–311). The

---

1. *Luc.* 7.197–200, on Luke 14:12ff.

impact of this was particularly clear in Rome, where, of the three popes who died during the period, the first weakened under persecution and the following two died after being banished from the city. Moreover, because of difficulties in securing replacements, during this period the church of Rome functioned without a bishop for over four years. It was a shaky start to the century, but early in the reign of Constantine the 'Edict of Milan' (313), which proclaimed full toleration of religion, was promulgated. With great speed, the Christian community moved from worshipping in house churches and catacombs to the imposing basilicas which were built, often with state funds. Imperial patronage combined with a strong sense of its own worth to make the standing of the church in society increasingly strong, particularly after the attempts of the Emperor Julian the Apostate (361–363) to revive the cause of paganism failed.

So it was that, from the vantage point of Ambrose, the history of the church appeared as a wonderful success story. While the martyrs held an important and in some ways growing place in its folk memory and cultic practice, by his time its leaders could look on the past with satisfaction and the present with complaisance. Despite the various waves and storms which sometimes assailed the church (*Noe* 1.1), Ambrose could interpret the request of the Gadarenes that Christ would depart from them as a prophecy that the whole earth would be filled with the fear of God (*ps.118* 10.22, on Luke 8:37): 'So great has been the progress of the church!' (*ps.118* 17.19). Everything had changed for the better, he believed. The church, seen as the moon in the Old Testament, had at first been hidden in the darkness, but little by little, as she waxed, she had come to shine brightly.[2]

There were good grounds to accept such optimistic assessments. Further, the balance of power between the church and the state was changing, the latter being often awkward in its dealings with strong bishops. Athanasius, the bishop of Alexandria (328–373) who was a strong leader of the Nicene party, emerged triumphant in his struggles against emperors, despite being exiled five times. Moreover, cracks were appearing in the facade of Roman political power. To the persistent

---

2. *Ep.* 73(=18).23f; cf. *patr.* 3.13. Ambrose frequently uses the moon as an image of the church, e.g. *exa.* 4.7.29, 8.32.

problems of rebellions led by generals and tensions between emperors, which sometimes boiled over into war, was added the defeat of the Romans by Germanic troops at the battle of Adrianople in 378. This triggered a series of interconnected events which were to culminate, just under a hundred years later, in the deposition of the last emperor in the West. No-one in the fourth century could have foreseen this outcome, but a sense of unease was already developing during the episcopate of Ambrose.

. . .

THE STATE

In its own right, the empire did not particularly concern Ambrose. To be sure, he saw its interests and those of the church as sometimes coinciding. Towards the end of his life Queen Fritigil of the Marcomanni, a tribe living near the Danube, wrote to him asking what she should believe. Ambrose sent her a catechism and advised her to persuade her husband to keep peace with the Romans, whereupon the king handed himself and his people over to the Romans (*VAmb.* 36). But in general Ambrose was nonchalant about the empire, as his treatment of the census held by the Romans referred to in the second chapter of Luke's Gospel shows. In the early third century the census had been discussed by Hippolytus, who stressed the opposition between the kingdom of Christ and the Roman empire, while conversely Origen, at about the same time, saw a providential connection between the coming of peace to the Roman world and the birth of Christ. Although Ambrose touches on the latter theme,[3] his handling of the topic suggests a view of the empire which was neither negative nor positive.[4] Doubtless this degree of coolness was more easily attained after Christianity's recent successes, but Ambrose's treatment of the biblical passage points towards a fundamental lack of interest in the Roman empire.

---

3. Commenting on the words 'He maketh wars to cease unto the end of the earth' (Ps. 46:9), Ambrose observes that when Augustus came to power wars ceased, which allowed the sending of the apostles throughout the world (*ps.* 45.21).
4. Buchheit (1984). Ambrose discusses the census at *Luc.* 2.36f.

His loyalties were directed elsewhere. As we have seen, he saw bishops as having a nobility which placed them before those holding the highest offices of the state (above, page 35); for him, Job was a witness more considerable than he would have been had he been master of the Roman empire (*interpell.* 2.3.9). His imagination loved to dwell on the heroism of the martyrs, like St Pelagia, when persecuted by the state (below, page 134), and at different times in his life he identified himself with the biblical figures of Elijah, Nathan and John the Baptist, who had all sturdily rebuked kings guilty of injustice. Nothing could bestow greater honour on an emperor than his being called a son of the church, Ambrose informed one emperor in language which would have astonished earlier sovereigns; the emperor, he felt, was within the church and not above it (*ep.* 75a(=21a).36). Such a line enabled enemies to accuse him of wanting to be more powerful than the emperor (*ibid.* 30). They could take a more diplomatic tone: 'You rule over all things', a pagan senator soothingly wrote to Valentinian II (Ambrose *ep.* 72a(=17a).18).

The visible weakening of the military position of the empire during Ambrose's episcopate caused him little alarm. Indeed, such was his lack of interest in earthly structures that the possibility that the end of the world was at hand was a matter of small concern. He felt that the biblical name Gog was to be identified with the Goths and that, with the Goths and Armenians having come to believe, the gospel had been preached throughout the world, and so the end of the world might be anticipated (*Luc.* 10.14, an unexpected comment for the Goths had been converted to Christianity in an anti-Nicene form; *fid.* 2.16.138; cf. *Luc.* 10.10). Wiser heads disagreed with Ambrose on both these matters,[5] but the coolness with which he could contemplate the destruction of the whole earth and the end of the world (*exc.fr.* 1.30) suggests a degree of distance from it.

---

5. His identification of Gog with Goth was accepted by neither Jerome (*CCSL* 72:11; 75:480, the latter passage contradicting an unnamed Ambrose) nor Augustine (*civ.dei* 20.11). Similarly, Augustine was more cautious about the spread of the gospel (*ep.* 199.46f; cf. 197, citing Matt. 24:14). Augustine identified the signs in the sun, moon and stars (Luke 21:25) with the church (*ep.* 199.38f).

THE CHURCH AS FEMALE

While Ambrose was not greatly concerned about the institution of the state, he had a lot to say about the church, in common with other early Christian thinkers. For some of these, such as Cyprian and Augustine, the subject was one for reflection in its own right. In the works of Ambrose the church is not examined systematically, but the topic occurs frequently and is treated consistently. Two themes are recurrent.

The first of these involves the identification of individuals mentioned in the Bible with the church. There is a large crop of such people in Genesis, the first of them being Eve, and it will be worth our while examining closely a passage, dense with biblical quotations and allusions, in which Ambrose considers her in relation to the church.

After the creation of Eve, Adam referred to her as 'bone of my bones and flesh of my flesh', and said 'she shall be called woman, since she was taken from man' (Gen. 2:23). This was a great mystery (Eph. 5:32), that the two will be one flesh and that a man shall leave his father and mother and be joined to his wife (Eph. 5:31, Gen. 2:24, Matt. 19:5), just as we are members of his body, of his flesh and of his bones (Eph. 5:30 referring to Christ's body). Who is this 'man', on account of whom the 'woman' leaves her parents? The church left her parents when she was brought together from among the gentiles, in accordance with the words of the prophet, 'forget your people and the home of your father' (Ps. 45:10), and the man is he of whom John the Baptist spoke: 'After me comes a man who was made before me' (John 1:30). God took a rib from Adam's side as he slept (Gen. 2:21), and this man is the one who slept, was quiet and rose again, since the Lord received him (Ps. 3:5). The rib stands for power, since, when a soldier opened up the side of the crucified Christ, water and blood poured out (John 19:43) for the life of the world (Mark 14:24, John 6:51). And, Ambrose continues after developing another point which need not concern us, this rib is Eve, the mother of all the living (Gen. 2:22, 3:20). Christ's words after the resurrection, 'Why seek ye the living among the dead?' (Luke 24:5), mean that those who are without him and do not share in life are dead; they do not participate in him, he being life (John 14:6). Hence, the church is the mother of the living (Gal. 4:26; *Luc.* 2.86).

It cannot be denied that this is a difficult passage. The argument is jumpy, compressed and allusive, its force is weakened by Ambrose failing to render a key word in a way which would capture an important pun in the original Hebrew,[6] and at one stage it simply fails to work, for the argument depends upon it being a woman who leaves her parents, but the passage in St Paul which Ambrose is following (Eph. 5:31) indicates that it is a man who leaves his parents and is joined to his wife. Yet the structures of Ambrose's thinking are clear. Adam is identified with Christ. The sleep of Adam during the creation of Eve is connected with a reference in a psalm to sleep, which early Christian commentators saw as a prophecy of the death of Christ, and the flowing of life-giving water and blood from the pierced side of Christ is paralleled by the emergence of the mother of all the living from the rib of Adam. Hence Ambrose can assert that Adam is to Eve as Christ is to the church, Eve and the church having being 'built' to help Adam and Christ (*Luc.* 2.87); that Eve had been formed to help the human, just like the church (*ps.* 39.11); that Adam and Eve symbolize, respectively, the soul and the body (see above, page 56f) and the church and Christ (*Luc.* 4.66, where the latter pair of items seem in the wrong order); and that, just as Eve did not take a second husband, so the church cannot know a second husband (*vid.* 14.89).

Eve is not the only person in the Bible Ambrose sees as symbolizing the church. We have already encountered Bathsheba in this role (see above, page 82f), and to her may be added other figures from the Old Testament.[7] The commentary on Luke is full of such people, foremost among them Mary. Indeed, just as St Paul suggested that Christ was

---

6. The common English translation of Gen. 2:23, 'She shall be called woman because she was taken out of man', reproduces a pun in the original Hebrew (*ishshah . . . ish*), but the play on words could not be brought out in the Greek of LXX, from which Ambrose would have been working. This is a pity, for the Latin of the Vulgate catches it (*virago . . . de viro*).
7. Sarah: *Abr.* 1.5.38; Rebekah: *Abr.* 1.9.90, *ps.118* 4.14; Rachael: *ps.* 37.10; the widow of Zarephath: *vid.* 3.14. The list could be extended.

the last Adam (I Cor. 15:45), Ambrose felt that Mary was the second Eve, from which it followed that she would have inherited Eve's status as representing the church. If the church was noteworthy for being without spot, despite being married (Eph. 5:27), so was Mary (*Luc.* 2.7). When Christ commended Mary to John, whom Ambrose sees as the youngest of his followers, she resembled the church, who had earlier been joined to the older people but had now chosen the society of a younger people (*Luc.* 10.134). 'How beautiful,' Ambrose exclaims, 'are the things which are prophesied concerning Mary in the figure of the church!' (*inst.virg.* 14.89). In his commentary on Luke, Ambrose sees the woman with the flow of blood, the woman who entered the house of Simon the leper, the woman who was bent over, the woman who placed yeast in the flour, the woman who lost a piece of silver, and the wife who was not to be put away by her husband as representing the church. If the widow who contributed two mites to the treasury of the Temple is not so interpreted in this work, where she is scarcely mentioned (at 7.157, out of sequence), she is in a letter (*ep.* 68(=26).5). Persistently, Ambrose sees the sinful woman who anointed the head of Christ as the church.[8] Revelling in paradoxes, he describes the church as a chaste prostitute, a sterile widow and a fruitful virgin (*Luc.* 3.23). The images may seem chaotic, but Ambrose's thinking on this topic is structured. Every one of the biblical personages he sees as denoting the church is a woman.

Female identity was shared by another person in the Bible Ambrose came to identify with the church, the bride in the Song of Songs.[9] After drawing on this book in his first work, the *De virginibus*, he showed no particular interest in it until the mid-380s, when he wrote commentaries on two portions of it.[10] One of these was in a book on Isaac and the soul, half of which Ambrose devoted to commenting on the greater part of the Song of Songs (2:1–8:6). Here he followed an interpretation developed by Origen, who treated the female character of the Song as standing for the soul. But she could

---

8. *Ep.ext.coll.* 1(=41).12; *Hel.* 10.37; *Luc.* 6.14.
9. See on this Dassmann (1966).
10. The *De virginitate*, another work probably written at this time, also includes a commentary on part of the Song (4:7–5:2).

be understood in another way. The theme of Yahweh being the bridegroom of his chosen people Israel, already found in some parts of the Old Testament (Ps. 45, Hos. 2), came, in some currents of Jewish thought, to be imposed on the man and woman in the Song, whose mutual love was felt to represent that between Yahweh and his people.[11] The notion of the chosen people being the bride of Yahweh was reworked by St Paul, who, in a famous passage, described the church as being married to Christ (Eph. 5:31f). The way was therefore open for Christian writers to go back to the Song and read it in this light, and this was done in the third century by Tertullian and Hippolytus. Ambrose was particularly indebted to the latter.

Despite his tendency to be cool towards wives, Ambrose relished this interpretation. It occurs in some of his earliest writing (*exc.fr.* 2.118f), and was sustained. The *Exameron* alludes to various passages of the Song which mention the woman, all but one of which Ambrose takes to refer to the church.[12] The interpretation finds its fullest expression in the massive commentary on Psalm 119. When Ambrose reached the last verse, 'I have gone astray like a lost sheep', he added, as a coda to the work, a commentary on part of the Song (8:5–14, taking it up at almost exactly the point where he left it in the *Isaac*, even though he goes on to offer a different interpretation). Here, although Ambrose sees the last verse of the psalm as indicating both 'the soul and the church', he tends to identify the female figure of the Song with the church. The commentary concludes by discussing words which Ambrose, following the translations of Symmachus and Aquila against the Septuagint, believes were addressed to the woman in the Song, 'Thou that dwellest among the gardens' (Song 8:13). He observes that the church began in a garden, Eve having been created in Eden, whereas Christ later suffered in a garden (John 19:41). Coming at the

---

11. Hence the use of the Song in IV Ezra: 'Out of all the flowers I have chosen thee one lily... out of all the birds that have been created thou hast chosen for thyself one dove' (IV Ezra 5:24, 26; cf. Song 2:2, 1:15 and 4:1).
12. The exception is at 6.6.39, where the 'beautiful among women' of Song 1:8 is seen as the soul. The commentary of Basil, on which Ambrose drew extensively, applies none of these texts to the church.

end of a long commentary, the conclusion may have an air of bathos, and it certainly constitutes an awkward touchdown, but the point is a neat one. It allows the church and Christ to be brought together by means of gardens.

We have already seen Ambrose apply to virgins the sexual longing described in the Song of Songs (above, page 53f). Now he applies its opening verse to the church:

> Think of a virgin, long betrothed and fittingly on fire with a passionate love. She has learned from trustworthy people of the many and outstanding exploits of the one she loves. Often, as her desires remained unfulfilled, she found the delays intolerable, and she did everything in her power to see the one to whom she was betrothed. One day she obtained what she had desired. Full of joy at the unexpected coming of her betrothed, she was not interested in formal greetings or exchanging words, but immediately demanded what she wanted. In the same way the holy church, betrothed in paradise at the beginning of the world, prefigured in the flood, announced through the law, and called by the prophets, had been awaiting the redemption of humans, the beauty of the gospel and the coming of her beloved for so long. Impatient at the delay she rushes at his lips, saying 'Let him kiss me with the kiss of his mouth', and, delighted with his kisses, adds 'The wonderful things you give are better than wine!' (*ps.118* 1.4, quoting Song 1:2)

Ambrose's view of the church was one which may seem strange today. He did not see it primarily as an association of people who chose to come together because of shared beliefs, nor as an institution to be defined in terms of a hierarchical structure, although the status he attributed to its clergy, particularly its bishops, points in that direction.[13] The female personages who, time and time again, are identified with the church, point to its fundamental and objective reality, that of being the wife or bride of the Lord. It is a powerful concept, although as we shall see, these female figures were not the only ones of religious significance in the time of Ambrose.

---

13. 'Where is the church except where the staff and grace of bishops flower?' (*Is.* 8.64, with an implied reference to the staff of the priest Aaron, cf. Num. 17:8).

POLEMIC AGAINST ANTI-NICAEANS

The doctrine promulgated by the council of Nicaea concerning the relationship between the Father and the Son was destined to become the standard Christian position. But in the fourth century many found it difficult to adopt a thoroughgoing Nicene approach, and recent work has demonstrated both the variety of positions adopted by anti-Nicene thinkers, who cannot by any means all be termed 'Arians', and their numerical strength,[14] things for which the triumphalist writings of the pro-Nicene authors of the period had not prepared us. Constantius II, the emperor when Auxentius became bishop of Milan, was sympathetic to an anti-Nicene position, and gatherings of bishops at Sirmium (357) and Rimini (359) had produced statements of belief contrary to that expressed at Nicaea. The emperor in the West when Ambrose became bishop, Valentinian I, was easy-going in matters of religion and disinclined to take a strong stand, while his brother Valens, the eastern emperor, increasingly came to sympathize with the anti-Nicaeans. Ambrose's caution when he became bishop was therefore prudent. He accepted the validity of the ordinations conducted by his predecessor, and his early writings, while pro-Nicene, are by no means polemical. Only as time passed did Ambrose come to express a strong position on the Trinity, and this was because of circumstances beyond his control.

As far as we can tell from the biography written by Paulinus, Ambrose's becoming bishop of Milan was an act of communal consensus, and he did not seek to disturb this. His early commentaries on Genesis reveal him as Nicene in his convictions, but by no means strident. He corrects Philo when he considers him to minimize the importance of the 'word' Christians took to refer to the Son,[15] and he let his feelings be known in an intrusive passage within his first oration on Satyrus (*exc.fr.* 1.12–14), yet the context is not polemical.[16]

---

14. See in particular Williams (1995).
15. At *Cain* 1.8.32, for example, he asserts, on the basis of John 5:17, that the Word of God is not a work, 'as a certain person maintains', but one who works (see further *SAEMO* 2/1: 229 n. 10).
16. It has widely been believed, on the basis of a passage in Paulinus (*VAmb.* 11), that he visited Sirmium in the early years of his episcopate

But by 381 an anti-Nicene bishop, Julian Valens, was active in Milan, and when another bishop of that persuasion, Palladius, wrote shortly afterwards that there had been no successor to Auxentius in the see of Milan,[17] he implicitly denied Ambrose's status as bishop of the city. In an unambiguous show of independence, Valens conducted ordinations (*ep.ext.coll.* 4(=10).10). Another unwelcome clerical interloper was Ursinus, the defeated candidate in the bitter struggle for the papacy in 366, and Ambrose was later to claim that Ursinus and Valens had plotted against the peace of the church in Milan (*ep.ext.coll.* 5(=11).1).

Other arrivals were more important. On 17 November 375 Valentinian I died of a stroke, angered beyond endurance by the arrogance of envoys sent by a Germanic people. Power in the West passed to his elder son in Gaul, the sixteen-year-old Gratian, who had already been proclaimed emperor in 367. Elsewhere, a group of officials proclaimed his younger brother, the four-year-old Valentinian II, emperor, although he was destined never to enjoy effective power. The Nicaeans had no reason to welcome the accession of Gratian, whose religious position was unclear, and their opponents could be cheeky. According to Paulinus, during Gratian's reign two chamberlains posed Ambrose a question concerning the incarnation while he was preaching. They promised to return another day to hear his reply, but when the day came and the bishop and people were waiting for them they left town in a large carriage, from which they fell to their deaths. Nevertheless, Ambrose gave his discourse, which Paulinus states was later published as his work on the incarnation of the Lord (*VAmb.* 18). By telling this story Paulinus may have been seeking to provide a plausible context for the origin of this book, but, whatever the origin of the work may have been, it reveals Ambrose's need to argue for the Nicene position in Milan.

Military developments strengthened the position of the anti-Nicaeans in the city. In the spring of 378 Gratian marched eastwards to help Valens fight the Goths, who were causing problems after being admitted onto Roman territory

---

to consecrate a Nicene bishop for that see, but it is highly likely that no such visit occurred (Williams (1995): 122–26).

17. *Scolies*, ed. Gryson, 322.

two years previously. But in August, while Gratian was still at Sirmium, the battle of Adrianople was fought, and Valens was killed. There were immediate short-term results. On 19 January 379 Theodosius, a military man in his early thirties, was elevated to be the new emperor in the East, while in the West the young Valentinian and his mother, Justina, left the now exposed city of Sirmium to take up residence at Milan. Justina was a strong supporter of the anti-Nicaeans, and one of the city's churches was made available for their use.

It was against the background of the accession of Gratian and the coming to Milan of Bishop Valens, Ursinus and, in particular, Justina and Valentinian, that Ambrose wrote his most sustained purely theological work, the *De fide*. He wrote in response to an initiative of Gratian, which he saw in biblical terms. Just as the queen of the South and King Hiram came to Solomon, so now the 'holy emperor Gratian', imitating the royalty of ancient times, wished to hear of Ambrose's faith. But Ambrose recoiled from the implications of his comparison: while he was no Solomon, Gratian was not the ruler of one people but the emperor of the whole world, who had decreed that Ambrose was to express his faith in a book, not with a view to acquiring knowledge but to give his approval (*fid.* 1 prol. 1). We may take these words at face value: Gratian had commissioned the work not to be instructed by a great bishop, but to learn of the faith of Ambrose. Indeed, Gratian may have commissioned the *De fide* in response to charges of heresy which enemies in Milan or elsewhere had laid against the bishop.[18]

The first two books of the *De fide* were probably presented to Gratian in March 380.[19] Never one to pull his punches, Ambrose expressed his convictions in a robust way, asserting that the bishops meeting at Nicaea had taken heresy away from the whole world (1.1.5). But the anti-Nicene community in Milan itself disproved this hearty claim, and Bishop Palladius of Ratiaria published a refutation of Ambrose's arguments. As so often, the arguments advanced by a loser within the Christian tradition are hard to establish, but we know that Palladius sought to refute Ambrose's charge that anti-Nicaeans held that the Father and the Son were 'unlike',

18. So Williams (1995): 145f.
19. McLynn (1994): 102.

and accused him of failing to distinguish the things which belonged to the Father and to the Son as individuals. Hence, Ambrose produced what are now books three to five of the *De fide*. They present a theologically more sophisticated case. Having read books by anti-Nicene authors, Ambrose abandons the argument that 'Arians' teach that Christ is unlike the Father, and expands on the application of the key notion of substance to the debate, even if it is not worked through clearly (esp. 3.14.122ff). But the presentation of material in these books is confused, doubtless because they are based, as Ambrose's written work often was, on sermons.[20] While Gratian was in Milan for Easter in 381, Ambrose produced a work on the Holy Spirit which the emperor had sought, the *De Spiritu sancto*, in which he drew on the best available Greek scholarship, in particular the writings of Athanasius, Didymus, Origen and, most remarkably, a book by Basil on the Holy Spirit which had only been written in 374/75.

It must be said that the *De fide* fails to engage with its opponents. While it abuses Arius it fails to cite him, nor does it discuss the thoughts of subsequent anti-Nicene thinkers such as Aetius and Eunomius. Ambrose claimed he could not be bothered to read these authors, as they all said the same things (*fid.* 1.6.43ff). But this was quite untrue, for while his opponents were united in their dislike of the theology of Nicaea there was a good deal of variation in their thinking. Ambrose's opponents were not impressed, and his thinking on the Trinity has attracted the scorn of some modern scholars.[21] Some of the knock-down arguments from the Bible on which he relies are remarkably forced. Seeking to show that there was not a time when Christ did not exist, he quotes words spoken of Jesus after he had died: 'Truly, he was the son of God' (Matt. 27:54), and comments '"He was", says the centurion, and the Arian says "He was not!"' (*fid.* 1.17.113f). When someone addressed Christ as 'good teacher' he replied 'Why do you call me good? No-one is good except God alone.' This exchange may be thought to

---

20. See 3.17.142, 4.10.119, and perhaps 5 prol. 8f. Such carelessness in preparing a work destined for the eyes of the emperor is striking.
21. Hanson suggests that 'too often his arguments are, as rational discussion, beneath contempt' (1988): 669. Homes Dudden was more positive (1935): 195.

create difficulties for those arguing for the deity of Jesus, but according to Ambrose, by not denying the title 'good' Jesus indicated that he really was God (*fid.* 2.1.15–2.32, on Luke 18:19; also *Luc.* 8.65; *virgb.* 3.1.3). In another work, Ambrose argued that Peter's reply to those who accused him of being a follower of Jesus, 'I do not know the man' (Matt. 26:72), showed that Peter did not know him as a man but as God, just as he correctly denied being a disciple of the man (John 18:17), for he was not a disciple of a man but of Christ.[22]

If Ambrose's writing on this topic has any strength, it arises from the qualities we have observed in his writing on other topics. His way of approaching the Bible allowed him to see it as being full of pointers to the Trinity. As early as the creation, the spirit of God 'which moved upon the face of the waters' (Gen. 1:2) was not air or breath, but the Holy Spirit, and the statement that 'In the beginning God created heaven and earth' (Gen. 1:1) necessarily referred to Christ, given that 'all things were made by him and without him was not anything made that was made' (John 1:3). Hence, in the very making of the world, the working of the Trinity shone forth (*exa.* 1.8.29). In one of his earliest works, Ambrose discusses an incident when Abraham lifted up his eyes and saw three men. He invests the event with Trinitarian significance: it was God who appeared to Abraham and shone before him, and the person in whose presence God shone saw the Trinity (*Abr.* 1.5.33; cf. *Cain* 1.8.30). Yet Ambrose's remorseless piling up of such data can weary the reader. Points which seem to be unrelated are forcefully adduced, one after the other, perhaps reflecting Ambrose's experience in the courts. As so often, the heart of his case is to be found not in the evidence but in the structures which underlie it. His understanding of the Trinity, and the difficult notion of how one being and two others derived from it could be equal, is expressed in three recurrent images.

'How many things has Jerusalem the virgin made!' asserted Jeremiah, according to the translation Ambrose read. 'Her

---

22. *Luc.* 10.82. In his commentary on Matthew, Jerome dismissed this point as frivolous (*CCSL* 77:262), while Augustine thought it perverse (*PL* 35:1810). Elsewhere, Ambrose accepts that Peter erred in denying Christ (*ob.Theod.* 19).

breasts, fed from the rock, will not be lacking, nor snow from Lebanon, nor will the water which is carried by a strong wind depart from her' (cf. Jer. 18:13f). Ambrose took this opaque text to refer to the virgin's being refreshed by the springs of the Trinity, for according to the apostle 'the rock is Christ' (1 Cor. 10:4), while brightness is from God and a river is from the Spirit (*virgb.* 1.5.22). As so often, Ambrose's words have more force than is immediately obvious, for when St Paul spoke of Christ as the rock he had in mind the rock struck by Moses, from which flowed water (Ex. 17:6), and elsewhere Ambrose discusses Christ's description of himself as a source of water (e.g. *ps.* 35.22 on John 4:14) and suggests that Christ was the fountain which watered paradise (*para.* 3.13). The image is thus one of the Son and the Spirit flowing like water, while God, that is the Father, is seen as snow, from which water flows as it melts. Elsewhere, Ambrose sees the Spirit as a river flowing from the throne of God (*Spir.S.* 3.154), and both the Father and the Son as springs, the Spirit being water coming from a spring, or a river. Nevertheless, Ambrose was aware that this image could be pressed too far: all three persons of the Trinity could be said to be both springs and rivers (*Spir.S.* 1.15.152–16.161).

Another image worked in the same way. Ambrose thought of the deity as shining forth in the incidents of the Bible,[23] and if it were true that a spring produces a river but a river does not produce a spring, it was also true that light produces brightness but brightness does not produce light; yet brightness and light have one nature in common (*fid.* 4.8.95). Hence, when the prophet spoke of the 'brightness of the eternal light' (Wisd. 7:26), by 'brightness' he meant the shining quality of the light of the Father in the Son (*fid.* 1.7.49; see further 13.79). Neither has priority in time; it could not be said that brightness came after light, nor that light came before brightness (*fid.* 4.9.108).

In a third image, Ambrose sees Christ as the Father's arm (*virgb.* 3.3.3), or right hand (*Spir.S.* 2.7.69 fin). In the creation, the Son acted as the arm of God and the Spirit as his finger; when the psalmist described the heavens as 'the work of thy fingers', the plural alluded to the Spirit's sevenfold nature (*apol.alt.Dav.* 12.63 on Ps. 8:3, cf. Is. 11:2f). Or the Son could

---

23. E.g. *'eluceat'* (*exa.* 1.8.29), *'refulget'* (*Abr.* 1.5.33), discussed above.

be seen as the right hand of God and the Spirit as his finger. What was the finger with which God inscribed the tablets of the Law but the Holy Spirit?[24] That the Spirit is God's finger is made clear by the parallel expressions 'the finger of God' and 'the Spirit of God' (*Luc.* 7.92 and *Spir.S.* 3.3.11 on Luke 11:20, Matt. 12:28). Yet Ambrose is again aware that the image is an inadequate one, for the Spirit is also the hand of the Father and of the Son (*Spir.S.* 3.16.114, taking the hand of John 10:29 to apply to the Spirit; see further 3.5.34).

These images point in the same direction. A river originating from a spring and brightness from a light are derived, yet in substance identical to that from which they are derived, just as, more precisely, the notion of the Son and Spirit respectively as the arm or hand and the finger of the Father suggests that the Spirit comes from the Father by way of the Son, a position which foreshadows a later emphasis in western theology. Ambrose recognized that the images were not entirely satisfactory, but valuable as attempts to express the inexpressible. Behind them stood the one substance common to the three persons, something shown in the practice of baptizing in the one name of the Father and the Son and the Holy Spirit, and this was not to be wondered at, given that there was one substance, one divinity and one majesty (*sacr.* 2.7.22). The son of Love was himself love, possessing this not because of something that happened (*ex accidentibus*), but always in his substance (*Is.* 5.46).

Why then did the Bible sometimes seem to imply the inferiority of the Son? Numerous passages could be used against Nicene theology, as: 'And of Zion it shall be said, This and that man was born in her' (Ps. 87:5), and 'The Lord created me, the beginning of his ways' (cf. Prov. 8:22). More worryingty, many incidents in the life of Jesus seemed to suggest that the Son was less than the Father, and he himself had said 'But of that day and hour knoweth no man, not the angels of heaven or the Son, but my Father only' (Matt. 24:36). Opposed as he was to any notion of subordination in the Son, Ambrose argued that such texts only applied only to Christ in his incarnate nature, not that

---

24. *Spir.S.* 3.3.11–4.17, where other examples of the Spirit as a finger are given. See further 2.7.69, where the Son is also seen as the right hand of the Father.

which he shared forever with the Father (e.g. *fid.* 3.11.83ff). The situations they described arose, not from the begetting of Christ before all ages, but from the humanity which the Son took upon himself in time.

While Ambrose was writing with theological intent, his work also has a political edge, for he argued that the welfare of the empire and correct belief were linked. Pagan emperors had been accustomed to sacrifice to Fortuna, and now Ambrose tells Gratian that victory is won by the faith of the emperor rather than the strength of warriors (*fid.* 1 prol.3). More pointedly, towards the end of the second book, and so of the entire work as it was initially envisaged, he states that he must not detain Gratian, who was intent on war and planned to bring trophies of victory back from the barbarians. This victory was already predicted in the Bible, for Ezekiel spoke of Gog coming from the north (Ez. 38:14–16), and Ambrose, responding to a verbal similarity in his customary way, had no doubt that 'Gog' meant 'Goth' (Ez. 39:10–12). The matter was one of urgent relevance, for the defeat at Adrianople had been inflicted by Goths, dealing with whom had suddenly become important for the empire. Ambrose suggests to Gratian that the anti-Nicene convictions of the emperor Valens had been responsible for the defeat, in strident words: 'There can be no doubt, holy emperor, that we, who have paid the penalty for another's misbelief, will be helped by the catholic faith which is strong in you.' Indeed, the areas where sacrilege was strong were just those where barbarians were making incursions. Uttering a principle dangerously susceptible of verification, Ambrose tells Gratian that the name and worship of the Lord Jesus would lead the army (in general, *fid.* 2.136–43; similarly *Spir.S.* 1 prol.17).

. . .

PERSECUTION OF ANTI-NICAEANS

As time passed the wind turned against the anti-Nicaeans. As early as 20 August 379 Gratian issued from Milan a law against heresies, a category which probably included anti-Nicene belief.[25] In 380 Valens' successor Theodosius was baptized into

---

25. *Cod.Theod.* 16.5.5. Williams, following Gottlieb, argues that the law was directed against Donatists (1995: 157–161). But some of his evidence

the Nicene faith, and the anti-Nicene bishop of Constantinople was deposed and replaced by one of the outstanding thinkers of eastern Christianity, Gregory of Nazianzus. The following January a law was issued from Constantinople in support of the practice of the Nicene faith and opposing heresies, those of Photinus, Arius and Eunomius being named. Their adherents were to undergo the savage penalty of being branded, and were denied the right to worship (*cod. Theod.* 16.5.6).

Following a meeting between Gratian and Nicene bishops, a council was held at his behest at Aquileia, in northern Italy, in September 381. It came after a council which took place in Constantinople from May to July 381, the second ecumenical council, at which about 150 eastern bishops produced an extended version of the Nicene Creed. The western council was to be on a smaller scale. Ambrose suggested to Gratian that there was no need to trouble many bishops with attendance at it, and only 25 bishops were on hand when it opened, about half of them from northern Italy. Palladius, the leader of the anti-Nicaeans, had anticipated that bishops from the East, where his theology was better represented, would attend, but when the council opened he found himself with only two allies, Bishop Secundianus of Singidunum (Belgrade) and the priest Attalus of Poetovio (Ptuj). It met not in a basilica but in a room in which the bishop of Aquileia, Valerian, sat in an elevated position beside Ambrose, with two stenographers ready to record what was said. The setting must have resembled that of a court of law, a familiar one to Ambrose, and Palladius found himself in a situation not unknown at other times in the history of the church, that of arriving at what he had thought would be a discussion to find himself on trial.

The council of Aquileia is unusual among early church councils in that we have a verbatim report of the discussions. They are not edifying. The proceedings were opened by Ambrose, who had read out a letter written by Arius in which he said that the Father alone was eternal. The anti-Nicaeans were asked how they stood on this question: if they thought

---

supports the view that it was aimed at anti-Nicenes; moreover, its reference to those who claimed clerical titles recalls Ambrose's '*audis aliquem sacerdotem dici*' (*Luc.* 7.52).

the Son was not eternal they could make their case, and if they thought the proposition was to be condemned, they could condemn it. Palladius said that he was not obliged to answer, for Ambrose had seen to it that the council was not general and full, and in the absence of their fellow bishops his side could not speak of their faith. Ambrose brushed away the point, demanding to know whether Palladius agreed with Arius that the Father alone was eternal and whether this was said according to the Scriptures. Palladius refused to reply, and after other bishops had intervened he again raised the question of the eastern bishops whose attendance he had expected. Ambrose cut him short:

> Forget about the matter of the easterners; today I want to know what you think. The letter of Arius has been read out to you, and your practice is to deny that you are an Arian. Today, defend Arius or condemn him.

Palladius replied: 'You don't have the authority to ask this of me.' The exchange showed that the council was really a clash between Ambrose and Palladius, and indicated who was in the dominant position. As the latter continued to refuse to speak, Ambrose and his allies began to anathematize opinions with which they credited him, and ultimately Palladius was drawn into discussion of matters of detail.

Doubtless the application of a technical vocabulary was a good way to clear up suspect theological understandings, but as the discussion continued both sides revealed themselves as wearisome and pedantic. At one point, for example, Ambrose asked Palladius to assent to the words that Christ was 'true God, the son of God' (*'verum deum filium dei'*). Palladius said that, according to the Scriptures, he was 'the true son of God, God' (*'verum filium dei deum'*). The reply was ambiguous, for the adjective 'true' could refer to either the 'son' or the word 'God' at the end of the phrase. An exchange ensued:

> Bishop Ambrose said: 'Do you say he is true God, the son of God?'
> Palladius said: 'When I say he is the true son (of God), what need is there for more?'
> Bishop Ambrose said: 'I'm not asking whether you say he is the true son (of God), but for you to say he is true God, the son of God.' (*Gesta*, Acta 18 (ed. *SAEMO* 21))

There was nothing new in such verbal manoeuvres,[26] but behind Ambrose's skirmishes it is possible to detect the tactics of an expert in judicial procedure. Palladius describes him as having clerics skilled at taking notes copy down unconsidered remarks, and as acting as though he was trying to extort something by the kind of terror one would associate with a censor, like a public authority.[27] Unsurprisingly, the council concluded by condemning the three anti-Nicene clergy. A document was dispatched to Gratian, Valentinian and Theodosius, summarizing what had occurred and asking them to take steps against the heretics.

The council is not only unusual in that a report of its proceedings survives. Remarkably, the proceedings have survived in a manuscript of the fifth century which contains the first two books of Ambrose's *De fide* as well as other pro-Nicene material, which was annotated by an anti-Nicaean who added critical comments in the margins, yet another sign of the persistence of anti-Nicene beliefs. Palladius also wrote a bitter rejoinder to the council, which makes it clear that he regarded Ambrose as the prime mover. Any sympathy one might have for him as the underdog is not likely to survive the reading of this document, in which Palladius accuses Ambrose of, among other things, knowing nothing about the Bible and being a blasphemer, a servant of Antichrist and a man of lascivious and sordid life.[28] He suggested that Ambrose spend thirty or forty days expounding his faith before the senate of Rome. For his part, Palladius was prepared to send works he had written which could be read out in public, before an audience which would include pagans and Jews as well as Christians.[29] But a person in Ambrose's position had no need to respond to this proposal.

The council of 381 was Ambrose's council, revealing both his power and the forceful way in which he exercised it.

---

26. Ambrose's predecessor in Milan, Auxentius, had agreed with Hilary of Poitiers that Christ was '*natum ex patre Deum verum filium ex Deo patre*', but the expression was ambiguous. It could be taken as either 'True God born of the Father, the son of God the Father', or 'God born of the Father, the true son of God the Father' (*Contra Arianos* 14, *PL* 10:617f).
27. *Scolies*, 282; cf. a later reference to Ambrose as 'judge', 304f.
28. *Scolies*, 294–300.
29. *Scolies*, 322.

Doubtless his sway was not as great as he would have wished. An awkward situation had developed in the church of Antioch, where two pro-Nicene bishops, Paulinus and Melitus, each claimed the see. The former was backed by the churches of Rome and Alexandria, among others, but Melitus enjoyed overwhelming local support, and the council of Aquileia attempted to resolve this delicate situation by decreeing that, on the death of one of the rivals, the other was to assume control over the whole church in the city. But Antioch is a long way from Aquileia. The proposal came to nothing, and a letter sent in the names of Ambrose and other bishops of Italy to Theodosius, the emperor in whose territory Antioch lay, laments that on the death of Melitus another bishop had been imposed, despite what had been decided by the council of Aquileia, attendance at which had been prescribed for the bishops of the whole world (*ep.ext.coll.* 6(=12)). This estimate of the scale of the council and its importance was breathtaking in its chutzpah. It was precisely on the issue of the limited attendance that Palladius based his initial refusal to speak, and the Antiochenes could hardly have been expected to accept instruction from what was little more than a local council in northern Italy. But the proposal reflects the confidence and ambition Ambrose had come to possess in the early 380s.

. . .

PAGANS

Ambrose knew funny stories about the gods worshipped by the pagans.[30] He knew of a king who took a gold cloak off a statue of Jupiter and replaced it by one made of wool, saying that the golden one would have been too cold in winter and too hot in summer! He also removed a beard made of gold from a statue of Aesculapius, saying that he should not have a beard while his father, Apollo, was beardless (*virgb.* 2.5.36). But laugh as he might, Ambrose was faced with the puzzling obstinacy of adherents of the traditional religion who remained content to follow the way of their ancestors, and their strength may well have been greater than our sources,

---

30. His critique of classical mythology and cults is well summarized by Jenal (1995): 518–22.

overwhelmingly Christian by the end of the fourth century, would have us believe. In 383 they profited from a political change. While Gratian was campaigning in the Alpine province of Rhaetia, Magnus Maximus, the military commander in Britain, was acclaimed emperor, and led an army onto the Continent. Deserted by his troops, Gratian was killed on 25 August, an awkward fate in the light of Ambrose's recent claim that correct belief would bring him victory. The rise of Maximus complicated the political situation. Theodosius continued to hold the East; in the West, Valentinian II retained control of Italy, Pannonia and Africa, while Maximus now held the Gauls. At one stage Ambrose, in circumstances which remain mysterious, travelled to Trier, the city of his birth, to negotiate with Maximus on behalf of Valentinian. We do not know the outcome, but the regime of the young Valentinian was precariously placed.

It is therefore not surprising that it made overtures to non-Christians, such as the Frankish general Bauto, who held a consulship in 385. More significant were its advances towards the old Roman aristocracy, which were reflected in appointments to high office. In 384 the pagan Praetextatus became praetorian prefect, although he died before the year was out. The last known vestal virgin, Coelia Concordia, erected a statue in his honour. The most substantial figure to receive preferment was Quintus Aurelius Symmachus. A famed orator who held various pagan priesthoods, Symmachus was saddened by the number of people becoming Christians, and complained, doubtless with justification, that some people had been led to desert the altars of the gods by their ambition (Symm. *ep.* 1.51). His involvement in a project to edit the voluminous history Livy had written of republican Rome reveals an antiquarian enthusiasm far from the concerns of Ambrose. Towards the middle of 384 he was appointed prefect of the city of Rome. This was a major office, which carried with it the presidency of meetings of the senate. However, it was usually held for a short time; we know of seven people who had already held it in the 380s. Symmachus' tenure was therefore a brief window of opportunity for the adherents of the old religion, and he made the most of it. While he was broad-minded enough to write letters of recommendation for bishops (*ep.* 1.64, 7.51), he would happily use the patronage at his disposal to advance the interests of non-Christians. Hence, when asked in the autumn of 384 to appoint a teacher of rhetoric for Milan, his eye fell on a non-Christian, Augustine. But by then, Symmachus had embarked on a more substantial project.

The first emperor, Augustus, had placed a statue dedicated to the goddess of Victory in the recently completed Curia Iulia, and he probably dedicated in her honour an altar later known to have been located near the entrance to the senate. As the fourth century advanced, the attitudes emperors took towards the altar became a clear pointer to their religious convictions. Constantius removed it, Julian the Apostate restored it, and Gratian removed it again. Members of the senate who appealed for the restoration of the status quo on that occasion were thwarted by the lobbying of Pope Damasus and Ambrose. However, Valentinian's need for support and Symmachus' coming to office meant that another attempt to restore it could realistically be made, and in a formal report written to Valentinian II in 384, the prefect argued for the restoration of the altar and state subsidies for the pagan cult.[31]

Symmachus lavished on his report the eloquence for which he was renowned. His approach was formal, as evidenced by his use of a ceremonially full way of addressing the emperor which he suppressed when he revised his correspondence for publication,[32] and prudent, being circumspect as to the worship of the traditional Roman deities. Symmachus, whose report attributes eternity to Valentinian, the city of Rome and the empire,[33] was prepared to argue for a long-term view. Against the 'fame' of the most recent period, he looks back to the ways of his ancestors and asks that old men like himself be able to transmit what they had received as boys, the love of custom being great. If a long passage of time confers authority on a religion, the faith which has lasted for many centuries should be maintained; we should follow our parents, who were happy to follow their own parents. Symmachus has the figure of Rome speak, a poignant touch,

---

31. Ambrose *ep.* 72a(=17a)). On the political background, Matthews (1975): 205–10.
32. Ibid., 1 ad fin; see further *MGH* edn, p. xvii.
33. Ibid., 3,7,14; eternity was an imperial attribute, and Rome had for centuries been referred to as the eternal city.

given the minor role the city had come to play within the empire. The ploy was in accordance with a fashion in the literature of the time for Rome to be depicted as interceding before powerful figures, and Symmachus' use of the convention was appropriate, for Rome was generally seen as being elderly,[34] a circumstance well suited to the argument he had her make: thanks to the ancestral ceremonies, the laws of Rome had been spread through the world and invaders driven away, and it would not be fitting if she had been saved only to be censured in her old age. In any case, old age is difficult to correct. Shifting his ground, Symmachus argues that there were sensible reasons for restoring subsidies to traditional forms of worship, a withdrawal of subsidies from the vestal virgins having been followed by famine and a poor harvest. All he was seeking, he maintained, was the restoration of the situation which existed in the reign of Valentinian's father, Valentinian I, who was now looking on the tears of the priests from the starry arc of heaven. His son should correct what Gratian had been led to do by bad advice, so that times past would be well thought of.

Polite in its address, stately in its expression and beguilingly irenic in its content, the report of Symmachus stands in contrast to the methods of Ambrose, who dealt with the possible restoration of the altar and subsidies in two letters to Valentinian. The first (*ep.* 72(=17)) was written before he had seen Symmachus' petition. It is uncompromising. Whereas Symmachus had adopted a conciliatory approach, writing calmly of two ways of thinking and two points of view and enunciating a view famous in the history of religious liberalism, 'We cannot arrive at so great a mystery by one path', Ambrose operated with categories which were more sharply defined. Valentinian, whom he addresses as 'most Christian emperor', is told that his welfare depends upon the worship of the true God of the Christians. Unlike Symmachus, Ambrose is prepared to name the other side, to whom he persistently applies the hostile term 'pagans'.[35] He asks for a copy of Symmachus' report and proceeds to engage in a

---

34. Cf. Claudian *De bello gildonico* 1.25; an aged Rome is also implied at *ob.Val.* 20.
35. Latin 'gentiles'; Ambrose usually uses a different word, '*gentes*', for gentiles as distinguished from Jews.

rhetorical ploy which was to serve him in good stead years later: if Valentinian came to the wrong decision and went to church, he would find either no bishop, or one who resisted. The words he puts in the mouth of such a bishop again suggest the black and white of Ambrose's perspective: 'The church does not seek your gifts, because you have adorned the temples of the pagans with gifts. The altar of Christ spits out your donations, because you have made an altar to idols.' Given that Valentinian II had made his headquarters in Milan, the statement bluntly indicated how Ambrose would act should Valentinian attempt to make donations to the church after acceding to Symmachus' request. Worse follows: his murdered brother Gratian is made to ask Valentinian whether his enemies could have done anything worse: 'You have abrogated my decrees, which the person who lifted up arms against me has not yet done.' Ambrose's tactic was to browbeat Valentinian, a teenager, but when he made a sly allusion to the sound policies of Maximus, who threatened the regime of the young emperor, he was hitting below the belt. Finally, Ambrose has the young emperor's father express disappointment, in a comparatively low-key speech. His son, who in the concluding sentence is addressed by the unadorned word 'emperor', is warned not to injure God, his father and brother, but to act before God in a way beneficial to his salvation.

Ambrose's request for a copy of Symmachus' report was a manoeuvre common among political operators. He was successful, and when he had read his opponent's case he wrote a lengthy rejoinder (*ep.* 73(=18)). His reply was a polished piece of writing, which contains far more reminiscences of the poetry of Vergil than any other letter he wrote. Style, however, did not conceal forcefulness. The first sentence, while politely referring to Valentinian as 'your clemency', is sharply addressed to 'you, emperor'; Ambrose disdained Symmachus' elaborate courtesy. Valentinian was bluntly told to consider not the elegance of the words Symmachus had employed but the strength of the argument. As Ambrose saw it, his opponent had advanced three arguments on behalf of what he called 'the sect of the pagans'. Responding to the proposition that Rome needed her old cults, he adopted a tone of heavy sarcasm, while arguing that history could be used to prove the contrary. The point is made in a hectoring style, with a remorseless flow of short sentences, many of them aggressively interrogative. Rome herself then launches into a speech, arguing that the trophies of victory were won by the strength of soldiers, not the entrails of animals. She was not ashamed to be converted, together with the whole world, in her old age, for there was no shame in moving on to better things. When Symmachus stated that one could not arrive at so great a mystery by one path, he was showing his ignorance of the voice of God. Ambrose's response to the request for the restoration of old altars is firm: as a Christian emperor, Valentinian II has learned to honour the altar of Christ alone. As for the vestal virgins, they were inferior to Christian virgins, and Symmachus' second argument, concerning the allocation of stipends to them and the priests, is refuted with reference to the inability of the church to gain property from wills. Ambrose finally turns to the argument which blamed Christians for recent misfortunes in the empire, one which would later evoke Augustine's *City of God*. He sets his face against this in terms which contradict the thesis he had set before Gratian a few years previously, that faith was more important than the strength of warriors:

> What they believed to be a goddess and victory, is only a gift, not a power; it is something donated, it does not dominate; it comes from legions, not the power of religions.[36]

Whereas Symmachus repeatedly emphasized the claims of antiquity, Ambrose urges the possibility of improvement: all things are making progress and getting better. When he states that the coming of the church is like the harvest and vintage which occur at the end of the year, we again see the church finding itself at home in a world it saw as changing for the better.[37]

---

36. *Ep.* 73(=18).30; cf. 7. Ambrose's prose is emphatic: '*donatur non dominatur, legionum gratia non religionum potentia*' (*ep.* 73(=18).30). Yet a few years earlier Ambrose had argued the contrary when writing for Gratian (above, p. 118).
37. Ambrose's response to attempts to blame Christians for contemporary problems is significantly different from that of Cyprian, who stressed the aging of the world: Mazzucco (1980). Yet elsewhere he describes the world as getting old and laying aside the vigour of its youth (*bon.mort.* 10.46).

The clash between Ambrose and Symmachus shows on one side aggression, sharpness of categories and belief in progress, and on the other politeness, indefiniteness and nostalgia. Another difference lies in their use of rival feminine personifications. As we have seen, the images Ambrose had of the church, in whose interests he campaigned, were feminine, while Victory, whose altar Symmachus defended, was a female figure, as was Rome, whom he represented as speaking on her behalf. The identification of tutelary responsibilities with female figures was deeply rooted in the ancient world, and the tradition remained alive: when Alaric the Goth came up to the walls of Athens in 395 he was believed to have seen Athena walking about them, armed and ready to resist.[38] Against a living tradition of female guardians, Ambrose placed a feminine church.

His success came quickly. The fate of the altar and subsidies was discussed at a meeting of the emperor's advisory council, the consistory. Not all its members were Christians, but Ambrose's arguments prevailed. As he recalled some years later, 'the counts acquiesced' (*ep.ext.coll.* 10(=57).3), and it was determined that the altar and subsidies would not be restored. By February 385 Symmachus was out of office, having been replaced by a man almost certainly a catholic Christian, and the window of opportunity he had sought to exploit had closed.

Ambrose had reason to feel content. Within a few years he had been victorious over heretics and pagans, two of the three enemies of catholic Christianity. His main involvement with the remaining one, the Jews, would occur later. Before then, his resolve was to be tested in affairs of a very different kind.

---

38. Zosimus 5.6.

Chapter 5

THE BISHOP AND THE CITY

. . .

MILAN, SINFUL OR CHRISTIAN?

Some of the inhabitants of Milan were complacent about sin. One man responded to Ambrose's suggestion that at his age he should be baptized with the assertion that there was no need, as he had never sinned (*sacr.* 3.13). Yet Ambrose saw the city as full of sinners. Some were all too interested in fine clothes. Barely able to tolerate wool, they decked themselves out in silk as far down as their feet.[1] Others were quarrelsome and seekers of revenge; to guard against these tendencies, Christ had sent his disciples to preach the gospel without gold, silver, money, or a staff (*Jos.* 13.78). Others were drunkards, whose vice Ambrose attempted to combat by preaching a series of sermons which he turned into a book.[2] Yet others, Ambrose claimed, were capable of walking straight past their own parents as they stood begging at the entrance of the church (*Luc.* 8.76). But human sinfulness, however varied its manifestations, found certain basic expressions. Discussing the statement of Jesus that 'Everyone who sins is a slave to sin', two examples came to Ambrose's mind: surely every avaricious person and everyone subject to lust was a

---

1. *Luc.* 5.107. Adam wore skins after the expulsion from paradise, not silk (*paen.* 2.11.98).
2. The *De Helia et ieiunio*. References to passages of the Bible 'you have heard today' (19.70, 20.75, 21.77) show its origin in preaching. Yet in addition to the drunkenness which brings about stumbling, unsteadiness and sensory change, there is another, spiritual kind which warms the mind with the grace of virtue and turns aside every infirmity (*Noe* 29.111), as well as the sober intoxication provided by the eucharist (below, p. 146).

slave? (*Ios.* 4.20). Similarly, Christ's refusal to reveal the time of his Second Coming and the Last Judgment was a device to keep adulterers and robbers on their toes (*fid.* 5.17.210). Doubtless other ways of schematizing sins were possible.[3] But when Ambrose contemplated the propensity of humans to commit sins, just two, lust and avarice, came persistently to mind.[4]

The first of these could be indulged in private,[5] yet it disfigured public life. The temptation posed by prostitutes is a theme never far from Ambrose's mind; he can describe pleasure as a prostitute, restless at home and wandering in public squares.[6] Against the temptations posed by such women, whose eyes constituted a trap for their lovers (*paen.* 1.14.73), he set the figure of the patriarch Joseph, who firmly resisted the advances of Potiphar's wife. In admiration of his saintly nature, Ambrose frequently styles him 'holy Joseph'.[7] But the defeat of lust could allow avarice to flourish unchecked, for the latter vice was not only common among laypeople, who could at least claim that their behaviour was prompted by concern for their children and relatives, but among celibate clergy as well.[8]

Two of Ambrose's books are devoted to avarice and its implications for society. In one he discusses the biblical story of Naboth, who was killed by King Ahab when he refused to give up his small vineyard, and denounces in vehement terms the oppression of the poor by the rich.[9] It was a theme with urgent contemporary relevance, for the period was one during which small holdings were being concentrated into ever larger estates and small farmers continually oppressed.[10]

---

3. Almost all sins could be seen as originating in delight of the flesh, the display of glory or the greed for power (*Luc.* 4.33–35); lustfulness, avarice and treachery are given at *fug.* 4.17.
4. E.g. *off.* 3.6.37; *patr.* 7.33; *ps.118* 5.30, 16.45.
5. Temptations which befall people as they sleep are discussed at *ps.118* 8.46.
6. *Cain* 1.4.14. See too e.g. *apol.alt.Dav.* 3.14; *bon.mort.* 6.24, 9.40; *Luc.* 4.63; *paen.* 1.14.68, 73. On loose women, cf. above, p. 44.
7. As at *off.* 2.11.59, 15.74, 16.83, 3.6.42; *ps.118* 12.31.
8. *VAmb.* 41.1f; see further below, p. 161f.
9. Ambrose's social thought is widely discussed; see for example Colombo (1974) and Vasey (1982). That these studies point in different directions suggests the unsystematic nature of Ambrose's thinking.
10. Ambrose's opening sentences bring out the contemporary applicability of the text; for the social context, see Ruggini (1961), esp. 23–28.

Ambrose knew of those who joined house to house and estate to estate, as if they could live alone in the earth, wanting to make their own something which was common to all.[11] Another work, which deals with the book of Tobit, a text contained in the Septuagint but not in the Hebrew Bible, attacks usury in memorable terms, and its heavy reliance on puns (*Tob.* 4.13–5.17) indicates that Ambrose was aiming at a wide audience. Money, he suggests, is like the waves of the sea. But whereas the sea can be calm, the waves of interest never rest. They are always driven to and fro, sinking the shipwrecked, casting forth the naked, stripping those who are clothed and receding from the unburied (*Tob.* 5.16). Like the sea, the usurer absorbs the properties of all in his waves yet is never filled (*Tob.* 13.44). Ambrose has only scorn for those who sold grain for great profit in times of scarcity and were saddened by a good harvest (*off.* 3.6.37–44).[12]

More generally, the public life of the ancient world was enacted in places which remained largely impervious to Christianity. Ambrose encouraged young women to flee the forum and streets for the desert which led to the kingdom (*virgt.* 8.46–9.52). Circus games, theatrical shows, pantomimes, wrestlers and horse-racing were no more than vanities (*ps.118* 5.28; cf. *fug.* 1.4), a sentiment which may have been as popular as the encouragement Ambrose gave to virginity. Believers were easily distracted from going to church by the rival attractions of circus games and the theatre (*ps.118* 16.45; others enjoyed a quiet life in the less Christianized countryside). Yet some of these diversions were of structural importance in Milan's civic life, for sometimes people paid for circus and theatrical shows, or gladiatorial and hunting shows, to win popular favour (*off.* 2.21.109). Ambrose's anti-urban polemic had complex roots, among them a Roman tradition of moralizing. When Pompey erected the first stone theatre in Rome in the first century BC he was so afraid of criticism

---

11. *Ps.118* 12.42 (where a borrowing from Is. 5:8 should be added to the textual apparatus in the *SAEMO* edition); *exa.* 6.8.52. See too *Abr.* 1.3.12, *ps.118* 6.32, and more distantly *exa.* 5.5.14, 10.27.
12. Yet Ambrose did not particularly sympathize with the poor. His commentary on Luke seems to soften the ethical teachings of Jesus; see for example *Luc.* 5.64 on 6:20 (although in fact Ambrose gives the text in the milder form of Matt. 5:3), *Luc.* 5.69–71 on 6:24, and *Luc.* 8.70f on 18:25.

that he installed within it a temple built so that the steps would seem to lead to it, and such authors as Horace firmly located vice in the city. Another influence was Christian, for the monastic movement which had recently sprung up exalted the desert over the classical *polis*.

But the city was not entirely lost. In some ways it was becoming more Christian, as its rapidly changing skyline showed. In a city already boasting an impressive cathedral, Ambrose erected three new churches. To the west of the city was the large Basilica Ambrosiana, 50.4 metres long and 26 in breadth,[13] a building so identified with the bishop that people were calling it the 'Ambrosiana' while he was still alive (*ep*. 77(=22).2). On the main road to Rome he dedicated the Basilica Apostolorum, also known as the Basilica Romana, now called San Nazaro, after the saint whose body Ambrose placed there in 395. It was even larger than the Ambrosiana, being 56 metres long by 45.3 across. Constantine had erected a basilica dedicated to the Holy Apostles in Constantinople, and Ambrose's building imitated both its cruciform shape and dedication, perhaps to assert the status of Gratian's capital, Milan, at a time of rivalry between him and Theodosius, in Constantinople.[14] Finally, he began work on the church of San Simpliciano. Ambrose's building activities, undertaken at a time when the erection of buildings for secular purposes was slowing down over most of the western empire, were an impressive sign of wealth and confidence, and made the powerful presence of the church in the city manifest.

. . .

A SKIRMISH OVER CHURCHES

It was probably late in 384 that the anti-Nicene community in Milan gained another bishop, when Auxentius Mercurinus, a pupil of the great Bishop Ulfilas, arrived in the city. Not surprisingly, Ambrose was hostile, accusing him of adopting his second name to deceive people (*ep*. 75A(=21a).22). Ambrose's congregation would have thrilled to his description of false prophets in sheep's clothing who were wolves

---

13. I regret not having been able to consult Perer (1995).
14. McLynn (1994): 227–32.

within, when, slyly alluding to Auxentius' origins within the modern Romania, he mentioned a certain person with the title of bishop whose limbs were hardened by the Scythian snow (*Luc.* 7.52).

Early in 385 Ambrose was invited to a meeting of the emperor's consistory at which he was asked to make a church, probably the Basilica Portiana outside the city, available for Auxentius and his community to celebrate Easter.[15] Alas, he had many enemies at court. Commenting on a passage in Luke's gospel concerning a rich man dressed in purple, he invited his 'reader', presumably standing for those who heard the passage when delivered in a sermon, to imagine 'Arians' intent upon worldly concerns, seeking the company of royalty and desiring to attack with military might the truth of the church as they reclined in the midst of purple (*Luc.* 8.17). Presumably Justina would have celebrated Easter with Auxentius and the anti-Nicene community in any church Ambrose made available. But, Ambrose states in a letter, when the people found out that he had been asked to a meeting in the palace they rushed there, and when a count tried to drive them away they all said they would die for the faith of Christ (*ep.* 75A(=21a).29); Ambrose's claim of popular support and the theme of martyrdom would be frequently reiterated in the months to come. The government did not press the point, and Justina and Valentinian spent Easter outside Milan. But on 23 January 386 a law was issued guaranteeing the right of assembly to those who accepted the faith promulgated at both the anti-Nicene council of Rimini (359) and the Nicene council of Constantinople (381). Moreover, if people who supposed that the right of assembly was granted to them alone tried to provoke agitation, 'they should know that as authors of sedition and as disturbers of the peace of the Church, they shall also pay the penalty of high treason with their life and blood'.[16] The law, clearly drafted with Ambrose in mind, caused a stir; the official asked

---

15. The following events present problems of interpretation which are well-nigh intractable; Nauroy (1988) is particularly useful. A *Life of Athanasius* known to Photius (*Bibliotheca* 482a) has that bishop agreeing with Constantius in 346 that one church in Alexandria would be made available to Arians and one in Constantinople to Nicenes, a fascinating detail of uncertain relevance.
16. *Cod.Theod.* 16.1.4 (trans. Pharr).

to draft it, Benivolus, resigned in protest. As the government prepared for the following Easter, Ambrose's thoughts turned towards martyrdom.

. . .

MARTYRDOM

More than half a century after Constantine brought about the peace of the church, the cult of the martyrs flourished.[17] Although Ambrose was part of the establishment, who was accused by enemies of persecuting them just as Roman officials had the martyrs,[18] they played an important part in his imagination. He admired St Pelagia, who saved herself from rape by jumping to her death out of a window, although the words he attributes to her, 'I am dying willingly; no-one will lay a hand on me', could be held to suggest that she was a suicide more than a martyr.[19] Fascinated as he was by persecution,[20] Ambrose's enthusiasm for the martyrs led him to look a little disdainfully at the Christians of his own time.[21] After describing the torments suffered by the martyrs, he can exclaim: 'Would that I deserved to be such!' (*ps.118* 21.8f; cf. *ep.* 23(=36).4).

A sign of Ambrose's feeling is given by a passage in the *De officiis*, a work which reached its final form towards the end of the 380s although it may have been based on earlier material, in which a discussion of the virtue of fortitude culminates in an enthusiastic encomium of the bravery of the martyrs. The section follows a passage on bravery in warfare, but Ambrose did not find this topic congenial, for after a perfunctory description of three brave warriors mentioned

17. Dassmann (1975).
18. He was accused of acting towards the anti-Nicaean Bishop Palladius in the way a Roman judge had towards the martyr Cyprian: *Commentaires de Maximus*, ed. Gryson, *Scholies* 201f.
19. *Virgb.* 3.7.33–36, with *ep.* 7(=37).38, from where these words are quoted. Whereas Augustine was uncertain whether such conduct was proper (*civ.dei.* 1.26), Ambrose felt that when the chance of a praiseworthy death offered itself it should be snatched (*off.* 2.30.153; see further *exc.fr.* 1.18).
20. Christians glory in blood, Ambrose informed Valentinian (*ep.* 73(=18).11). In one of his interpretations of the parable of the Good Samaritan, the man who went down from Jerusalem on the road to Jericho is a person who declined martyrdom (*paen.* 1.11.51).
21. See for example *ps.118* 14.17, with 11.21.

in the Bible he asks, using a form of words which will resonate throughout this section: 'What shall I say of the Maccabees?' The bravery the members of this family displayed against King Antiochus is powerfully evoked: Judas Maccabeus uttered the words 'Let us not leave any charge against our glory!' and found an occasion of death more glorious than a triumph in arms. 'But what shall I say of the passions of martyrs?' Ambrose later inquires, as he turns again to the triumph of the Maccabees over the proud King Antiochus. But other martyrs occur to Ambrose: 'What shall I say of the mother? . . . What shall I say of the two-year olds? . . . What shall I say of St Agnes?' He goes on to describe the martyrdom of St Laurence, providing a lively speech in which Laurence asked Pope Sixtus to allow him to accompany him to his martyrdom. Sixtus refused to take his disciple with him: Laurence's triumph over the tyrant would be more glorious! So it came to pass, and Ambrose quotes Laurence's joke to those roasting him, 'This side is cooked, turn it over and eat.' By his strength of mind, Laurence overcame the nature of fire (*off.* 1.40.196–41.207).

Ambrose's feelings on martyrdom are also apparent in the conclusion of a work based on sermons quite possibly preached in the first months of 386, the *De Iacob*.[22] While it ostensibly deals with the biblical account of the patriarch Jacob, its real theme is the power which a mind directed by reason can exercise over the passions. It opens with the story of how King David desired to drink water from a source behind the lines of the enemy he was fighting. Yet when men brought him some of it, at the risk of personal danger, he poured it away, for although desire had preceded reason, reason resisted desire. It had been human of David to desire in a way contrary to reason, but he laudably cheated a desire devoid of reason in a reasonable way (*Iac.* 1.1.3, on IV Macc. 3:6–18). This account sets the scene for the entire work. One

22. Well discussed by Brown (1992):111. The date is briefly and inconclusively discussed in *SAEMO* 3:215f, to which I would add that the powerful concluding section on the Maccabees may be connected with the celebration of their festival on 1 August, in which case the themes of resistance to illicit power would have been exercising Ambrose well into whichever year the addresses were given in. Typically, Ambrose mentions a biblical text 'which you have heard read out today' (2.5.23), yet at the beginning of the second book he refers to the preceding book and the one which follows.

of Ambrose's sources for this teaching is the Neoplatonist author Plotinus (cf. below, page 169ff), whom he follows late in the first book when he discusses what he calls a perfect man. For such a person, who seeks only the one, outstanding good, such things as the body and its health, and his children, will be of little concern; in fact, the body will be of no interest to him (1.8.36ff). When Ambrose finally turns in the second book to the ostensible topic of the work, Jacob and his happiness, he makes the point that, whereas passion enslaves, a person who is the overseer of his own will and coerces the appetite of bodily passion is free (*Iac.* 2.3.12). The life of a perfect person is marked by the use of reason.

Towards its end, this work lurches in an unexpected and exciting direction. Observing how happy Jacob was at the end of his life, Ambrose comments on the happiness of Joseph in prison, of Isaiah when he was being cut in half, of Jeremiah when he was being drowned, and of Daniel when he stood amid the lions. These curious examples of human felicity lead to a discussion of the supreme example of happiness, that of the mother of the Maccabees who experienced the happiness of seeing her seven sons die and being killed herself (*Iac.* 2.9.42). Ambrose gives a strongly felt account of the persecution of this family by the tyrant Antiochus, in which he closely follows account given in the deutero-canonical book of IV Maccabees. This text, written in Greek in the last century BC or the first century AD, is preserved in a number of manuscripts of the Septuagint, which is doubtless the context in which Ambrose read it, and it provides a version of the story of the Maccabees more strongly expressed than the better-known one given in II Maccabees. Ambrose puts powerful speeches into the mouths of the scribe Eleazar, each of the seven brothers, and their mother. The second brother, in intense pain as the skin is pulled off his head, is made to exclaim 'How sweet it is to die for religion!' Ambrose simplifies, and de-judaizes, his source, which has the brother say 'How sweet is every form of death on behalf of the religion of our fathers' (IV Macc. 9:29), his words recalling a line in a poem by Horace, who wrote of how sweet and fitting it was to die for one's fatherland.[23] The dichotomy of

---

23. With Ambrose *Iac.* 2.11.47 ('*quam dulce est mori pro religione*') compare Horace *Carmina* 3.2.13 ('*dulce et decorum est pro patria mori*').

the claims of religion and those of the state, one of the chief themes of Ambrose's episcopate, was nowhere more clearly expressed than in the events of 386.

. . .

EASTER 386

Events began to move quickly as Easter drew near. Our source for them is a letter Ambrose wrote to his sister Marcellina (*ep.* 76(=20)), which provides his version of what happened, but because it cannot be verified against other sources its reliability is uncertain. On Friday 27 March an important group, made up of counts from the consistory, approached Ambrose, asking him to hand over not the Basilica Portiana but the cathedral, and insisting that he would see that the people did not cause a disturbance. The demand was arrogant, for the cathedral was the church in which Ambrose presided as bishop of the city, the surrendering of which would have compromised his standing. The counts' concern for the behaviour of the people reveals a difficulty the consistory foresaw, for the cathedral was located in the heart of a densely settled part of the city,[24] and Ambrose may have been able to manipulate the people of the area. He refused: 'I answered, as was suitable to one of my rank, that the temple of God could not be handed over by the bishop.' His emphasizing, perhaps in a prickly way, the dignity of his episcopal rank is not surprising. Another concept was more important. In earlier times the charge of 'handing over' (*traditio*) had been levelled against bishops who surrendered copies of the sacred texts in times of persecution. Behind this usage lay that of the gospels, which use this word for the handing over of Jesus to Roman power by the Jews and, worse, the handing over of Jesus to the Jews by Judas. The word Ambrose used for what was asked of him was therefore one with remarkably sinister connotations. On the following day he was acclaimed when he entered the church. Then Eusignius, who had recently been appointed praetorian prefect, entered, to make a more modest proposal, that Ambrose cede the Basilica Portiana, but the people responded by crying out, and he withdrew. On Palm Sunday, while

24. Arslan (1982): 204.

Ambrose was 'handing over' the Creed to candidates for baptism,[25] word came that some of the people had rushed to the Basilica Portiana, having heard that the church was being prepared for the arrival of the emperor. Ambrose remained where he was and began to say mass, in the midst of which he was distracted by news that an anti-Nicene priest was in danger of being lynched by the people. A posse of clergy was dispatched to save him. Ambrose wept bitterly as he proceeded with the liturgy, praying that if blood were shed it would be his.

Shortly afterwards heavy penalties were imposed on merchants, suggesting the collusion between them and Ambrose was suspected,[26] while members of the palace staff were told to desist from activities which could be thought to indicate involvement in rebellious strife. In Ambrose's words, 'persecution was boiling'. On Tuesday a group of counts and tribunes asked him to hand over the basilica quickly, but he replied that, while they were welcome to his own possessions, things which were divine were not subject to the power of the emperor. Did they wish to carry him off to his death in chains? He assured them that he was willing to be sacrificed before the altars. After making more fruitless appeals the delegation departed, leaving the self-dramatizing bishop to pray that he would not live to see the ruin of the great city, or of all Italy. Before dawn on Wednesday, news came that the Basilica Portiana had been surrounded by soldiers. In the midst of confusing reports and tension, Ambrose preached to the people.

A passage from the book of Job had been read, and as usual Ambrose tried to relate the lesson to current circumstances. God had delivered Job into the power of Satan (Job 1:12), but, knowing that Ambrose was weak, he had not given the Devil power over his body, even though Ambrose longed for this to happen and was prepared to offer himself. Job had been told by a woman 'Say something against God and die' (Job 2:9); Ambrose had been told 'Hand over the basilica.' His audience would immediately have seen the

---

25. The formal language '*symbolum . . . tradebam*' (4) picks up the '*traderem*' of (2).
26. We lack evidence which would supply a helpful context for this occurrence.

implied reference to another woman, Valentinian's mother Justina, a point which Ambrose strengthened by reminding his hearers of how Eve led Adam astray, and how Jezabel and Herodias persecuted Elijah and John the Baptist. He represented himself as talking sharply to Valentinian: 'Don't trouble yourself to think, emperor, that you have some imperial right over things which are divine.' After telling him that, if he wished to have a long reign, he should be subject to God, he asserted a general principle: 'Palaces belong to the emperor and churches to the bishop. Rights have been given to you over public buildings, but not sacred ones.' If Valentinian wanted a church, Ambrose could only answer, in words which showed he saw himself playing the role of John the Baptist to the emperor's Herod, 'It is not right for you to have it, for what have you to do with an adulteress?'[27]

The language was strong and brave. But before he finished speaking, word came that the royal curtains in the Basilica Portiana had been gathered together. These were the curtains which screened a ruler from his subjects, of the kind to be seen in late-antique mosaics at Ravenna, and their removal constituted a retreat by the authorities. Moreover, the basilica was said to be full of people demanding the presence of Ambrose. Meanwhile a messenger came, asking on behalf of the emperor why Ambrose acted against the order which had been given. Was Ambrose, he asked, a tyrant? This was an extraordinary suggestion, for the word implied that he was setting himself up as an illegitimate ruler, and shows how seriously the government took his stand.[28] Ambrose protested that he had not acted in such a way: when he had heard that troops had occupied the basilica he had said that, while he could not hand over the basilica, he ought not fight, and he had expressed the belief that the emperor would join them. Far from being a tyrant, such power as Ambrose had was that of offering his life. Moreover, the Old Testament showed priests bestowing power, not claiming it. His implied claim to bestow power was not

---

27. Compare Ambrose's '*Non tibi licet illam habere*' with John's '*non licet tibi habere eam*' (Matt. 14:4, Vulgate). The adulteress referred to by Ambrose is the anti-Nicaean community.
28. Ambrose will later speak of illegitimate emperors as tyrants (e.g. *ob.Theod.* 53).

conciliatory, and towards the end of his discourse Ambrose played his trump card, just as he had towards the end of his letter to Valentinian during the controversy over the altar of Victory. But now Ambrose boldly named the person who could destroy Valentinian's regime: 'Maximus doesn't say that I'm a tyrant!' It was a dangerous stroke, but it sufficed. On the next day the emperor ordered the withdrawal of troops from the basilica, and the return of the fines the merchants had paid. The soldiers who had been carrying out Valentinian's orders rushed to the altars and kissed them. Ambrose emphasized the popular response: what happiness there was among all the people! His letter to his sister concludes with the restatement of a central theme, his willingness to die a martyr: 'May the Lord turn them aside from the church, may they aim all their spears at me, may they slake their thirst with my blood.'

Valentinian had been forced to back down. He continued to refer to Ambrose as a tyrant, and, in an unexpected reprise of the theme of handing over, complained to his counts that if Ambrose told them to they would hand him over, bound. An unpleasant exchange of words took place between Ambrose and the chief of Valentinian's bedchamber, the eunuch Calligonus. Ambrose distrusted eunuchs, believing that they often turned the mind of a king towards what was in their own interests rather than the public good (*exa.* 5.21.68). He told his sister that Calligonus said to him, with a significant look, 'Do you despise Valentinian while I am alive? I'm taking away your head!' His reply was rude: 'May God allow you to do what you have threatened. May I suffer what is appropriate for a bishop, and may you do what is appropriate for a eunuch.' The exchange can hardly have pleased Calligonus. Valentinian had quit Milan by 20 April,[29] leaving the city to its bishop.

. . .

MUSIC AND HYMNS

Music was important to Ambrose. He approved of the practice of Pythagoras, who hired a musician to play something that would soothe his heart, made anxious by worldly cares,

---

29. On that date he issued a law from Aquileia: *cod.Theod.* 13.5.17.

before he went to bed (*virgb.* 3.4.19). He thought of the great story of the Bible as having being played out to music. At its very beginning, the gathering of the waters (Gen. 1:9) made Ambrose think of the singing of psalms, something which rivalled the gentle sound of lapping waters, for the sound of waves could be heard when men, women, virgins and children sang the psalms responsorially (*exa.* 3.5.23). The two canticles in the books written by Moses resembled the two ages of the world and the two lights of heaven, and cast a radiance over Moses' whole work (*ps.* 1.4f, on Ex. 15, Deut. 32). Ambrose took pleasure from the story of Miriam, the sister of Moses, and her tambourine (*exh.virg.* 7.47, *virgb.* 2.2.15–17), and observed that the singing of David cast out the spirit which oppressed Saul, that Solomon had singers in the temple, and that Christ himself sings to us in the gospel (*ps.118* 7.26).

It was therefore fitting that Ambrose's two works on parts of the Psalms both begin with discussions of singing. He felt that the pleasures of psalm 119 and the sweetness of singing delighted the ears and caressed the mind (*ps.118* prol.1; see further *Iac.* 2.9.39). More detail was provided in a passage which, being placed at the beginning of his commentary on psalm 1, reflects his approach to the entire psalter. Within the Bible the book of Psalms is especially sweet, and after running through various songs to be found in the Bible, from which he typically omits those in the New Testament, he observes that in a psalm teaching and beauty contend with each other: it is sung for delight and learned for instruction, its sweetness penetrating deep down. Yet there was a danger that delight in its sweetness would arouse the passions of the body, and when Ambrose mentions young women singing a hymn to God with sweetness of voice one hears an echo of the sweet voices of another group of women, the Sirens, whose sweet singing was to be resisted (above, page 59f). Again, one feels that he may be playing with fire.

At some stage during the controversy over the basilicas Ambrose hit upon a practice new to Milan. As Augustine described it, to prevent the people from suffering weariness and sorrow, he introduced the eastern practice of singing hymns and psalms (*conf.* 9.7.15). His innovation is also mentioned by Paulinus, who states that antiphons, hymns and vigils then began to be celebrated in the church of Milan

(*VAmb*. 13.3), and both authors state that his innovation was quickly imitated by other churches. But Ambrose went beyond instituting an influential custom, for he was the author of some of the hymns which were sung. There were ample pre-Christian precedents for the writing of hymns, as for example the pieces written by Horace; the Greek word '*hymnos*' originally referred to a composition in praise of gods or heroes. Hilary of Poitiers had recently composed hymns in Latin for the use of Christians, and now Ambrose set out to do the same. Many hymns have come down to us in his name, of which fourteen have a good claim to authenticity. All are written so as to be appropriate to some point in the passing of time. Four, those for the crowing of the cock, dawn, the third hour and the lighting of the lamps, are connected with the time of day; another three are concerned with feasts of the church year, Christmas, Epiphany and Easter; while another group, which concerns martyrs whose feasts were kept on particular days, again shows the importance of the martyrs for Ambrose. He designed the hymns for insertion into public worship at a time when his congregation may have needed something to boost its morale.

They are very simple in style. In such ways as an avoidance of subordinate clauses they share in the characteristics of Ambrose's writing when it seeks to represent the spoken word (above, page 66). Each hymn consists of eight verses of four lines, almost always made up of eight syllables. The words in each line usually make sense when taken as a unit, making the hymns easily understood as they were sung. While Ambrose composed according to the classical laws of metre, using iambic dimeters, the metrical rhythm often coincides with the accentual rhythm of everyday speech, which again facilitated congregational use. Augustine was aware of the danger that people would not understand what they sang in church, in which case their singing was like that of birds (*Enarrationes in Psalmos* 18.2.1; *CCSL* 38:105), but this was unlikely to happen when his hymns were sung. Like other church leaders of his time, Ambrose was an intellectual communicating with a wide public to a degree unusual in the ancient world.

We have two nearly contemporary responses to Ambrose's hymns. One is that of Augustine. In 386, at a time of spiritual crisis, he may have been particularly susceptible, but there can be no mistaking the impact the hymns had on him: 'How I wept during your hymns and canticles!' (*conf.* 9.6.14, cf. 7.16). He had a similar experience in the following year when, after the death of his mother, he could not cry. Not even the offering of the eucharist brought tears to his eyes, and a bath he took to relieve his tension brought no relief. Only after remembering the words of one of Ambrose's hymns could he weep (*conf.* 9.12.31–33). Their ability to induce tears left Augustine in no doubt as to the power of Ambrose's hymns. Neither did Ambrose's enemies in Milan doubt it. He summarizes their attitude: 'It is said that I beguiled the people by the songs of my hymns.' He did not deny the charge: what was more powerful than a great song, or the daily confession of the Trinity in the mouths of the whole people (*ep.* 75A(=21a).34)? But the accusation, as transmitted by Ambrose, cut deep, for while the noun '*carmen*' has as its primary meaning 'song', it can also mean 'magical chant',[30] and a suggestion that Ambrose's hymns acted on the people as spells seems to lie behind this accusation. Ambrose replied by pointing out their educational use: 'All those who had scarcely been disciples before were turned into teachers.' The claim that Ambrose's hymns were spells was an acknowledgment of their power over the people of Milan, and, indirectly, of his ability to strike a genuinely demotic tone.

The hymns therefore contributed to the unity and morale of the worshipping community which other kinds of singing were already building up. How could other pleasures available in the city compete? The lascivious music of the theatre and the sound of reed instruments had nothing in common with the concord of the people singing together. For this was true harmony, when people of different ages and diverse virtues sang a psalm together in complete concord (*Luc.* 7.237f). Those worshipping with Ambrose would display a unity of which his enemies had best beware.

. . .

THE SIGNIFICANCE OF EASTER

The setback suffered by Valentinian was given added impact by the approach of Easter. This was the climax of the church's

---

30. Cf. Vergil *Aeneid* 4.487, *Eclogae* 8.68. Ambrose himself uses the word in this sense: *exa.* 4.8.33.

year, and Ambrose avoided going far from Milan even during the forty days of Lent which preceded it.[31] Throughout the world, new believers were baptized and sacred virgins veiled during the Easter vigil (*exh.virg.* 7.42); across the whole world, concordant prayer was poured forth (*ep.ext.coll.* 13(=23).7); in Rome, Alexandria, Antioch and Constantinople, indeed in the whole world thousands were cleansed on the one day by the sacrament of baptism (*Spir.S.* 1.17f). The universality of the observance indicated its importance. Ambrose saw Easter as being connected with the biblical Passover. This was a standard position in early Christianity; indeed the biblical word for Passover, '*Pascha*', was used by Christians for Easter. But he also saw the feast as reaching back beyond this to the very beginning of the Bible. 'This month shall be unto you the beginning of months', God said to Moses and Aaron of the first month of spring, in which the Israelites left Egypt (Ex 12:2). Ambrose developed this notion by identifying that month with the one in which God made heaven and earth. So the turn of the seasons, when the rays of spring shone after the ice and fogs of winter and the reproductive cycle of plants began again, provided an image of the birth of the world. Building on Paul's remark that the Israelites who left Egypt and passed through the sea were baptized in the cloud and sea (I Cor. 10:1f), and assigning these events to spring, he concludes that they took place at the time when the Pascha of the Lord Jesus Christ was celebrated every year, a time of passing from vices to virtues. This made it appropriate for an exposition of the biblical words concerning the first month to be addressed to those who had been regenerated in baptism (*exa.* 1.4.13f, based on sermons preached in Holy Week). The creation and Exodus were at the centre of Ambrose's view of Easter.[32]

But the significance of Easter was more than purely theological. The law provided that all prisoners, except those guilty of the most serious crimes, were to be released on Easter Day.[33] It was turning into an occasion of social cohesion,

---

31. *Ep.* 36(=2).27. A study of the significance of Easter in the urban life of late antiquity would be welcome.
32. Helpful material in Cantalamessa (1979).
33. For the release of prisoners, see *cod.Theod.* 9.38.8, issued in time for Easter 385; Ambrose's '*venit pascha, venit indulgentia, advenit remissio*

when communities which were increasingly contoured by religion would go to the cathedral to welcome into the church new believers, some of whom would have come to town from the surrounding countryside for baptism.[34] For Ambrose, whose Easter hymn is full of words denoting water,[35] baptism was a key aspect of the season. Cathedrals built in the fourth century had large baptisteries, in which ceremonies of extraordinary power would be enacted on the night before Easter. These owed something to the community rituals of public bathing, and when Christians referred to the place where baptisms were carried out as a *'baptisterium'* they were using what had been for centuries the ordinary Latin word for a bathing place. The candidates for baptism would be anointed, a practice familiar from the baths, and descend into the font, which had the dimensions of a small swimming pool. There, in a ritual suggestive of burial, they would be immersed three times, once for each person of the Trinity. When they emerged they would be anointed again and the bishop would wash their feet. Such nocturnal ceremonies recalled the rites of initiation into mystery religions. When Rufinus described Ambrose's baptism in terms of his being 'initiated into sacred things' (*HE* 11.11), he registered, at least on a verbal level, correspondences with pagan practice.[36]

The newly baptized would then proceed from the baptistery to the spacious cathedral, where the bishop would celebrate the eucharist and they would take communion for the first time. Doubtless some were incredulous at what they were told was the transformation of bread and wine into the body and blood of Christ,[37] but Ambrose replied that the heavenly words of consecration showed that this indeed happened, the 'transfiguration', as he tended to call it, being effected by the words of Christ himself. Psalm 23 was sung while

---

peccatorum' (*Is.* 4.35) may be ambiguous. A letter of Cassiodorus on the freeing of prisoners, probably at Easter, deals with '*indulgentia*' (*Variae* 11.40; ed. *CCSL* 96:458).

34. As did Augustine for his baptism on the night of 24/5 June 387 (*conf.* 9.6.14).
35. '*Diluit*', '*refundens*', '*abluat*', '*mundans soluat*'.
36. See further below, p. 168.
37. Ambrose notes the comments 'It's my usual bread!' and 'It doesn't look like blood to me!' (*sacr.* 4.4.14, 20).

communion was administered, its references to a table and a cup running over being taken to refer to the eucharist. Ambrose saw participation in the sacrament as a kind of sober intoxication, a paradoxical notion which had already been used by Philo, Origen and Plotinus.[38] While Ambrose was aware of the evil of drunkenness, one of his hymns contains the words 'let us joyfully drink the sober intoxication of the Spirit', a wording precisely reflected in Augustine's description of Ambrose distributing the sober intoxication of God's wine to the people.[39]

The Easter vigil was thus a night of impressive ceremonies and heady experiences, and at both font and altar the central figure was the bishop. He also gave addresses to those preparing for the sacrament and the newly baptized. Ambrose's *De sacramentis* contains six addresses given to the newly baptized on the days of Easter Week, explaining things it would not have been proper to have explained to them previously, and the text which has come down to us almost certainly reproduces verbatim the spoken words of Ambrose.[40] The work is characterized by such features as a word-order similar to that of modern English, parataxis, short propositions, repetitions, questions and indeed puns, as well as the use of words in senses which point towards usage in modern Romance languages.[41] Few intellectuals of antiquity took it upon themselves to communicate with the wider public in such a way, yet Ambrose, like his near contemporaries Cyril of Jerusalem, Gregory of Nyssa and Augustine, delivered simple addresses

---

38. Lewy (1929), Dassmann (1965): 190–92. Ambrose knew of a good intoxication which leads to good and pleasant things and brings about an ecstasy of the mind (*mentis excessus*; *ps.118* 13.24). The wine which 'brings joy to the human heart' (Ps. 104:15) gives the intoxication of sobriety (*fid.* 1.20.135).
39. Hymn 2 (*In aurora*). 23f, cf. *sacr.* 5.3.13 and *myst.* 8.43; similar expressions occur in Paulinus of Nola (*Poemata* 24.685, 27.106; *PL* 61:628, 650). More generally, the reception of communion can be seen as drunkenness (*ps.118* 15.28. Augustine's description: *conf.* 5.13.23).
40. Compare Augustine's sermon 37, which exists in identical transcripts by two independent stenographers.
41. Word order: 'You saw water. But not every water heals. But the water heals which has the grace of Christ' (*sacr.* 1.5.15, inverting two words). Puns: '*Iudaei . . . ius dei*' (4.3.10). Words used in new senses: '*vere totum ubi tota innocentia, tota pietas, tota gratia, tota sanctificatio*' (*sacr.* 1.3.9). See Lazzati (1955) and Mohrmann (1952).

communicating essential things to ordinary people. As do his hymns, the *De sacramentis* allows us to catch Ambrose attempting to communicate with as wide a section of society as possible. Some of his material was secret. The written-up version of his addresses, the *De mysteriis*, which would have been read by non-believers, omits direct reference to material involved in what modern scholars call the *disciplina arcani*, a practice of disclosing key teachings only to believers shortly before or after baptism; as expressed by Ambrose, explaining the mysteries to the unbaptized would be betrayal rather than explanation (*myst* 1.2). As late as the time of Ambrose, the Lord's Prayer and the Creed were not to be made public (*Cain* 1.9.37, *inst.virg.* 2.10), and such concerns must lie behind the failure of his commentary on Luke to discuss passages dealing with the Lord's Prayer and the institution of the eucharist. 'Now is the time and the day for us to hand over the Creed', Ambrose would announce on Palm Sunday to those awaiting baptism a week later (*expl.* 1; significantly in its written form this short work, an exposition of the Creed, does not reproduce the text in full). So too the texts of the eucharistic canon and the Lord's Prayer are given in the *De sacramentis*, but not its written-up version, the *De mysteriis*. An air of excitement would have accompanied the transmission of such important secrets.

So it was that Easter was when a bishop most clearly fulfilled his functions. Bishops who, by some chance, found themselves unable to officiate at the Easter ceremonies, were distraught. It is easy to imagine Ambrose presiding in 386, in the cathedral from which enemies had sought to dislodge him, surrounded by the faithful, the 'people' who had so loyally supported him in the recent days of turmoil and threatened martyrdom, with great satisfaction.

. . .

CONTROVERSY WITH ANTI-NICAEANS

After Easter his enemies struck back. Ambrose was summoned to debate with the anti-Nicene Bishop Auxentius on the Trinity before the constistory. If he declined the summons, he was told that he would be free to leave Milan. But he was not keen to participate, and responded to the imperial proposal by preaching to the people an address against Auxentius which is worth extended summary.[42] He assured his hearers that he would never desert the church, as he feared the Lord of the world more than the emperor of this age. He asserted that if the emperor were to act as royal power generally does, he would undergo what bishops usually do. This slightly melodramatic utterance, verbally similar to that Ambrose represented himself as having recently addressed to the eunuch Calligonus, may have been intended to convey the message that persecution would be met by martyrdom. Would that he were certain that the church would not be handed over to heretics! He would willingly have gone to the palace of the emperor to debate with Auxentius, but struggles in the palace rather than in the church did not comport with the office of bishop. Ambrose rammed home the familiar point about handing over: when he was asked to hand over the sacred vessels of the church he replied that he was prepared to hand over his own property, but he could not tear away and hand over that which he had received so that he would protect it, not hand it over. He was also concerned for the salvation of the emperor, a sentiment surely full of the affection a bishop owed an emperor.

As he often did, Ambrose turned to his purposes a lesson which had been read out during the liturgy, which suggested encouraging precedents for someone being persecuted by royalty. God had supported Elisha against the king of Syria, and Peter against both Herod and the pagans prior to his crucifixion. For his part, Ambrose had walked past the palace every day, even though he had been expecting that something important would happen, perhaps the sword or fire. It had been suggested that he leave the city and go elsewhere, but where would he go? Where was there? Everywhere were groans and tears, as the orders were given for catholic bishops to be cast out from the churches and for those who resisted to undergo the sword, and for all the functionaries to be outlawed if they did not carry out what was ordered. Just as the Lord Jesus had redeemed the world in one moment, in one moment Auxentius had slain many peoples, some by the sword and others by sacrilege. Now, with his savage mouth and bloody hands, he was seeking a basilica from Ambrose.

42. *Ep.* 75A(=21a), usually called the *Sermo contra Auxentium.* McLynn (1994): 186, whom I follow, dates it to after Easter, others to Palm Sunday.

Another portion of the Bible which bore on the present situation was the account of the holy man Naboth. When asked by a king to give up his vineyard, he replied bluntly: 'Far be it from me to hand over the inheritance of my fathers.' Thereafter the king, deceived by the advice of a woman, came into possession of the field by means of the death of Naboth. The reference to a woman was already pointed, given the role Valentinian's mother Justina played in the controversy, and that to handing over which Ambrose read into the text[43] made it even more applicable to present circumstances: if Naboth did not hand over his vineyard, should we hand over the church of Christ? Only one response was possible: 'Far be it from me to hand over the inheritance of Christ!' (cf. I Kings 21:3). In any case, to whom could he hand it over? The attitude of the Arians was like the hostility of the Jews to the children who sang the praises of Christ as he entered Jerusalem. And whereas Jesus had driven people from the temple with a whip, Auxentius deployed sword and axe. How could such a man of blood and savagery dare to suggest a discussion? He thought to compel people to believe by a law, asserts Ambrose, thinking of the law enacted that January, but against him Paul asserted that justification was not by the works of the law (Gal. 2:16–19, of questionable relevance). Turning to Christ's injunction to render unto Caesar the things which are Caesar's and unto God the things which are God's, Ambrose observes that, as the church is God's, it cannot be delivered to Caesar. The emperor would be most honoured when he was called the son of the church, for he was within the church, not above it. Fire, the sword and exile were threatened, but the servants of Christ should not fear. The sermon ends inconsequentially. Having responded to the proposal of a debate, by implication in the negative, Ambrose asks Auxentius a question: why did he believe in rebaptism?

As with so many of the works of Ambrose, this sermon lacks coherence.[44] It is held together by a powerful animosity towards Auxentius and intimations of ferocious persecution,

---

43. LXX renders 'give', rather than 'hand over'.
44. McLynn (1994: 206) sees this as evidence of Ambrose responding to audience participation, but changes of direction are typical of his works.

although no other source indicates that this occurred or was expected to occur. Ambrose was simply deploying rhetoric based on the great persecutions of pagan emperors, just as in the sixth century catholic authors would attribute persecuting zeal to the anti-Nicene King Theoderic. Before long Ambrose wrote to Valentinian, declining to appear before the consistory, on the grounds that bishops, not lay people, should judge bishops (*ep.* 75(=21)). Valentinian's father had not acted in this way, even though he was much older and, unlike his son, had been baptized. Then Ambrose changes tack: he would have come to the consistory had the bishops and people allowed him, but they said that matters of faith should be discussed in the church before the people. He had been told that it made little difference whether he left the altar of Christ willingly or handed it over, for were he to leave he would still be handing it over. With these restatements of familiar themes, and an odd reference to an order that all the other churches were to be taken possession of, Ambrose concluded his letter. Another letter Valentinian received at about this time may have unsettled him more. It came from Maximus, whose name Ambrose had invoked before Easter. Playing on the weakness of Valentinian's position, the emperor in Gaul reminded Valentinian of his presence and alluded to the troubles in Milan. And if this were not enough to intimidate Valentinian, Ambrose had another card up his sleeve.

· · ·

THE DISCOVERY OF RELICS

Milan was soon to witness more amazing scenes.[45] In a letter to his sister which is our main source for them, Ambrose states that he had a feeling something would happen.[46]

---

45. For what follows, Dassmann (1975).
46. *Ep.* 77(=22). Curiosity as to the kind of feeling Ambrose had is not satisfied by his vague language: '*Statimque subiit veluti cuiusdam ardor praesagii.*' Augustine wrote that God revealed the hiding place of the martyrs to Ambrose visually ('*per visum*', *conf.* 9.7.16, just as Paulinus has Ambrose appear to people '*per visum*' and '*in visu*' after his death, *VAmb.* 50f) or through a dream (*civ.dei.* 22.8). Other sources are less precise: Bishop Gaudentius of Brescia and Paulinus have the martyrs merely revealing themselves to Ambrose (*PL* 20:963; *VAmb.* 14; cf. 29,

On 17 June he ordered that the ground near a grille located before the shrine of the martyrs SS Felix and Nabor was to be cleared. Two bodies, those of men whose wondrous stature showed they had lived in an earlier time, were found, and a demon seems to have identified them as SS Gervasius and Protasius. The names were generally unknown, but some old men said they had once heard them and read them on an inscription. Their bones were unbroken, although there was much blood. A huge crowd gathered around, and the relics were taken to the basilica of Fausta for an all-night service and the laying on of hands, following which they were carried to the new Basilica Ambrosiana. Along the way occurred a miracle rich in metaphorical significance: a blind person was healed.[47] Ambrose then preached a sermon which he claims to have reproduced in the letter to his sister.

Earlier in the year, Ambrose had observed that he could only offer tears against Gothic soldiers (*ep.* 75a(=21a).2). Now, the Lord Jesus was providing more efficacious protection, in the persons of the martyrs:

> These are the defenders I have obtained for you, holy people, who may benefit all and harm no-one. Such were the defenders I wanted and such are the soldiers I have, soldiers not of the world but of Christ. I fear no ill-will from them, whose support is both great and safe. May they also aid those who bear me ill-will! Let them come and see my bodyguards, for I do not deny that I am surrounded by such arms. 'Some in chariots and some in horses, but we shall be made great in the name of the Lord our God'. (cf. Ps. 20:7)

Yet again, Ambrose had defiantly challenged the Roman state, whose actions against him had been carried out by soldiers. Again, he went on to draw attention to Elisha who, surrounded by the army of the Syrians, prayed that his servant's eyes would be opened, whereupon he saw armies of

---

where the martyrs Vitalis and Agricola revealed themselves to Ambrose), while Paulinus of Nola speaks of God revealing the martyrs to Ambrose (*ep.* 32.17; *PL* 61:339).

47. 'Where there is misbelief there is blindness' (*ob. Theod.* 10; a reference to the power of the martyrs follows shortly). Compare Ambrose's hymn 7 (*In die Paschae*), verse 6, 'illuminating the blind with sight'. On the healing of blindness and baptism, cf. e.g. *ep.* 67(=80).5f, behind which lies Acts 9:8–18.

angels beyond counting. He described the martyrs as 'patrons', these being people who defended the interests of others. His images were all confrontationalist. Turning towards a theme which had exercised him before Easter, Ambrose stated that, while he was not worthy of being a martyr, he had obtained these martyrs for the people, and proposed that their remains be interred beneath the altar of the new basilica. In this way he linked the cult of the martyrs with himself, for not only was that the altar at which he offered the eucharist, but he had planned to be buried there himself, thinking it proper for a bishop to rest where he had offered the sacrifice. But he would yield to the martyrs the right hand side. On this scarcely modest note the sermon came to an abrupt end.

Ambrose was keen to identify himself with the martyrs, perhaps because he was still uneasy. Paulinus and Augustine both seem to misdate the finding of the relics to Holy Week, an error which suggests they interpreted it in the light of the tensions of that period.[48] That tensions between himself and the court continued can be deduced from Paulinus' description of miracles associated with the martyrs. For some time Ambrose had thought that 'Arians' lacked proper respect for martyrs (*fid.* 2.15.135), and people associated with the court now claimed that those from whom unclean spirits had ostensibly been driven had been bribed to act a part. But one of the crowd was suddenly seized by an unclean spirit, and began to cry out that those who denied the authenticity of the martyrs or did not believe in the unity of the Trinity as taught by Ambrose would be tormented, just as he was. The warning was not heeded, for those who should have been converted murdered the embarrassing man by drowning him in a pool (*VAmb.* 15f).

Despite hostility from the court, Ambrose had the crowd on his side. The people cried out that the deposition of the relics should be postponed until Sunday, but Ambrose brought the ceremony forward to the following day, when he again addressed them. After complimenting his hearers on their enthusiasm he began to attack unnamed enemies. Envious people who could not tolerate the crowds which had assembled hated what they were doing, he declared. In their madness they denied the merits of the martyrs, something

---

48. Paulinus '*per idem tempus*' (*VAmb.* 14.1); Augustine '*tunc*' (*conf.* 9.7.16).

which the very demons confessed. Just as the Jews denied that Christ was the Son of God even when they heard the devil say that he was, now the Arians were denying the evidence of the demons, who cried out that the martyrs were torturing them, and of a blind man, well known in the city, who was healed when he touched the edge of the fabric in which their relics were wrapped. Ambrose briefly switches into a more informal style:

> Here I ask whether they envy me or the holy martyrs. If it's me, have other miracles been happened through me, through my work, in my name? Why, then, do they envy me something which is not mine?

The sentiments so vehemently expressed seem out of place in a discourse on martyrs, and remind us of the dapth of Ambrose's involvement. Against the testimony of the demons that the martyrs were genuine, the 'Arians' claimed that what were called miracles were false and contrived shams. Ambrose was scornful: he had heard of many things being made up, but no-one had gone so far as to pretend to be a demon! The best proof of the authenticity of the relics were the miracles which had occurred.

The importance played by the dead in Christianity was known to its enemies,[49] and it was growing. A few years earlier Pope Damasus had conducted digging campaigns which led to the discovery of martyrs' bodies in Rome, where the cult of Peter and Paul was increasingly important. Ambrose had been uneasily aware of Milan's lack of martyrs, a deficiency which he had now stunningly overcome. The stature of the church of Milan had been enhanced, in a way that enhanced Ambrose's authority within it. Something similar was to occur years later, when the body of the martyr Nazarius was brought from a garden beyond the city to the basilica of the apostles, as was the body of the martyr Celsus. When this was done, one of the people, possessed by an unclean spirit, began to cry out that he was being tormented by Ambrose, but the bishop rounded on him, telling him to be quiet. According to Ambrose, it was the faith of the saints and the

---

49. Julian the Apostate famously observed that the world was being filled with tombs and sepulchres (*Contra Galilaeos* 335B).

envy of the devil at seeing humans ascend to the place from which he had been cast down that was tormenting him. The possessed person fell to the ground and said no more (*VAmb.* 32f). Here again, we see the growing power within the community of its bishop as he brought relics to a place where they would be firmly under his control.

. . .

AMBROSE VICTORIOUS

In the short term, the importance of the discovery of relics lay in the harm it did the government.[50] Cumulatively, Ambrose's actions in 386 may have fatally weakened the position of Justina and Valentinian, while in Gaul Maximus was presenting himself as a friend of the church. The pose may not have been entirely convincing, given that he had murdered Gratian, but emperors were always prepared to cultivate whatever constituencies seemed promising. Early in 386 a rigorist Spanish bishop, Priscillian, had been tried at Maximus' court at Trier and found guilty of sorcery, a crime which carried the death penalty.[51] Priscillian was an old enemy of Ambrose, for not only had the bishop of Milan refused to see him when he came to Italy seeking support in 383, but such benefit as Priscillian derived from his visit arose from a document he obtained from the *magister militum* Macedonius, whose relations with Ambrose were poor (cf. *VAmb.* 37). Maximus supported mainstream ecclesiastical opinion, while Valentinian's court seemed determined to antagonize it. So when he invaded Italy in the summer of 387, in an expedition which is not well documented, he was able to pose as the avenger of the wrongs done the church (Rufinus *HE* 11.16). Valentinian and Justina did not linger. They took ship to Thessaloniki, whereupon Maximus established himself as emperor in Milan. He was not to last long. In 388 Theodosius invaded Italy, where he encountered Maximus in two battles. The latter was captured and put to death at Aquileia in August. Later in the autumn Theodosius

---

50. This is true despite a need to revise a received view, according to which Ambrose violated a recent law against the translation of relics (so e.g. McLynn (1994): 213), against which Markus (1990): 144f.
51. Chadwick (1976).

arrived in Milan, to join the list of emperors who had to deal with the turbulent bishop of the city.

Meanwhile, the eunuch Calligonus, with whom Ambrose had exchanged harsh words, came to a sad end, being put to death for immoral conduct.[52] This must have happened by about 388, when Ambrose alluded to it in his work on Joseph (*Ios.* 6.29–33). When he discussed the dreams which the officials of Pharaoh (whom he thought of as eunuchs) told Joseph in prison, Ambrose refused to comment on the dream of the second eunuch, which Joseph interpreted to mean that he would be put to death. He utters a rhetorical question: 'But what shall I say about those eunuchs?' This is a device which, as in his discussion of the martyrs (above, page 135), Ambrose uses to emphasize the material which follows. Eunuchs, he goes on to observe, are people of weak and feeble status, for all their hope is in the will of the king. Hence, if they commit a trivial offence, they are in grave danger, and Ambrose represents himself as recoiling in horror at the death of his enemy.

It was a good time for Ambrose. In a work written in the late 380s, he looked with satisfaction at the standing of the church. For what did the gathering of the waters on the third day of the creation refer to but the catholic church being filled up with heretics and pagans (*exa.* 3.1.3; cf. Gen. 1:9)? It was as if the season had turned:

> Behold the acceptable time, when the year is not stiff with the wintery frosts of murky unbelief and the unformed surface is not frozen by the deep snows of blasphemy, the ice remaining firm. Freed from the storms of sacrilege, the earth is now ready to give birth to new fruits, and produces old ones. Yes, the storm of all controversies has come off the boil: the heat of each worldly passion and every blaze which cooked the people of Italy through the fires of perversity, first that of the Jews and then of the Arians, is now tempered by a serene breeze. The storm is calmed, concord sails, faith breathes, and now the sailors seek again the harbours of faith which they had left. They place sweet kisses on the shores of their fatherland, rejoicing to have been freed from dangers and rescued from errors.[53]

Time would tell whether this would last.

---

52. Augustine *Contra Julianum* 6.14.41 (*PL* 44:845).
53. *Luc.* 9.32. The reference to Jews is puzzling.

THE CITY AND ITS BISHOP

We have considered a number of issues in this chapter. In many ways, the cities of late antiquity remained untouched by the church, human sinfulness and the structures of ancient urban life proving hard to uproot. Yet a glance at the skyline of Milan would have shown how important the church had become. Ambrose's struggle with the court over the use of churches reveals much of the standing of the church and its bishop in the city. He entered the fight with great assets, among them the strength of his conviction, expressed in the concepts of martyrdom and handing over, which he communicated in powerful sermons. This could not be matched by his opponents, whose situation was in any case threatened by Maximus. Yet other considerations were more significant. Ambrose enjoyed the support of an enthusiastic community, whose commitment he built up by the singing of hymns, the celebration of Easter, and the cult of relics. These observances united those who participated in them, were pitched at a populist level, and remained firmly under episcopal control. Doubtless Ambrose did not carry all with him, and his repeated references to 'the people' must refer to a committed element among Milan's Nicene Christians, perhaps especially the less well-off who lived near the cathedral. Such people may have had little in common with the wealthy families which provided the church with its consecrated virgins. But with their support Ambrose carried the day in the city, in a way which anticipates the role bishops would play for centuries to come.

Chapter 6

ON DUTIES

Towards the end of the 380s Ambrose produced his longest work on a non-biblical theme, a treatise on duties (*De officiis*). It is not an easy work to read. Not only does it suffer from Ambrose's failings as an editor, which caused him to juxtapose in a confusing way material originally presented orally with formally written elements,[1] but he was not clear in his own mind as to the audience for which the book was intended, for although the book is addressed to his clergy, large portions of it seem unrelated to their specific needs. We may assume that the work was undertaken with them in mind, but that Ambrose, never a systematic thinker, followed his own inclinations in developing themes which led him away from the concerns of those for whom the work had been initially intended. Yet the book which he found himself writing is full of interest. It provides important evidence for the status of the clergy, an increasingly significant group in society, towards the end of the fourth century, and beyond this its contents raise the issue of how Ambrose was able to reconcile his beliefs as a Christian with what he knew of the intellectual and philosophical traditions of antiquity. For most of this chapter we shall therefore be concerned with this theme, which will involve analysis of other works of Ambrose we have yet to consider in detail.

---

1. Towards the beginning of the book are references to parts of the Bible which have been read out 'today' (*off.* 1.3.13, 4.15; 1.8.25) and elements of an informal style which sit uneasily with a clear statement that he was composing a written work (1.7.23). Cohesion is argued for in the important studies of Steidle (1984, 1985).

THE *DE OFFICIIS*

Ambrose begins his work by pointing out the duty of teaching imposed on bishops, and goes on to discuss the danger of talking too much and the value of silence. He states that he had been thinking about psalm 39, when it came into his mind to write to his 'sons', as he calls the clergy of Milan, on the subject of duties. The movement from meditative reflection on a part of the Bible to exposition is a typically Ambrosian reflex. But the point which follows is unexpected. Ambrose observes that the topic of duties had received the attention of a number of students of philosophy, such as Panaetius and his son among the Greeks and Cicero among the Latins.[2] Just as Cicero wrote to instruct his son, so now Ambrose would write to mould his sons, not loving those whom he had borne in the gospel less than he would have had he received them in marriage, nature being no stronger than grace in provoking love. But, Ambrose wondered, was it appropriate for someone in his position to write on the topic of duties? The word was certainly suitable for philosophers, but it also occurred in the Bible, for the gospel said of Zacharias: 'When the days of his duty were completed, he went home' (Luke 1:23), and hence it could be used by Christians. Having made this defence, based as his arguments so often are on an identity of words rather than ideas, Ambrose moves onto the attack. The writing he was undertaking was not pointless, because he valued duty in a different way from the philosophers, who in any case were figures of the past.[3] Whereas they think that the goods of this world are to be prized, we count them as losses, since a person who receives good here will be tormented elsewhere. Ambrose concluded the introductory portion of his book with a standard rhetorical ploy which he may not have meant his readers to take seriously: his work would appeal to those who sought not fine writing but straightforward arguments (*off.* 1.9.29).

---

2. Panaetius' son is otherwise unknown; perhaps his existence was suggested to Ambrose by Cicero's having written on duties to his son Marcus.
3. Note the tenses, '*aestimamus ... aestimaverunt*'. But the distinction is weakened in the following sentence.

In this way Ambrose located his work with respect to the works of non-Christian writers, in particular Cicero. His debts to Cicero were enormous. Ambrose owed the very title of this work to his Roman predecessor, whose *De officiis* also provided him with much of his material and a structure. Cicero's very addressee, his son, was paralleled by the 'sons' for whom Ambrose represented himself as writing his book. We have already seen how comfortable Ambrose was in using non-Christian sources, whether Philo in his early biblical commentaries or Cicero and Seneca when he came to commemorate his dead brother. Now, writing a serious book in an area where the tradition of work was firmly non-Christian, it was appropriate for him to consider the issues which separated him from his predecessors in the field, such as the teachings of the philosophers that God has no concern for the world, a topic which he treats in an unusually non-biblical way (*off.* 1.13.47–50), that God does not know what happens, and the problem of apparent injustice in the world. The first book mainly deals with what is honourable (*honestum*). After examining the virtue of silence, Ambrose settles into a discussion of the four cardinal virtues, long praised in the ancient world. He sees the first among them as prudence (or wisdom), from which are derived the other three, justice, fortitude and temperance. The list is taken from Cicero, and the sequence in which it presents the virtues contradicts that which Ambrose presents in some of his other writings, where he places justice as the primary virtue.[4] From these four virtues are born the various kinds of duties (*off.* 1.25.116). The four cardinal virtues can be found in the lives of biblical characters, who, as usual in Ambrose, turn out to be figures from the Old rather than the New Testament, and he provides substantial discussions of each of them. The second book, which deals with what is useful, is less structured. A good deal of it is taken up with money. Ambrose stresses that people who are concerned with money or personal influence will be of doubtful reliability, and that a good reputation, especially in the church, is to be sought by other means. The clergy should seek to earn respect for their mercy, fasting, integrity, doctrine, reading, the praise they give the activities

---

4. *Para.* 3.18; *ps.118* 11.11. Yet prudence is explicitly given the primacy at *off.* 1.27.126, and comes first at *Abr.* 2.8.24; *Is.* 8.65.

of others and their avoidance of boastfulness, rather than seeking to obscure the merits of the bishop by affecting knowledge, humility or mercy (*off.* 2.24.122f). Avarice, Ambrose held, was an ancient evil, and money something which should be despised.

The third book, in which the honourable and the useful are brought together, begins with a reference to David teaching us to walk in our heart as in a spacious home.[5] Scipio had said that he was not alone when he was alone, and never less at leisure than when he was at leisure (Cicero *off.* 3.1.1), a paradoxical sentiment in which, Ambrose thought, he had already been anticipated by a host of people mentioned in the Bible. After a lengthy display of biblical one-upmanship Ambrose returns to the themes of the honourable and the useful, and asserts that what is honourable surpasses what is useful (*off.* 3.6.37). He concedes that the two qualities often go together. Some years previously those foreign to the city had been expelled from Rome in time of famine, but shortly afterwards Rome had to seek grain from the very people whose children had been banished. Not only was the expulsion of the foreigners wrong, but as it turned out it was to no avail, whence it followed that what was honourable was also useful and what was useful honourable.[6] But the superiority of the honourable was clear, as the manner in which the Israelites took the Promised Land (*off.* 3.8.53–56) and numerous other events described in the Bible showed. Nothing, Ambrose asserts, is to be placed before what is honourable, but neither should friendship be passed over (*off.* 3.22.126). He concluded his work by stating that he had given his sons things to keep in their minds and put to the test. His three books contained nearly all the relevant examples and many of the sayings of their elders so that, even if the writer's style was not attractive, good instruction would still be found there (3.22.139).

---

5. Ambrose's words '*David propheta docuit nos tamquam in amplo domo deambulare*' unexpectedly echo the words he used elsewhere to describe the activity of David, '*deambulans*' in his '*domus*' on the afternoon when he caught sight of the naked Bathsheba (*apol.Dav.* 1.2; *apol.alt.Dav.* 2.5).
6. *Off.* 3.7.45–52; the second half of this passage is a powerful piece of writing. The expulsion was the work of Symmachus, while prefect of the city. It would therefore have occurred at about the time of Ambrose's controversy with him over the altar of Victory.

An unusual work among the writings of Ambrose, the *De officiis* is interesting in more than one way. Most obviously, it gives insight into the life of the clergy in Ambrose's time.

. . .

THE CLERGY

Ambrose saw the clergy as people with dignity. He reminds his readers that he once refused to admit a friend into the clergy because his way of walking left something to be desired, while another person, already a cleric, irritated him by his insolent gait. Such people gave an impression of levity and of being men about town. Ambrose had clear ideas on how a member of the clergy should walk: he was to avoid being so slow that he looked like a statue and so quick that he resembled an acrobat. His style of walking should have 'an appearance of authority, a weight of gravity, an imprint of tranquillity' (*off.* 1.18.72–5). Such a man would be a person of self control. Concern for this resonates through the advice Ambrose gives. It lies behind the injunction that the clergy should avoid the company of intemperate people, for those who sought pleasure, especially in banquets, play and fun, would weaken their manly gravity. It was necessary to guard against any impulse to slacken one's resolve. The clergy should avoid the banquets of outsiders, involving as they did a love of feasting, the telling of stories and the possibility of drinking too much.[7] Young clergy were only to go to the homes of widows and virgins for the sake of visiting, and then only in the company of their elders, the bishop or, in case of need, priests, for even those of faultless conduct could be held in suspicion. Free time could be profitably spent in reading the Bible and prayer (*off.* 1.20.87f). Jests were inconsistent with the discipline of the church, and could not be found in Scripture, while the telling of stories could weaken one's gravity (*off.* 1.23.102f). Ambrose has little to say on any temptation women might pose the clergy, being rather concerned with the gossip which innocent behaviour could cause. Avarice, which may have been in an obscure way

---

7. *Off.* 1.20.85f. One of the lessons Augustine learned from Ambrose was not to attend banquets held by one's fellow citizens (Possidius *VAug.* 27).

linked with chastity, was more of a problem. Writing to an emperor, Ambrose observed that the first victory of chastity was the defeat of desire for possessions, because desire for gain was a temptation for modesty (*ep.* 73(=18).12), and that he saw avarice as a problem for celibate clergy is implied by Paulinus (*VAmb.* 41). He knew that some who restrained themselves from sexual activity were seized by avaricious yearning (*ps.118* 16.45), which meant that avarice could be a particular temptation for chaste members of the clergy (*Luc.* 4.53).

The clergy were to be separate from the familial and social lives of those around them. Among such men, deprived of other relationships, friendship would be important:

> Preserve, my sons, the friendship into which you have entered with the brothers. Nothing in human affairs is more beautiful than this. For it is the solace of this life for you to have someone to whom you may open your heart, with whom you may share private things, and to whom you may entrust your innermost secret. You then have in place a faithful man who will rejoice with you when things go well, suffer with you in times of sorrow, and encourage you when you are attacked. (*off.* 3.22.132)

The language is powerful, and that Ambrose was proposing a dauntingly high estimate of friendship did not escape the notice of medieval readers.[8] But Ambrose's sentiments are borrowed, being a paraphrase of the sentiments of Cicero (especially *Laelius de amicitia* 6.22), and they need not imply anything about himself. Indeed, we may speculate whether they had any relevance to him at all, for there is scarcely any evidence for friendship in his life. The solitary reference to an unsatisfactory friend whom he refused to admit to the clergy is scarcely compelling, and close personal relationships of the kind Jerome and Augustine enjoyed, and which can be documented from sources of a similar kind to those we have for Ambrose, in particular letters, are unknown in his

---

8. Ailred of Rievaulx quotes a passage from *off.* 3.22.136 fairly accurately, but his disciple Walter found the doctrine so sublime and perfect that he did not dare to aspire to it, and was willing to settle for the concept of friendship suggested by Augustine, which seemed less demanding (*De spirituali amicitia* 3.83–85, ed. *CCSL Continuatio medievalis* 1; cf. Augustine *conf.* 4.8.13).

case. The biography of Paulinus breathes no hint that he had a friend.

Ambrose saw the job of the clergy as one of high status. The very word 'duties' he applies to their tasks indicates this.⁹ It was also suggested by his implicit comparison of the duties of the clergy for whom he wrote his book with those of the person for whom Cicero wrote, his son Marcus, whose career was distinguished. By basing himself on Cicero's text, Ambrose was saying something about his own status and that of his 'sons', the clergy. It was true that only a few followed their physical fathers into the clerical ranks, an unusual circumstance in a society where sons often followed fathers in a field of employment. But Ambrose pointed out that the work was burdensome and abstinence was difficult for the young, who did not find a life of obscurity attractive. The clergy were not to be downhearted in the face of this, for Ambrose told them that the service in which other people were engaged involved things of the present, whereas theirs was was to do with future things.¹⁰ At one point, after following Cicero, Ambrose comments:

> If those who exhort people to enter public life give these precepts, how much more ought we, called to duty in the church, do such things as may please God, so that the power of Christ might be in us? Hence we may be looked on with approval by our Emperor, so that our members may be the arms of justice, not arms of flesh in which sin reigns but arms strong for God by which sin is destroyed. (*off.* 1.37.186)

The emperor served by the clergy is superior to the one served by those who enter public life, Ambrose implies, yet again valorizing the church at the expense of structures of the Roman world. Moreover, his comparison of the clergy with members of the imperial civil service again raises the general question of the connections between classical antiquity and a new world increasingly coloured by Christianity. It will be worth our while to return to this topic.

---

9. See above, p. 45 n. 11. Duty is also an important theme in Ambrose's one letter to his clergy (*ep.* 17(=81).
10. *Off.* 1.44.218. The verb he uses, '*militare*', is often applied in the Theodosian Code to the activity of those in the civil service, as it may have been by Ambrose at *ep.ext.coll.* 10(=57).6.

AMBROSE AND CLASSICAL THOUGHT

When he began writing the *De officiis*, Ambrose followed Cicero's work of the same name closely, but as he proceeded he steadily became more original. Whereas in the first book Ciceronian reminiscences occur largely in bunches, in the second they occur with less density, often at the beginning or the end of a passage, while apart from one solid block they are thinly sown in the third book.[11] As his work advanced Ambrose increasingly adopted a biblical and exemplary tone; indeed, he ended by drawing attention to his use of a great number of examples (*off.* 3.22.139), which he drew from the Old Testament twice as often as the New. A book which began by locating itself against a background of classical philosophy had become steadily more biblical as it advanced.

One might see here a representation of the intellectual trajectory of late antiquity. Yet Ambrose was not prepared to write off non-Christian thought. Indeed, he asserted a direct connection between the Greeks and the Bible. Early in the *De officiis* he asks whether Panaetius and Aristotle were earlier than David, and states that when Pythagoras, who came before Socrates, told his disciples to maintain silence, he was simply passing on the teaching of David in a garbled form (*off.* 1.10.30f). In his biblical commentaries, Ambrose had already staked out a claim for Christian ownership of the Old Testament. Here he went further, claiming with insistence that whatever was good in classical thought had biblical origins. The idea was not original. It occurs in earlier Christian authors[12] and, like so much else to which Ambrose was attracted, it had developed in the Judaism of the Hellenistic period, for Philo had stated that Heraclitus drew on Moses (*Quaestiones in Genesin* 3.5). Oddly enough there was even a parallel to this position in Cicero, who held that a number of Greek philosophers had visited Egypt for instruction in intellectual matters (*de fin.* 5.29.87). Such a belief is implied in one of Ambrose's earliest works, when he spoke of the wise of the world having drawn their teaching from 'our laws' and derived it from the fountain of the divine law

---

11. Testard (1989): 118. Note a recent argument that Ambrose sought to replace Cicero's work: Davidson (1995).
12. See briefly Moorhead (1983).

(*exc.fr.* 1.42), and he went on to assert it with confidence. Cicero, Panaetius and Aristotle are said to have taken over the teaching of Job,[13] who is elsewhere said to have been older than Plato and Cicero (*off.* 1.12.43f). The same argument occurs in others of his works. Plato, he asserts, went to Egypt to learn the oracles of the law of Moses and the sayings of the prophets (*ps.118* 18.4), whereas David lived long before Plato; indeed, not only Plato's teacher but the grandparents of his grandparents could not have seen him, for David came at the beginning of the kingdom of the Jews, while Plato lived after the time of the captivity, when the Jewish monarchy had already been undone (*ps.* 35.1). One of Plato's borrowings was the idea of a garden which, among other things, he took from the Song of Songs (*bon.mort.* 5.19, 21).[14] Ambrose felt that such borrowings could even have occurred at a verbal level, for when Vergil used the noun '*puer*', which usually means 'child', to mean 'slave', whether directly or indirectly he may have been following the use of Scripture.[15] Ambrose asserts that he used the writings of Esdras in one of his books so the pagans might know that the things at which they marvel in the books of philosophy were taken across from ours (*bon.mort.* 10.45; an interesting sign that Ambrose anticipated a readership for this work outside the Christian community). Yet the pagans could not be trusted to have comprehended what they took: 'The orators of the world placed the things which they stole from our books in theirs, but he who first said it has the right way of understanding it' (*off.* 1.21.92). In a curious way, this strategy of attributing good things in pagan writings to the influence of the Bible may have worked in favour of the pagans, by guaranteeing the validity of some of their ideas. But as this was only achieved by placing them in the context of the Bible, Ambrose's strategy irretrievably undermined their autonomous value. His position was an easy one for someone who

---

13. *Off.* 1.36.179f; the verb '*transtulerint*' may also contain suggestions of 'translated', one of its meanings in classical Latin. Ambrose frequently uses it for the activities of pagan scholars confronted with the Bible, as at *bon.mort.* 10.45, 12.55; *fuga.* 8.51.
14. See further *off.* 1.21.94, 1.28.131–33, 1.29.141.
15. *Abr.* 1.9.82, referring to Verg. *Eclogae* 1.45, with which compare Gen. 42:2 (where Ambrose's '*puer*' translates the '*pais*' of LXX; Vulg. reads '*servus*').

had access to many of the writings of the philosophers to take; for future generations whose intellectual horizons were narrower, Ambrose's position may have come dangerously close to legitimizing ignorance.

We may use the *De officiis* as a point of departure for further discussion of Ambrose's intellectual culture. Just as he was coy in acknowledging his use of Philo in commentaries written at the beginning of his episcopate, Ambrose is understated as to his indebtedness to Cicero, whom he mentions just five times (1.7.24bis, 1.12.43, 1.19.82, 1.136.180). Today, many would see issues of intellectual honesty being involved here, and Ambrose has been accused of being 'an unscrupulous plagiarist' of Cicero in the course of one learned critique. But the charge is not well founded in detail,[16] and may miss the extent of the changes Ambrose made to Cicero. For example, considering the virtue of modesty, he recalls the case of Ham, who laughed when he saw his father Noah naked. Ambrose holds that from this arose an ancient custom, in Rome and many other cities, for adult sons not to bathe with their fathers, nor sons-in-law with their fathers-in-law, lest the authority which comes from the respect due to a father be lessened (*off.* 1.18.79). His discussion of the prohibition of inter-generational bathing takes its origin from Cicero, who handles it differently and, obviously, provides a different reason for it (*off.* 1.35.129). Again, writing of the duties of young men, the Roman author observes:

> A young man should respect those who are older, and choose from among them some fine people who are well thought of, on whose advice and authority he may rely; for the ignorance of someone just beginning should be set on a firm footing and ruled by the prudence of older men. In particular, this age is to be protected from desires and exercised by the toil and endurance of both mind and body, so that activity in the duties of war and politics may be successful. (Cicero *off.* 1.34.122)

16. Hagendahl (1958): 346–72 (the words quoted are at 372). Concerning *off.* 1.25.118, '*Primi igitur nostri definierunt prudentiam in veri consistere cognitione*', Hagendahl notes: 'In spite of the literal agreement with Cicero's definition . . . Ambrose pretends to follow Christian authorities (*nostri*)' (350). Yet it is clear from what follows that the authorities to whom Ambrose refers are those of the Old Testament, who came before Cicero.

Ambrose is much more to the point:

> Good young men should have the fear of God, defer to their parents, hold older people in honour, preserve their chastity, not scorn humility, and love clemency and modesty, which are as an ornament to the age of youth. (*off.* 1.17.65)

The two passages are very different. Not only is the syntax of Ambrose less complex, but the virtues which are commended are dissimilar and the purposes for which Cicero states they are to be exercised find no echo in Ambrose. Ambrose uses Cicero's work as a starting point from which he can go on to express his own ideas, rather than a body of ideas to be engaged with. The apparently careless manner in which he appropriated Cicero may have been connected with his having to read his work in scrolls rather than the codices which were generally used for the works of Christian authors, which would have caused him technical problems of a kind familiar to users of microfilms.[17]

Yet, however haphazard his use of Cicero, Ambrose remained open to the pre-Christian past. This was even true at the level of language. In some ways his Latin is very Christian. For example, he persistently refers to the first day of the week as the Lord's day, although laws issued at the time by Christian emperors still use the classical expression 'Day of the Sun'.[18] A description of David fighting against the Titans of classical mythology does no more than add an elegant touch to his prose, an appropriate one given the gigantic stature of David's opponent Goliath (*off.* 1.35.177). But when he writes of himself offering the sacrifice of the eucharist the terminology which came naturally to him was that which classical authors had used for pagan sacrifices.[19] Similarly,

---

17. Suggested, not conclusively, by Testard (1989): 75f.
18. Ambrose uses (*dies*) *dominica* at *Luc.* 8.26, *ps.* 47.1, *sacr.* 4.6.29; cf. *cod.Theod.* 2.8.1f and 8.8.3 (with 11.7.13), referring to 'the Day of the Sun, which our ancestors rightly called the Lord's day'. The term used by Ambrose was the one with a future in the Romance languages (cf. Italian *domenica*, French *dimanche*, Spanish *domingo*).
19. With '*nobis adolentibus altaria*' (*Luc.* 1.28), compare '*adolere altaria*' (Vergil *aen.* 7.71, Lucretius 4.1237). Ambrose's vocabulary was not precise: at *ep.* 72(=17).14 *ara* is used of both Christian and pagan altars, doubtless for rhetorical effect; *altaria* of pagan and *ara* of Christian at *ep.* 73(=18).10; *altare* and *ara* both used of Christian altars at *virgb.* 1.11.65.

Ambrose applied language drawn from non-Christian religious practice to baptism. In his funeral orations, he spoke of people being 'initiated into sacred mysteries' (*ob.Val.* 23, cf. 51) and 'initiated into the more perfect mysteries' (*exc.fr.* 1.43; cf. 1.44.49), and in a formal letter to Valentinian he wrote of the initiation of the emperor Constantius into the sacred mysteries (*ep.* 73(=18).32). Even in semi-formal works, he spoke of mysteries which it would not have been right to make known to those not yet initiated (*myst.* 1.1.2) and young women initiated into the sacred mysteries (*virgt.* 5.26). Such terminology, while it had long been used by Christians, would not have raised an eyebrow had it been used among pagans, for they employed it to describe their own rights of initiation into mystery religions.[20]

It would be ridiculous to suggest, on the strength of such verbal similarities, that Ambrose saw himself as doing the same things as officiants at pagan ceremonies. In various works he persistently uses the explicitly Christian noun 'baptism' for the sacrament, so his preference for language of initiation in some works is a sign of the level at which he was writing, and of a tendency to use different vocabularies for different audiences. Similarly, when he compared heresy to two monsters of classical mythology, the Hydra and Scylla (*fid.* 1.6.46), the learned allusion was not well received by his enemy Palladius, who urged him to desist from useless story-telling. Indeed, Palladius made the cutting suggestion that Ambrose brought up matters concerning monsters in his long-winded address simply to flaunt his literary knowledge (Palladius *apol.* 87; *Scolies*, ed. Gryson 272). Such allusions were appropriate only in works written for learned readers, and those to which Palladius took exception occur in a work addressed to the Emperor Gratian, himself a student of the scholar and poet Ausonius. Yet Christian and non-Christian discourses were permeable enough to operate at all registers. When Ambrose, in a hymn designed for popular singing, described the apostle John as standing motionless, he was using an expression derived from Vergil which a pagan contemporary, the historian Ammianus Marcellinus, applied to the Emperor Julian the Apostate, so fragile was the

---

20. Cf. Cicero *Tusculanae disputationes* 1.29.

division between ancient and Christian spirituality.[21] At the level of vocabulary Ambrose was happy to adopt explicitly non-Christian usage. To what extent was this also true of non-Christian thought?

. . .

NEOPLATONISM

Ambrose liked to think that the simple truth of the fishermen stood in the way of the words of the philosophers (*inc.* 9.89). He exuded a gruff, matter-of-fact air of common-sense realism. As in political life, so in intellectual life Ambrose saw the tide as flowing strongly in the right direction:

> The philosophers remain alone in their colleges. See how faith with its arguments is of greater weight:
> those who dispute at length are deserted each day by their comrades;
> they who believe simply grow each day.
> The philosophers are not believed; the fishermen are.
> The dialecticians are not believed; the publicans are.[22]

These comments are not borne out by his own practice.

It is one of the great achievements of modern scholarship on Ambrose to have discovered that at some points he drew upon the works of a great non-Christian philosopher, Plotinus.[23] A Greek-speaker born in the East, he had taught in Italy during the third century of the Christian era, and after his death his writings were published by his disciple Porphyry as the *Enneads* ('groups of nine'). The founder of a tradition now usually referred to as 'Neoplatonism', since it involved what its participants thought of as a revival of the teachings of Plato, Plotinus developed a complicated

---

21. See on his use of '*immobilis . . . stetit*' (*aen.* 12:398–400) Fontaine (1982), with an intriguing query as to the applicability of the expression '*Antike und Christentum*', given that Christianity developed as a part of antiquity (551 n. 81).
22. *Fid.* 1.13.84; philosophers and fishermen are also played off at *inc.* 9.89, while philosophy and dialectic are criticized at *fid.* 1.5.42 and *ps.118* 22.10. In all cases, Ambrose's comments occur in the context of attacks on 'Arian' thinking; hence he is making a point about heresy as well as philosophy.
23. See especially Courcelle (1950) and (1963).

philosophical system in which he posited the existence of the One, from which proceeds the world of ideas, from which in turn proceeds the spirit of the universe, this last being responsible for the creation of material things. Plotinus' thought is difficult and it is not expressed clearly, but Christian thinkers and those on the fringes of Christianity in late antiquity were fascinated by the points of contact it seemed to offer with their own beliefs. It was through reading Plotinus that Augustine, philosophically far more acute than Ambrose, thought himself advised to return to himself, and found himself far from God in what he termed a region of unlikeness (*conf.* 7.10.16, a passage full of reminiscences from Plotinus). Similarly, it was from 'the books of the Platonists' that he learned to seek an incorporeal truth (*conf.* 7.20.26). After his conversion to Christianity he drew on Neoplatonic teaching in his attempts to give expression to the mystery of the Trinity, and a long section of the *City of God* is devoted to delineating the common ground and the differences between the 'Platonists', by whom he chiefly means Plotinus and Porphyry, and Christianity. At the very end of his life, when the town of Hippo was besieged by the Vandals, Augustine's biographer Possidius describes him taking comfort from the opinion of 'a certain wise man', as he circumspectly terms Plotinus, that 'He is not great who thinks it is great that wood and stones fall and those destined for death die' (*VAug.* 28, quoting *enn.* 1.4.7). The impact of Plotinus on Christian intellectuals such as Augustine made him an important element in the second of the three major encounters which have taken place between Greek philosophy and a monotheism of Semitic origin.

It is not clear how Ambrose came to know of Plotinus, although the lack of allusions to his ideas in early works may indicate that he only discovered him some time after he had become a bishop. He may have been introduced to him by his 'father in grace', the scholar Simplicianus, who had Neoplatonic leanings. In one of his letters to Simplicianus, Ambrose credited him with showing how far from the truth the 'books of philosophy' were (*ep.* 2(=65).1), but this may reveal how Ambrose wished to understand his learned correspondent, or perhaps how Simplicianus wished to be understood. When Augustine was in Milan Simplicianus gave his approval to his reading of Neoplatonic books, and told him of Marius Victorinus, a formidable scholar of African origin who included Neoplatonism among his intellectual interests, and in whose conversion to Christianity he had been involved (*conf.* 8.2.3–5).[24] But Ambrose made very little use of Neoplatonic texts in his early works, when the influence of Simplicianus on him is likely to have been at its strongest, and we must be sceptical as to the existence of a Neoplatonic circle at Milan.[25] Moreover, Ambrose's knowledge of the writings of Plotinus was not wide, for his borrowings from Plotinus in specific works tend to come from a very narrow range of the *Enneads* in each case,[26] and it is possible that his access to Plotinus was by way of an intermediate source or sources.[27]

One of the phrases in Plotinus which made the greatest impact on Christian readers was his observation that one should flee to one's true country. Intimations of it, perhaps not reflecting conscious recollection of it, occur in contexts where one would not expect to see the influence of Plotinus on Ambrose. Discussing the biblical story of the wise men who worshipped the infant Jesus, Ambrose points out that they came to him by one way and went away by another. He links this circumstance with the teaching of Jesus on the two ways, one of which leads to destruction and the other to life (Matt. 7:13f). But Ambrose replaces 'life' with 'kingdom', which allows him to suggest that the former is the way of sinners which leads to Herod, while the latter way is Christ, by which one goes back to one's country. By being on guard against Herod we may gain an eternal dwelling place in the heavenly country (*Luc.* 2.46; *ep.* 11(=29) is saturated with the language of Plotinus).

---

24. See further *civ.dei* 10.29 fin. Many of Victorinus' works survive.
25. Madec (1987).
26. The index of ancient authors appended to the *SAEMO* edition of the *De Isaac* indicates eight borrowings, but all but one of them are from a short section of the *Enneads* (1.6.7–1.8.8), and the other may be from Origen rather than Plotinus directly (*SAEMO* 3:51 n. 35); all but three of the ten passages used in the *De bono mortis* are from the first book of the *Enneads*; and of the nine passages drawn on in *Iac.*, seven fall in the range 1.4.2–1.4.16.
27. Madec (1974), together with Savon (1977b). The narrow range of the *Enneads* on which Ambrose draws in his various works could be held to support this hypothesis.

Ambrose's use of Plotinus is particularly striking in three works which seem to have been written within the space of a few years, *De Isaac vel anima* (On Isaac or the soul), *De bono mortis* (On the Good of death), and *De Iacob et vita beata* (Jacob).[28] Hence, an influence on Ambrose's thinking from outside the Judeo-Christian tradition apparently came to operate in a significant way after he had been a bishop for over a decade. One of these works, that on Jacob, we have already examined (above, page 135ff); we shall now consider the other two, which as it happens are closely linked.

The *De Isaac*, as its subtitle suggests, is largely concerned with the soul, a topic on which Ambrose believed the Song of Songs had a good deal to say. In this work he interprets the bride of the Song as the soul. He sees her as being set on the chariots of Aminadab (Song 6:12), which were drawn by horses. These could be good, in which case they stand for the virtues of the soul, or bad, in which case they represent bodily passions. Ambrose identifies the good horses with the cardinal virtues, here itemized as prudence, temperance, fortitude and justice, and names the four bad horses as wrath, ardent desire, fear and iniquity (*Is.* 8.65; the four bad horses are identified as wrath, cupidity, enjoyment and fear at *virgt.* 15.95). The good horses, which fly upwards as they raise themselves from the earth to higher things, lifting the soul with them, behave in a very Neoplatonic way, and Neoplatonic themes are particularly clear in both the argument and the expression given to it as the book moves towards its climax. 'Let us take the wings which, like flames, head towards higher regions!' exhorts Ambrose, following Plotinus (*Is.* 8.78; cf. *enn.* 1.6.7). When he asserts that the fount of life is the highest good (*summum bonum*) and that we should flee to our true country he appropriates concepts readily to hand in Plotinus, even though he immediately Christianizes the latter point

---

28. Courcelle (1950a, 1963a) has argued that the *De Isaac*, *De bono mortis* and the *Exameron* are versions of sermons which Augustine heard in 386 and which led him to accept a Neoplatonist interpretation of Christianity. His theory is exciting but remains unproven, for not only does the dating of these works remain open, but what Augustine later remembered as having learned from Ambrose was a general principle of biblical interpretation, already widespread, that 'the letter kills but the Spirit gives life' (II Cor. 3:6), rather than any doctrine which can be traced to Neoplatonic sources (*conf.* 6.4.6).

when he observes that Jerusalem is the mother of all.[29] But what does this flight consist of, Ambrose asks? He answers in terms drawn from Plotinus. When he asserts that the fatherland cannot be reached by feet, chariots or horses but rather by mind (*animus*), eyes and interior feet (*Is.* 8.79) he closely follows his source, according to whom feet, carriage and boat will not suffice (*enn.* 1.6.8). The 'good' (*bonum*) we seek is God, who is the only good, for there is no-one good but the one God (cf. Mark 10:18). We know this good in a spiritual way: just as only a healthy eye can look at the sun, so only a good soul can see the good. Life is a good, but death is not to be feared, for while it is rest for the body it brings freedom and release for the soul. We are not to fear the one who kills the flesh but not the soul (cf. Matt. 10.28), for someone who takes away our clothing can steal what is ours, but not what we ourselves are. Having already delivered himself of the opinion that the pleasures of the body are evil enticements, from which the soul flees like a sparrow from a broken snare (7.61), Ambrose is definite in his identification of individuals with their souls: 'We are souls . . . we are souls; our limbs are (just) clothes' (*Is.* 8.79).

We have already seen Ambrose taking a negative view of the human body (above, page 56ff), but this scarcely prepares us for the finale of the *De Isaac*. Ambrose's identification of individuals with their souls and his understanding that these are released by death are views for which there is scarcely any support in the Judeo-Christian Scriptures, just as his implication that the body will be discarded is hard to square with the teaching on the resurrection of the body found in the Apostles' Creed. His view represents the triumph of Greek speculation over any dignity Christian thought has vested in the body.

Ambrose developed his position in a book on the good of death, *De bono mortis*, in which he deals with a question posed by Plotinus: 'If life is a good, how is death not evil?'[30]

---

29. *Is.* 8.78; see Plotinus *enn.* 1.6.7 (*summum bonum*), 1.6.8 (flight to true country; but Plotinus has himself borrowed the language of Homer, *Iliad* 2.140). A comment by Plotinus shortly afterwards that we should flee to where the Father is assisted in a Christian interpretation of this passage.
30. *Enn.* 1.7.3. Ambrose had already discussed the topic in the second oration on the death of his brother, *exc.fr.* 2.39, within a section with

He replies that there are three kinds of death: a death arising from sin, a mystical death by which one dies to sin and lives for God, and that by which we complete our journey through life, which he follows Plotinus in defining as 'a separation of soul and body'.[31] What, then of the body? Ambrose is blunt: 'The body is your enemy, which makes war on the mind.'[32] Another image derived from Plotinus (*enn.* 1.4.16, cf. 1.1.3), suggested a less negative view: the body could be seen in a neutral way, as a means by which virtues could be displayed, for the soul was able to use the body as an instrument or organ on which it could play the tunes of chastity and temperance, the song of sobriety, the sweet sound of bodily integrity, the pleasantness of virginity, and the seriousness of widowhood.[33] One way of understanding Christ's words concerning two or three gathered together in his name was to see them as referring to the soul and the body or the flesh, the former bringing the latter under control, just as Paul castigated his flesh and brought it into slavery.[34] The third kind of death, when the soul is separated from the body, brings pleasure to few, but this is the fault not of death but of weakness: 'Taken captive by the pleasure of the body and delight in this life, we dread the end of the journey, in which there is more bitterness than pleasure' (*bon.mort.* 2.3). The categories of pleasure and delight, which Ambrose elsewhere saw as having been involved in the Fall and in the light of which he interpreted the singing of the Sirens, make their return, yet again linked with the body. As life is so full of hardships, Ambrose is not surprised that the book of Ecclesiastes, having praised the dead above the living, went

---

overtones of Plotinus (e.g. the notion of 'returning to that country' at 2.33).
31. *Enn.* 1.6.7; consult *SAEMO* 3:131 n. 6 on the notion of the three kinds of death, which goes back to Origen, and n. 9 on the Platonic background to the third death (which is similarly defined at 8.31, but note that Courcelle, cited here, errs in seeing Macrobius writing before Ambrose).
32. *Bon.mort.* 7.26; see in general Seibel (1958).
33. *Bon.mort.* 6.25; see too *Iac.* 1.8.39: *Luc.* 6.10.
34. *Inst.virg.* 2.10f, on Matt. 18:19f. There is more here than meets the eye, for Paul's 'enslavement' of his body (1 Cor. 9:27) recalls the rulership exercised by the man over the woman (Gen. 3:16); for Ambrose's association of the body with women, see above, p. 58.

on to say that 'above both these is the one not yet born, who does not see this evil'.[35]

Ambrose argued his case with the forcefulness of a schoolboy debater: if life is a burden, its end is a relief. A relief is good, death is the end; therefore, death is good (*bon.mort.* 2.5). When Simeon, having taken the infant Jesus into his arms, said 'Lord, now lettest thou thy servant depart in peace' (Luke 2:29) he meant a release from the chains of the body, an image which recalls that of the body as a prison. Seeing death in this way, Ambrose praises it as a freeing from the chains of the body, and argues that we should flee evils and lift up our soul to the image and likeness of God (5.17). This expression combines the notion of flight, borrowed from Plotinus, with an allusion to the biblical teaching that humankind was created in the image and likeness of God (Gen. 1:26), the latter replacing a reference in Plotinus to Plato's notion of humans 'being made like God' (*enn.* 1.2.1; cf. Plato *Theaetetus* 176). Ambrose's amendment Christianizes the vocabulary, but scarcely the thought. The Song of Songs again makes an appearance, the bride again being seen as the soul (5.18–20). But Ambrose's argument seems to point away from the sense of the Christian Scriptures, and he makes heavy weather of them. To make a quotation from Paul fit his argument he takes a reference to his members warring against the law of his mind as applying to the soul (7.26 on Rom. 7:23), while a reference by Jesus to his 'life' is changed to make it apply to his soul (10.43 on John 10:18). IV Ezra, a Jewish work written in the early Christian period, is altered, a reference to souls that have striven to 'overcome the innate evil thought that it might not lead them astray from life unto death' (IV Ezra 7:92) being amended so that the souls have 'overcome the flesh and have not been bent over by its allurements' (11.48). Paul's teaching on the resurrection of the body, difficult to square with Ambrose's emphases, makes only a fleeting appearance (8.33), while conversely Ambrose praises the teaching of 'the Greeks' (8.34). He goes on to write of the soul:

35. See Eccl.4.2f. The thought is a commonplace with Ambrose. In his second oration on Satyrus he had commented favourably on such an opinion (*exc.fr.* 2.30, quoting the same text from Ecclesiastes), and elsewhere he stated that a dead person is esteemed above the living, and one who has not been born above the dead (*ps.118* 18.3).

Let that part which is on good terms with the virtues, a friend of the disciplines, zealous for glory, a follower of the good and subject to God, fly to that elevated place and remain with that undefiled, perpetual and immortal good. Let it hold fast to Him and be with the one from whom its kinship is derived, just as a certain person says: 'Whose offspring we are.' It is evident that the soul does not die with the body, because it does not come from the body. (9.38)

The image of the flight of the soul is Platonic in origin (*Phaedo* 79D), and the statement attributed to 'a certain person' is from Aratus, a Greek writer of the third century BC. Ambrose borrowed it from St Paul, who quoted it in a sermon (Acts 17:28). But as the book moves towards its end it becomes far more Christocentric. Ambrose turns to the figure of Christ, and speaks of following him, the one without whom no-one goes up (12.55). The biblical and liturgical notion of going up was important to Ambrose (above, page 92ff), and it was also easy to link with Neoplatonic thought, according to which the soul, when freed from the prison of the body, flies upward to the higher place whence it had come.[36] The point is neatly made, just as a reference in a psalm to finding good things in the land of the living (Ps. 27:13) is used to Christianize the Neoplatonic notion of the good. Indeed, such are the similarities between Neoplatonism and Christianity that Ambrose, using a standard ploy, states that the philosophers gained their idea of the 'highest good' from the Bible. We should advance with confidence to life, he concludes, seeking the risen and ascended Christ.

The use to which Ambrose put Plotinus is of a different order from that to which he put Cicero in the *De officiis*. In the latter case his debts, while substantial, are largely in terms of words and the organization of material, and in any case the material Ambrose drew from Cicero concerns ethics rather than doctrine. The things which Ambrose found Plotinus saying came closer to the heart of Christianity. When we consider the thinking of Plotinus now, it seems in some ways to express and in other ways to subvert Christian doctrine. But as Ambrose understood Plotinus, his teaching could

---

36. Cf. *Cain* 2.10.36. Hence Ambrose can describe the soul of the departed emperor Theodosius as returning to the place whence it came down (*ob.Theod.* 36).

be assimilated very easily into the structures of Christianity. Indeed, some of what he says in passages influenced by Plotinus he had already said in earlier books, in particular when he discussed the body. Hence there is no need to see Plotinus as a determining influence on the thought of Ambrose. To be sure, he went through a period of enthusiasm for him, but this meant nothing more than the addition of Plotinus to the list of Ambrose's intellectual enthusiasms. Just as he drew on Philo in early works, but disdained to do so in some of his later commentaries on Genesis, and just as he felt free to interpret the figure of the bride in the Song of Songs in various ways, for a while he was captivated by what he found in Plotinus.

. . .

SYNTHESIS

Yet there was no escaping the reality that Plotinus, and the current of Neoplatonism he represented, was hostile to Christianity. Despite this, Ambrose was happy to take and exploit what he found there. It has been well said that Ambrose has an extraordinary and disconcerting aptitude to empty formulae of their substance.[37] An example of this, which also reflects his interest in words rather than ideas, is furnished by his use of the word '*conscientia*' (perhaps 'self-awareness') in the *De officiis*, which suggests his difficulties in integrating biblical incidents with the sense he found in the word.[38] But Ambrose's ability to bring together such disparate materials as those he encountered in Cicero and Plotinus point to one of his strengths as a thinker which we have already encountered in our discussion of his work on the Bible, his synthesizing power. Ambrose had an ability to take what seem to be very dissimilar things and make them fit categories already established in his mind. We shall return to this theme, taking as an example things that come in fours.

---

37. Madec (1974): 175, who goes on to observe that one is dealing here with a process of substitution and not doctrinal synthesis.
38. Testard (1973), who makes the interesting suggestion that the diminishing number of occurrences of the word as the book proceeds indicates Ambrose's awareness of the problem and his inability to overcome it (247).

As we have seen, Ambrose felt that the four virtues could be seen in various parts of the Bible. Indeed, they were represented by the four rivers of paradise mentioned in Genesis 2. In this context they carried an additional layer of meaning, for they also stood for the four ages of the world. Hence the Phison represented wisdom and the period before the Flood, the Gihon temperance and the time of the patriarchs, the Tigris fortitude and the time of the law and the prophets, and the Euphrates justice, a quality which is connected with the Gospel (*para.* 3.15–22). This understanding of the rivers of paradise involves taking the four virtues in an unusual order (cf. above, page 159), but it is partially corroborated when Ambrose discusses God's promise that the land from the river of Egypt to the great river Euphrates would belong to the descendants of Abraham (Gen. 15:18). The river of Egypt, which Ambrose identifies as the river Gihon, stands for earthly things, such as chastity of the body, patience and temperance, whereas the Euphrates stands for virtues of the soul, among which is justice, the pre-eminent virtue upon which the proper exercise of prudence and bravery depend (*Abr.* 2.10.68).

Another part of the Bible contained the prophet Ezekiel's description of four living creatures which had the faces, respectively, of a human being, a lion, an ox and an eagle, and four wheels which were associated with them. Ambrose held that the prophet wished to describe the soul, whose motions are as four horses. Naming them in Greek, he identifies them as reason, passion, desire and discernment, each of them being signified by one of the living creatures. The wheels with which they were associated turn out to be the virtues of prudence, temperance, fortitude and justice. Elsewhere he interprets the human being as standing for prudence, the lion for fortitude, the ox for temperance and the eagle for justice.[39] Another reference to the virtues, as we have seen, was implicit in the chariots of Aminadab, where the contrary vices were also indicated (Song 6:12; see above, page 172) The virtues could also be discerned in the beatitudes declared by Christ, for the poor in spirit have

---

39. *Abr.* 2.8.54, on Ez.1 (Ambrose believes that Plato drew some of his teaching from this part of the Bible); *virgt.* 18.114f. Good discussion in Jenal (1995): 528–31.

temperance, those who hungered and thirsted for justice obviously possess that virtue, those who weep are prudent and those who are hated have fortitude (*Luc.* 5.62–68). In all these instances Ambrose reads the four categories into biblical passages; in some cases he uses them as a tool to suggest other four-way schemes of itemization. Another four-way patterning was suggested by the four parts into which Ambrose believed, going beyond the accounts in the gospels, that Christ's garment was divided by the soldiers who crucified him: he connects these with four colours, and the different qualities of the four evangelists (above, page 84).

The ancient notion of there being four elements out of which the body was made offered another way of understanding the data of the Bible. Aaron's ephod was made of gold, and then blue, purple, scarlet and flax (Ex. 39:2). Given that blue is like the air, purple water, and scarlet fire, while flax comes from the earth, Ambrose felt that this combination of colours indicates the four elements which constituted the human body (*fid.* 2 prol. 11f). An identical point is made concerning the bed of Solomon. It was constructed from the wood of Lebanon, its columns were made of silver and its base of gold, while its back was strewn with gems (Song 3:9f). What does this bed reveal but our body, for the gems stand for air, gold for fire, silver for water and wood for earth, the four elements which make up the body (*virgb.* 3.5.21)? It must be said that here, as in the case of Aaron's ephod, there is a degree of straining: the ephod's having also been made of gold, and additional information concerning the middle of Solomon's bed, each of which would have introduced an awkward fifth category into the discussion, are understandably passed over. Sometimes the strokes of Ambrose's brush are uncomfortably broad, as when he asserts that the statement that in the beginning God created heaven and earth really comprehends all four elements (*exa.* 1.6.20), and that while Christ hung on the cross all the elements did him service, even though he only mentions the sun, presumably doing duty for fire, and the earth (*fid.* 2.11.96).

Ambrose, then, loved to make connections. His intellectual world was one of synthesis. Not for him the company of those who sought for exact knowledge:

> What is so obscure as the investigation of astronomy and geometry, which they carry out? And to measure the great extent of the air, and to imprison the heaven and sea with numbers, to leave the causes of salvation and to seek errors? (*off*. 1.26.122)

At this point he engages with a passage of Cicero, who had named scholars who excelled in astrology and geometry (*off*. 1.19; Ambrose alters Cicero's 'astrology' to 'astronomy'). It must be said that the Romans themselves were not particularly adept at scientific work, and Ambrose's coolness may represent a Christianized version of an attitude already widespread in his society, but Cicero had mustered more enthusiasm than Ambrose could manage. Synthesis, rather than analysis and measurement, interested him. His mind was happy placing things together and seeing connections between them, and it was in this context that, as a Christian, he approached the ideas of Plotinus.

. . .

CONCLUSION

The themes we have considered in this chapter are diverse, but they share a common characteristic. Ambrose's locating the position of the clergy in society by comparison with that of a Roman noble entering public office was a sensible strategy in the fourth century, but it was to have little resonance in the following centuries, for before long western Europe was to see the emergence of political structures in which the figure of the Roman noble would be of little direct relevance. Similarly, his using a work of Cicero as the basis for a discussion of the duties of the clergy must have given readers in the following centuries a feeling that his work was part of an outmoded discussion, for they would have expected a more explicitly Christian framework. In the same way, the theory that the Greeks borrowed their good ideas from the Hebrews was not destined to endure. While Augustine noted with approval in one of his early works the discovery of 'our own Ambrose' that Plato travelled to Egypt when Jeremiah was there, whence he came to know 'our literature', as time passed he turned against the theory.[40] It was to have a very

---

40. Jeremiah: *doct.christ.* 2.28.42. Turns against theory: *civ.dei* 8.11f; *retr.* 2.4 (*PL* 32:632).

limited life in the West, doubtless because the insecurity of Jewish and then Christian thinkers faced with the attractiveness of classical thought, which may have prompted the creation of the theory, ceased to be a problem for Christians as their faith triumphed. Indeed, the tenses Ambrose uses in the expressions 'they thought' and 'we think' (above, page 158) suggest a feeling that pagan thought was a thing of the past with which there was no real need to engage. Even Plotinus, however attractive Ambrose found him in the years of his intellectual maturity, posed no great threat to his equilibrium. He assimilated ideas and expressions into his own writing and calmly went on. Works written late in his life show Ambrose steadily becoming more Christian and biblical in his approach.

The mid-380s therefore emerge as an interesting stage in Ambrose's intellectual development. We have already seen that it was then that he set about comparing translations of parts of the Old Testament, and how the thinking of earlier commentators then led him to develop extended commentaries on sections of the Song of Songs. To these signs of intellectual activity we may add his interest in Plotinus. That this was a time of heavy involvement in affairs of state can only heighten one's sense of the energies which Ambrose had at his disposal in these years. The period which was to follow would confront him with problems which were less tractable, yet Ambrose's responses were to be as creative as ever.

Chapter 7

THE ELDERLY BISHOP

The victory of Theodosius over Maximus in 388 meant the end of various tensions in Ambrose's political life. But circumstances changed quickly. Before long he picked two fights with Theodosius, one over an incident concerning Jews and the other over reprisals the state exacted after an incident in Thessaloniki. Other developments, in particular the murder of Valentinian, which led to a civil war, and the death of Theodosius, which brought a Germanic general to power in Italy, demanded appropriate responses from the bishop of what was effectively the capital city of the West. The first of these events involved a topic of great interest to Ambrose. We shall approach it by way of the broad contours of Ambrose's thought on Jews.

. . .

THE JEWS

Ambrose saw all kinds of continuities between the world of the Old Testament and that of his own day. The Latin word he used for a priest of Old Testament times, '*sacerdos*', was the very word he tended to use for a Christian bishop, and he thought of his office in the church in terms of the Jewish priesthood (*ep.ext.coll.* 14(=63).48ff, esp. 59, written to the church of Vercelli). It was natural for him to feel he could rely on the biblical figure of Eleazar, a fellow *sacerdos*, to help him with his prayers.[1] Similarly, for much of the Old

---

1. *Iac.* 2.10.43, a bold stroke given that Eleazar was merely a scribe (II Mac. 6:19), although of priestly family (I Mac. 5:4). Ambrose almost always uses the word '*sacerdos*' to mean bishop should he use it for

Testament the Septuagint rendered the Hebrew noun for the 'community' of Israel by the Greek word *'ecclesia'*, the word used in Latin as well as Greek for 'church', a translation Ambrose was perfectly content to follow (e.g. *Luc.* 3.30; *ps.118* 10.3). He was happy to identify the prophet Elisha as a disciple of Christ (*ep.* 51(=15).6). It was therefore legitimate for him to see the Jews of biblical times as 'our ancestors' and 'our fathers'.[2]

Yet Genesis, the Psalms and the Song of Songs, the books of the Old Testament to which Ambrose continually returned, are secondary to the story of the Exodus and the giving of the Law in the understanding Judaism has of itself. For all his interest in the Jewish scriptures and some Jewish exegesis of them, Ambrose found little to detain him in the parts of the Bible in which Jewish identity is most clearly expressed. His treatment of texts sometimes lessens their Jewish nature, as when he edits out the references to the Maccabees being the children of Abraham found in I Maccabees.[3] And whatever standing the Jewish people may once have had, Ambrose felt that it had been decisively replaced in God's favour by the Christian people. He persistently interprets the tales of sibling rivalry in which the elder is overcome by the younger, which are such an important and sustained feature of the book of Genesis, as referring to the synagogue and the church, or the Jewish and Christian peoples, respectively,[4] just as he displays an extraordinary ability to relate pairs of individuals mentioned in different parts of the Bible, one bad and one good, to Jews and Gentiles.[5] He often interprets the parables

---

priest, as at *off.* 2.15.69, another term is used nearby for bishop); Jerome and Augustine use it for both priest and bishop, while subsequently it tends to mean priest.

2. See for example *Cain* 1.8.31, 9.35; *ep.* 57(=6).2; *ep.ext.coll.* 14(=63).28; *ps.* 43.12; *sacr.* 1.4.11. St Paul described the Jews as 'our fathers' (I Cor. 10:1).
3. See above, p. 136 for Ambrose's replacement of 'the religion of our fathers' by 'religion'.
4. So his exegesis of Cain and Abel (*Cain* 1.2.5), Ishmael and Isaac (*Abr.* 1.4.28), Esau and Jacob (*Iac.* 2.3.10), and Leah and Rachael (*Iac.* 2.5.25). Compare Jacob's blessing of Ephraim and Manasseh (*Iac.* 2.9.37).
5. Hence the two children of David by Bathsheba (*apol.alt.Dav.* 7.38); two men in a city, one rich and one poor (ibid. 11.57); two brothers in the parable of the prodigal son (*Luc.* 7.239); two women at a mill (*Luc.* 8.48).

of Jesus as portraying the Jews negatively with respect to the Christians.[6]

The Jews, therefore, had been replaced by the Christians. Jesus once spoke of two women grinding at a mill. The mill could be taken to stand for the world, but Ambrose preferred to think of it as the human body which encloses the soul like a prison. In this mill the synagogue, or bad-living soul, is unable to separate the inner part of the grain from the husks, but the holy church, or the soul unstained by contact with sins, offers good flour to God (*Luc.* 8.48, on Luke 17:35). In this dense cluster of images, the soul is seen as being enclosed in the prison of the body; it is assimilated into the church, a move authorized by Ambrose's long meditations on the Song of Songs; and the church is compared, to its advantage, with another female figure, that of the synagogue. The failure of the Jews to follow the clear lead of their own Scriptures and join the church exasperated Ambrose. He found their unbelief, quite simply, damnable (*exh.virg.* 10.66). Commenting on a passage of Genesis, he accused the Jews of failing to understand what they read and not wishing to believe what Moses wrote. For what could be more obvious?

> In this place they are invited to pass over to the church of God, and those who were confined within the borders of Judaea to migrate to the people of God who have come together from the whole earth, from all nations and peoples, to become a great people. When Jacob was called by his sons, the Jewish people was invited to grace by Peter, John and Paul. (*Ios.* 14.82, on Gen. 46:2–4)

Ambrose's attitude to Judaism came to take a harder edge. In late works he explicitly blamed Jews for the crucifixion of Christ (*patr.* 2.9), and went beyond the contents of the Gospels to have 'the Jews' offer Christ vinegar (*Luc.* 10.124). He even turned the statement that God's law was the truth against them: because they did not receive the truth in the form of Christ, they did not really possess the law (*ps.118*

---

6. In addition to the parable of the prodigal son (above, n. 5) are those of the two debtors (*Luc.* 6.24) and the barren fig-tree (*Luc.* 7.160–72). The woman with the flow of blood, whom Ambrose identified as the church, could be seen as carrying away the kingdom of the synagogue by force (*Luc.* 5.113).

18.36, on Ps. 119:142)! Elsewhere, Ambrose sets up a syllogism: God is known in Judaea; God is truth; therefore truth is in Judaea. But this only applied to the Jews of the past; when the later Jews turned aside from the ways of their fathers, truth passed from them to the church (*ps.118* 12.19). The Jews, therefore, had no future: when St Paul said that God chose things which are not to destroy things which are, he meant that God chose the people of the Gentiles to destroy the people of the Jews (*Luc.* 7.234, on I Cor. 1:28). Many of Ambrose's hostile observations arise from biblical references to a synagogue or the synagogue. Following a loose translation in the Septuagint, Ambrose saw the whole synagogue as having put to death a lamb, whom he saw as representing Christ.[7] A man in a synagogue who had an unclean spirit could be identified with the Jewish people in their wickedness and shameless behaviour (*Luc.* 4.61). Chillingly, in one of his last works, he observed that the laughter of the Jews as they tormented Christ would set the synagogue on fire for ever (*exh.virg.* 11.76).

. . .

CALLINICUM

The phrase had contemporary resonance. The mood in the empire was becoming more hostile to Jews, as evidenced by a law of March 388, according to which marriage between a Christian and a Jew was to be taken as adultery (*cod.Theod.* 3.7.2). But an incident which occurred in the following summer showed that Ambrose was ahead of official opinion. A group of Christians, at the instigation of their bishop, burned a synagogue at Callinicum, the modern ar-Raqqah, just to the north of the Euphrates. In addition, a group of monks destroyed the meeting place of an heretical group, the Valentinians. They had been celebrating the feast of the Maccabees, and perhaps, like Ambrose, they felt a bond with those martyrs of biblical times. When a report from the count of the East reached Theodosius in Milan, he ordered that the bishop was to pay for the rebuilding of the synagogue and that the monks were to be punished. In this he reckoned without Ambrose.

---

7. *Ps.* 39.14 on Ex. 12:5f; LXX reads 'synagogue' for 'congregation'.

Our chief source for the following events is a letter Ambrose wrote to Theodosius at the end of the year from Aquileia, where he seems to have gone to participate in the election of a new bishop. It is a fine example of aggressive writing. Even its form of address, 'Ambrose to Theodosius the emperor', rudely placed the name of the author before that of the recipient and failed to use the honorific titles usually applied to emperors; when Ambrose later revised the letter, he changed it in these respects.[8] Taking up the concept of the eucharist as an offering, which he was among the first in the West to employ, Ambrose resorts to blackmail: if he were not worthy of being heard by the emperor he would not be worthy of offering the eucharistic sacrifice for him.[9] Opposing the freedom of speech appropriate to bishops to an improper silence, Ambrose suggests that the difference between good and bad rulers is that the good love freedom, the wicked slavery. He assures Theodosius that he was exercising his freedom of speech out of obedience to God and love for him, and that he knows him to be good, clement, mild and peaceable. With the preliminary pleasantries out of the way, Ambrose develops the argument in a dramatic direction: if a bishop agreed to pay for the rebuilding of a synagogue, as the emperor sought, he would become an apostate; if he refused, martyrdom awaited him! Either alternative would be foreign to Theodosius' times, and would recall the days of persecution, a period towards which Ambrose's imagination was always prepared to turn. In any case, he was prepared to plead guilty himself: 'I cry out that I set fire to the synagogue, certainly that I told them to do it, lest there be a place where Christ was denied.' Ambrose then adopts the rhetorical ploy of assuming that the order given to the bishop had been revoked, before suggesting that if the count of the East were to order the

---

8. The original letter is *ep.ext.coll.* 1a(=40); the revised version, *ep.* 74=(40), is addressed 'To the most clement prince and most blessed emperor Theodosius Augustus, Ambrose the bishop'.
9. Ambrose uses the term to refer to his offering of the eucharist: cf. *ep.* 77(=22).13; *ep.* 76(=20).5; *ep.ext.coll.* 1(=41).28, 11(=51).14; *off.* 1.41.205; see as well Paulinus *VAmb.* 10.1. He seems to have thought of himself as offering the eucharist on behalf of emperors in particular, e.g. *ob.Val.* 78, with *sacr.* 4.4.14 on prayers for rulers at the eucharist.

rebuilding of the synagogue from Christian funds he would be an apostate.

Changing direction, Ambrose goes on to consider events of the recent past. When the apostate Emperor Julian ordered the rebuilding of the Temple at Jerusalem, the workers had been burned by divine fire. The homes of prefects at Rome and that of the bishop of Constantinople had been set on fire, and no-one was punished; why, then, should people be punished for the burning of a synagogue, 'a place of unbelief, a house of impiety, a shelter of madness which God himself has condemned?' The Jews set many basilicas on fire at the time of Julian without being punished, and the judge who condemned a man who overthrew a pagan altar to martyrdom was thereafter regarded as a persecutor, and shunned. And anything said by the Jews, who had brought false witnesses against Christ, was bound to be false. They would take pleasure in seeing countless hosts of Christians persecuted and murdered, regarding it as a triumph similar to those they enjoyed in former times.

The letter then changes direction again. Ambrose represents the prophet Nathan reminding King David, a younger son just as Theodosius was, of all the benefits he had received. But the real speaker in this passage is Christ, the person being addressed is Theodosius, and the benefits which are described as being received by the latter, in particular the defeat of an enemy who clearly stands for Maximus, are tailored to Theodosius' recent past. Ambrose expresses himself with strength: of the ten sentences placed in the mouth of Christ, nine intimidatingly begin with the pronoun 'I'. He argues that Maximus was defeated because he posed as an upholder of public order after a synagogue was set on fire at Rome. Surely there was a warning here for Theodosius; and if this were not sufficiently alarming, Ambrose alludes to the danger to Theodosius' salvation. But the latter threat is left hanging, as Ambrose returns to a favourite theme. Many people were plotting against the church, and what answer would Ambrose give if orders from Milan led to Christians being killed by the sword, cudgels or balls of lead? When he revised the letter, Ambrose added a hectoring passage at the end, which included a dire threat: he had acted in as honourable a way as possible so that the emperor would hear him in the royal quarters rather than it being necessary for him to give him a formal hearing in church.[10] But this was no more than a case of prophecy after the event.

Yet again, Ambrose's letter to Theodosius demonstrates the difficulty he had in sustaining a line of argument, and the ease with which extraordinarily exaggerated images of persecution came to him. Its real significance lies elsewhere. At one point he addresses Theodosius:

> But public order concerns you, emperor. Which, then, is the more important, the display of public order or the interests of religion? Repression should yield to religion. (*ep.* 74(=40).11)

We have already seen Ambrose argue that the rights of religion were superior to those of family feeling (above p. 66ff); here he places them above those of the state. Again, Ambrose's polemic attacked an important part of the Roman world.

Perhaps there was safety in writing in such terms from out of town, but Ambrose rarely lacked courage, and on his return to Milan he spoke publicly when Theodosius came to church, delivering an address the words of which are included in a letter to his sister Marcellina (*ep.ext.coll.* 1(=41)). After commenting on the need for admonition to be harsh as well as mild, Ambrose discussed the biblical passage which recounted Christ's visit to the house of Simon the Pharisee, when a woman bathed his feet with her tears. When the Pharisee was asked whether one who was forgiven a little or one who was forgiven much loved his creditor more, he replied that it was the former. Christ praised his judgment (*iudicium*) but censured his feeling (*affectus*). These are the very terms Ambrose elsewhere applies to the attitudes Isaac and Rebekah displayed towards their son (above, page 41f), and the Pharisee was found deficient in the characteristic associated with women. Ambrose uses erotic language to express the lesson to be learned from this. Commenting on Jesus' words to Simon, 'You did not give me a kiss, but this woman has not ceased to kiss my feet from the time I came in', he observes:

> The synagogue does not have a kiss. The church has, she who waited expectantly, who loved, and who said 'Let him kiss me with the kisses of his mouth!' (Song 1:2). She wanted to put out her burning longing, which had lasted so long and become

---

10. The verb '*audire*' is used in the same way as it is at *fid.* 1 prol.1.

greater as she awaited the coming of the Lord, with his kiss, bit by bit, and to slake her thirst through this gift.

If the Pharisee had any kiss, it was no more than the kiss of the traitor Judas (*ep.ext.coll.* 1(=41).14, 16, on Luke 7:36–50). For the woman and Simon constitute yet another of the biblical pairs Ambrose sees as standing for the church and the synagogue: the woman who washed Christ's feet with her tears, wiped them with her hair, kissed them and anointed them with oil joined the many women in the Bible who represent the church.

After discussing God's kindness to the Jews in biblical times, Ambrose approaches the climax of his address by returning to a topic he had already developed in his letter to Theodosius, the rebuke the prophet Nathan addressed to King David. Again, it is clear that David stands for Theodosius.[11] Freely embroidering the biblical text, Ambrose makes God, speaking through Nathan, remind David of all that he has done for him, before asking:

> Will you, then, deliver my servants into the power of my enemies and take away what belonged to my servant, thereby branding yourself with sin and giving my enemies something to boast about?

As if this was not pointed enough, Ambrose then announced that he would go on to speak not about the emperor but to him. He advised him to imitate the woman in Simon's house who treated Christ's body so well. But Christ's body is the church, and hence Theodosius would do well to pardon and grant peace to those who had sinned, pay honour to people who were not important, and guard the one body of the Lord Jesus, so that he in turn would guard the empire.

After Ambrose came down from the apse into the main body of the church, words passed between him and Theodosius. At that point the liturgy should have proceeded towards the offering of the eucharistic sacrifice, but Ambrose had already indicated in his letter to the emperor that if he

---

11. Whereas Theodosius was described in Ambrose's letter to him as pious, clement, mild and tranquil (*ep.* 74(=40).5), here David is said to have been pious and merciful (*ep.* 74(=40).25). Mercy is also among the characteristics attributed to David at *off.* 1.24.114, and occurs among the clusters of virtues attributed to Theodosius at *ob.Theod.* 12, 33.

were unworthy of being heard he would be unworthy of offering the sacrifice. Theodosius remarked that he had been the topic of the address, to which the bishop replied that he had dealt with what was to the emperor's benefit. The emperor observed that he had been too hard in having the bishop rebuild the synagogue, a verdict which he had changed, and that monks committed many wrongs, a view few neutral observers of the period would have disputed.[12] Timasius, a distinguished general and close ally of Theodosius, began to speak strongly against the monks, but Ambrose silenced him: he was dealing with an emperor who had the fear of the Lord; it would be necessary to deal with Timasius, who spoke so harshly, in another way.[13] Ambrose stood for a while before the seated emperor, and asked Theodosius to allow him to offer the sacrifice for him with peace of mind.[14] The emperor said that he would alter the decision. But this was not enough: prompted by Ambrose, he promised that no harm would befall Christians because of an inquiry conducted by the count. Ambrose said 'I act in accordance with your good faith.' He then repeated the words, whereupon the emperor said 'Act.' Ambrose then made his way to the altar, having a sensation of the divine presence as he offered the sacrifice.

Ambrose represents his encounter with Theodosius as a confrontation which he won: 'All things were done to my liking' (*ep.ext.coll.* 1(=41).28). We only have his side of the story, and this as told to his sister; siblings have been known to exaggerate their triumphs to each other. But it is worth remembering that while Ambrose, as so often in his life, delivered his address from an elevated position, when he came down from the apse he was standing before a seated emperor who was doubtless surrounded by people ready to take his side. While Ambrose represents himself as having competently dealt with the impertinent words of Timasius, the general's intervention would have been an awkward reminder that there were always rivals for the ears of the

12. Concern about turbulent monks is relected in a law issued on 7 September 390, ordering that monks were to dwell in desert places and desolate solitudes (*cod.Theod.* 16.3.1).
13. Timasius' role in this incident recalls that of Caligonus in 386.
14. Such is the tension of this scene that in his letter to Marcellina describing the incident Ambrose uses the historic present (*dico*).

emperor; he was aware that, while there were many people in the Roman empire, those close to the emperor enjoyed greater favour (*Luc.* 5.61 fin.). Further, the body-language of their encounter may have suggested that Ambrose was making a request of the seated emperor. Indeed, it has been suggested that Ambrose was the loser in the affair, which enabled Theodosius to appear in a good light and cost Ambrose his good will.[15] Theodosius went on to spend at least part of the summer of 389 in Rome. Few people would choose to spend that season in Rome, and during his sojourn there he may have been bidding for the support of traditionalist circles not likely to have seen eye to eye with Ambrose. On his return to Milan a delegation in the pagan interest, representing part of the senate, came to the city. Ambrose spoke to the emperor face to face; for several days thereafter the bishop did not approach him (*ep.ext.coll.* 10(=57).4). We may well conjecture a falling-out.

At about this time Ambrose wrote a tract on penitence (*De paenitentia*). The question had arisen because of a rigorist group, the Novatians, who, while orthodox in doctrine, claimed that those who committed serious sins could not do penance and be received back into full membership of the church. Against them, Ambrose argued that the Spirit of God was more inclined to mercy than harshness (*paen.* 1.2.9). In a relatively original work, he marshalled a great volume of evidence from the Bible for God's mercy towards sinners. Essaying another interpretation of the parable of the Good Samaritan, Ambrose sees the person going down from Jerusalem to Jericho as having relapsed from the combat of martyrdom to the concerns of this life. Yet the Samaritan did not pass him by, but cared for him and cured him; and Christ said 'Go and do thou likewise' (*paen.* 1.11.51f). Ambrose's notion of penitence is a little imprecise, owing to a tendency of the Latin of the period to express verbal ideas by the use of a simple verb and a noun or adjective, which caused 'repent' to be expressed by 'do penitence'.[16] There

---

15. McLynn (1994), esp. 307f, against Brown (1992): 109, where Theodosius is seen as having been 'forced into the dangerous habit of giving way to bishops'.
16. '*Agere paenitentiam*'. The tendency is also reflected in the use of '*salvum facere*' for '*salvere*', 'save'.

is therefore an ambiguity in the expression, which sometimes must mean simply 'repent' (e.g. *paen.* 2.4.27) rather than carrying out some penitential practice. But whatever reality was expressed by the words, Ambrose's attitude was sunny. God, he held, was willing to forgive a sinner. It was an emphasis all the more significant for having been clearly stated just before he had another major falling-out with Theodosius.

. . .

REPRESSION AT THESSALONIKI

In 390 a riot broke out in Thessaloniki.[17] The sources are confused, perhaps hopelessly so, but as far as we can tell a charioteer was imprisoned after making improper advances in a tavern to a man in the following of the general in command of Illyricum. Rioting ensued, in which the general himself was killed. This was not something Theodosius could tolerate, and he seems to have ordered that citizens of the town were to be killed, up to a fixed number, as a reprisal. It was reported that 7,000 people were killed in the ensuing massacre, which lasted for three hours. Whatever the reality may have been, on 18 August Theodosius issued a law from Verona prescribing that unusually severe punishments were not to be exacted for thirty days after they had been decreed (*cod.Theod.* 9.40.13), apparently an acknowledgment that an overly swift and savage punishment had recently been carried out. When Theodosius returned to Milan, Ambrose failed to meet him. It was put out that this was because Ambrose was not well, but writing to the emperor (*ep.ext.coll.* 11(=51)) he made it clear that he had not wanted to see him, and explained why he was unhappy.

The letter is a famous one. It is a private communication between two people, so confidential that some and perhaps all of it was written in Ambrose's own hand, to be read by Theodosius alone. Voicing a familiar concern, Ambrose complains of having been excluded from the emperor's counsels. He states that he alone of the members of the consistory had been denied the right of speaking, and that sometimes Theodosius had been angry when Ambrose found out about

---

17. For what follows, see McLynn (1994): 315ff.

matters decided upon in the consistory in his absence.[18] But such exclusion may have provided a licence for boldness in correspondence:

> That you have a zeal for the faith I cannot deny, that you have the fear of God I do not doubt. But your nature is impetuous. If someone tries to calm it, immediately you turn to mercy; if someone encourages it, you stir it up the more so that you can hardly restrain it. If no-one moderates it, would that no-one would kindle it! Freely I entrust it to you; restrain yourself, and overcome nature by applying goodness.

This is firm language to use to an emperor.

Ambrose claimed that what had been done in Thessaloniki was without precedent. Yet the themes of the letter are familiar. Again he writes to Theodosius of David: when he was accused of having behaved wrongly the king admitted his sin, and, Ambrose admonishes, 'sin is not taken away except by tears and repentance'. An allusion to the goodness and clemency of Theodosius restates qualities he has already attributed to the emperor. When Ambrose comes to the heart of the matter, his threat turns out to be familiar: 'I shall not dare to offer the sacrifice if you intend to be present.' The letter concludes with a passage explicitly stated to have been written in Ambrose's own hand for Theodosius' eyes alone. One night, he says, he dreamed that when Theodosius came to church he found he was not allowed to offer the sacrifice; other things occurred, which he passes over. Christians, Ambrose feels, will condemn their sin rather than defend it. The letter concludes with a warm message alluding to Theodosius' two sons, Arcadius and Honorius: 'Most blessed and most flourishing, may you with your holy offspring enjoy perpetual tranquillity, august emperor!'

Ambrose's letter has often been interpreted as implying that he excommunicated Theodosius, although when read with care it can be seen not to.[19] His assertion that he would not dare to offer the sacrifice if the emperor were present does

---

18. Paulinus complained that counts acted in secret with the emperor while Ambrose was kept in the dark (*VAmb*. 24.1), and Ambrose blames Theodosius' sin which led to the massacre at Thessaloniki on the deceitful conduct of others (*ob.Theod*. 34).
19. McLynn (1994): 326f.

not entail this: if, some months after the massacre, Theodosius had not shown contrition, Ambrose might well have hesitated to offer the eucharist. A few years earlier he had threatened not to offer it if he were not heard by Theodosius, and he may now have been using the same tactic. To be sure, Ambrose later said that Theodosius did public penance and abstained from taking the sacrament until his sons came (*ob.Theod.* 34), but his withdrawal from the eucharist could have been voluntary, for he did the same thing a few years later after a military victory, and there is no reason to connect his behaviour then with Ambrose.[20] The account of Theodosius' penance supplied by Rufinus does not mention Ambrose: according to him, Theodosius was rebuked by the bishops of Italy, acknowledged his fault and, declaring his guilt with tears, did public penance in the sight of the whole church. Laying aside royal pride he patiently fulfilled the period prescribed for him (*HE*, 11.18). Later authors elaborated upon these events (below, page 212), but there is no need to accept their stories.

When Ambrose's biographer Paulinus came to write his account of the affair of Thessaloniki, he fabricated a dialogue between the emperor and the bishop. He has Theodosius assert, in an attempt to justify himself, that David was guilty of both adultery and murder, to which Ambrose replies 'You followed him going astray; follow him mending his ways' (*VAmb.* 24). This is a piece of fiction, for the reply attributed to Ambrose is copied from one of his works on virginity (*inst.virg.* 4.31). Nevertheless, Paulinus' story is a reminder of how important David had become important to Ambrose. Just as political developments in 386 had led him to consider the Maccabees, his difficulties with Theodosius now prompted him to reflect on King David.[21] He was a resonant figure in the early Christian period, whose victory over Goliath was depicted in both Jewish and Christian art. Ambrose, however, was interested in another aspect of his career. In about 388 he had delivered a series of addresses on King David. He recognized that aspects of the king's behaviour could easily be condemned, and his *Apologia* ('defence') of

---

20. Having defeated Eugenius and Arbogast, Theodosius abstained from communion until his sons arrived from Constantinople (*ob.Theod.* 34).
21. See Roques (1996).

David is largely taken up with inviting people to penitence. It was apparently intended for a wide audience, for it contains sections addressed to pagans, who were offended at the king's committing adultery and homicide, to Jews, who erroneously thought he was the son of God, and to Christians. Ambrose was struck by one aspect of David's behaviour: 'He sinned as kings generally do, but he did penance and wept, which kings do not usually do' (*apol.alt.Dav.* 3.7). And his description of David as 'noble in faith, outstanding in mercy, strong in his hand' (*apol.Dav.* 3.9), recalls the qualities he admired in Theodosius. Ambrose observed that there was no difference between the wrath of a king and that of a lion; but a person who incited him and became involved in it sinned against his own soul (*apol.alt.Dav.* 3.9). The harsh sentiment may be that of a person nursing a grievance at having been excluded from Theodosius' circle of advisers.

After the massacre at Thessaloniki Ambrose wrote up the text of his defence of David and published it in a revised form containing a commentary on psalm 51, which deals with the repentance of the king after he had committed adultery with Bathsheba and seen to the killing of her husband.[22] The second half of the work closely follows the writings of the Alexandrian authors Didymus the blind and Origen, which shows that Ambrose had reworked the defence he had originally delivered orally. We may ask why he did this. The oldest surviving manuscript for this part of the text contains a dedication to Theodosius,[23] which makes it highly likely that Ambrose wrote for him, to induce him to do penance. This would explain signs of haste in its composition.[24] Ambrose had already assimilated the figures of David and Theodosius when writing to the emperor and preaching before him after the troubles at Callinicum, and again in writing to him after the massacre at Thessaloniki. The revised version of his defence of David constitutes the final statement of this theme. To the continuities which Ambrose saw between the Old Testament priesthood and the Christian episcopate

---

22. This is the version entitled *Apologia* in modern editions; confusingly, the version which preceded it is called the *Apologia altera* ('other defence').
23. See the edition in *CSEL*, 32/2: 299.
24. *SAEMO* 5:47.

we may therefore add the way in which a Christian ruler could be assimilated into the figure of an Old Testament king. The theme was to have a great future in Christian Europe.

The affair of Thessaloniki was another victory for Ambrose, his most palatable to modern eyes. The aggressive tone he had earlier adopted towards Justina concerning the basilicas and Theodosius over Callinicum is here used against a harsh action of the state, from the overturning of which Ambrose and the church stood to gain nothing. In February 391 Theodosius, in a sign of good will, prohibited all pagan sacrifices and closed temples to the public (*cod.Theod.* 16.10.10). Shortly thereafter he returned to the East, from which he was only to return at the head of an army.

. . .

CHURCH AFFAIRS

At about this time Ambrose became involved in a church council which was held, for reasons which cannot be surmised, in the southern Italian town of Capua in 392. Among the matters discussed was the dispute within the church of Antioch, which the council of Aquileia had unsuccessfully sought to settle in 381. Like many such controversies, it comfortably outlasted the issues which generated it. The council decided to place the matter in the hands of the bishop of Alexandria, who was to consult with the bishop of Rome, thereby abandoning the line which Ambrose had pursued. The council also considered the case of Bishop Bonosus of Niš, who was held to have taught that Mary bore children after she gave birth to Jesus. Ambrose argued against this position in his work on the institution of a virgin (*inst.virg.* 5.35–9.62), and in a letter which he seems to have written on behalf of the council, but those present felt unable to act against Bonosus (*ep.* 71(=56a)). In 393 a council at Milan followed the lead of Pope Siricius in condemning another heretic, Jovinian, and those associated with him. Among other things, they taught that married people were not inferior to virgins. Ambrose dealt with this issue in familiar terms: the wife was bound by the chains of marriage, while the virgin was free of chains. While marriage, Ambrose still believed, was good, virginity was better. But another doctrine of the heretics, that Mary had not remained a virgin in the act of giving birth to Christ, called for something new in response. Ambrose's defence of the virginity of Mary in giving birth is heavily based on allegorical readings of biblical texts, although he argues on the basis of a precise reading of a text in the Septuagint translation of the Old Testament, 'Behold a virgin shall conceive and bear a son' (Is. 7:14), that Mary remained a virgin not only in conceiving but also in bearing her son (*ep.ext.coll.* 15(=42).5).

. . .

THE DEATH OF VALENTINIAN

While such activities reveal the stature Ambrose had acquired as an elder statesman within the church, the last years of his life were dominated by political tensions. They originated in Vienne, the town in Gaul where the young Valentinian lived. Ambrose looked on him as a person of sound views. In 391 a group of senators came from Rome to plead for the restoration of pagan privileges; according to Ambrose, while everyone in the consistory, Christians and pagans, supported their petition, Valentinian rejected it (*ep.ext.coll.* 10(=57).5; *ob.Val.* 19f, 52). But the emperor was under the tutelage of a powerful Frankish general, Arbogast, who felt sure of the favour of Theodosius, having supported him in his struggle against Maximus. Valentinian could not rid himself of his protector. Early in 392 a threat of barbarians prompted the sending of Ambrose to Vienne to ask Valentinian to come to Italy, at about the same time as Valentinian, for reasons of piety or statecraft, wrote to Ambrose asking him to come and baptize him. But as Ambrose journeyed across the Alps in the spring of 392 to undertake what had become a twofold mission, word came that Valentinian had been found dead. Some believed he had taken his own life; others alleged that he had been murdered on the orders of Arbogast. The body of the young emperor was taken to Milan for burial, and Ambrose delivered a commemorative address, the *De obitu Valentiniani*, perhaps late in July.

This work has a different feel from the two discourses Ambrose had pronounced on his dead brother nearly twenty years earlier. While it shares with the first of them an abundance of tears, there are few borrowings from classical authors, and at one point Ambrose, reflecting the more scholarly interest he had come to take in the biblical text, feels that his audience will be interested in a problem posed by the Greek of one passage. He begins with a lament for the dead emperor, which is heavily indebted to the Lamentations of Jeremiah, although Ambrose's verbal approach to the Bible continued to get in the way of clarity: a reference to tears running down cheeks (Lam 1:2) suggested Christ's instruction to turn the other cheek, which in turn prompted the reflection that the church had been struck on one cheek by the loss of Gratian and on the other when Valentinian had been snatched away. He had been a virtuous young man. On one occasion he ordered that an attractive actress for whom the noble youths of Rome had fallen was to be brought to the court, but when she came he disdained to look at her and merely sent her away. Was anyone else so much a lord over his own body? To be sure, he had not been baptized, but Ambrose told his mourning sisters not to worry, for his desire for the sacrament meant that he had possessed the grace which would have come from it. He proceeds to a eulogy of the deceased, whom he describes as 'my white and ruddy young man', praising his head, belly, lips, and mouth in terms drawn from the Song of Songs, only then going on to praise his soul. Here again, the use to which the Song is put is unexpected, but it is clever, for the verse 'I am my brother's and his desire is towards me' (Song 7:11, LXX) leads into the final portion of the work, in which the language of the Song is used to suggest Valentinian's meeting his brother, the murdered Gratian, in heaven. A passing reference to a brother sucking the breasts of the speaker's mother (Song 8:1), and an interpretation of the breasts as the sacrament of baptism, allows Ambrose to reiterate that Valentinian had, in a sense, been baptized. Ambrose hopes that, after his own death, he will be with Gratian and Valentinian.

When Argobast declared his choice of an emperor to replace Valentinian on 22 August, it was clear he was taking no chances. The successor was Eugenius, a teacher who had joined the civil service and come to hold a post overseeing imperial rescripts.[25] His appointment foreshadowed those of nonentities which generals sometimes made in the following century. Paulinus was later to claim that Arbogast boasted of

---

25. Kaster (1988): 403f.

being a friend of Ambrose and often sharing banquets with him (*VAmb.* 30), but when the emperor he had elevated wrote to Ambrose the bishop failed to reply (*ep.ext.coll.* 10(=57).11). Such caution was understandable until Theodosius showed his hand from Constantinople, but circumstances made it increasingly difficult for Ambrose to remain neutral.

In 393 Eugenius and Arbogast arrived in Milan. Ambrose was awkwardly placed, for if he remained in the city he would have to enter into relations with a government which had yet to secure its legitimacy. Hence, forgetful of a principle he had enunciated during the events of 386,[26] he felt an extended absence was called for. He retreated to Bologna, and thereafter Faenza and Florence, where he consecrated a basilica. Beneath its altar he placed the relics of two martyrs, Vitalis and Agricola, which he had exhumed from a Jewish cemetery at Bologna after their presence had been revealed to the local bishop in a vision. Before he returned home, Ambrose wrote to Eugenius (*ep.ext.coll.* 10(=57)). He explained that his departure from Milan was the result of his fear of God, not his fear of emperors: he had not been silent before other emperors and he would not be silent before Eugenius! Ambrose rehearsed events concerning the endowments of the pagan temples in earlier times, before accusing the new emperor of having given the endowments to pagan senators, a stratagem which would allow subsidies for pagan worship to be maintained. Ambrose reminded Eugenius of the power of God and drew his attention to a similar case mentioned in the Bible, when persecution ceased because of the faith of the fathers[27] and paganism gave way. No-one forced Eugenius to act as he did, no-one had him in his power: he should have consulted with a bishop before acting as he had.

The sting of the letter was in its convoluted concluding sentence: 'Wishing, as you do, for us to pay deference to you, allow us to pay deference to the One whom you would like to be thought of as the source of your authority.' Eugenius may have wished his authority to be seen as coming from God, but Ambrose was taking no chances. His attitude was distanced, as shown by the intitulature he used: while he applies the

26. 'I am not accustomed to flee and leave the church' (*ep.* 75a(=21a).2).
27. The 'fathers' were Jews. Ambrose's telling of this story is a remarkable example of his ability to strip a biblical passage of Jewish significance.

imperial characteristic of clemency to Eugenius, the epithets 'most blessed' and 'most Christian' which Ambrose used of other emperors are absent. His true feelings may be contained in a letter written to his clergy at a time which cannot be identified but may have been then (*ep.* 17(=81)). It is dense with biblical references, even by the standards of Ambrose, and coherent themes are hard to extract from it, which may be a sign that it dealt with sensitive matters it was not safe to broach directly. Ambrose begins by pointing out how bad it is for clergy to desist from their duties, perhaps a surprising comment if Ambrose were writing from outside Milan. He goes on to observe that Christ, despite being a child, is greater than an old and foolish king whom he does not name:

> Let us therefore live under [Christ], so 'the old and foolish king' (Eccl. 4:13) may have no power over us. Wishing to reign as the lord of his own will and not to be under the chains of the Lord Jesus, he grows old in his sins and passes into a deformed foolishness. For what is more foolish than to be intent upon earthly things, having abandoned the things of heaven, and to choose things which are weak and fragile, looking on everlasting things as inferior? (*ep.* 17(=81).12)

We have no evidence for the age of Eugenius, but the reference to an old and foolish king who turned away from heavenly things could have been a coded reference to an emperor who was building bridges to pagan opinion.

The refusal of Ambrose to support the new regime made it, in turn, more inclined to cultivate non-Christians. Later Christian polemic may have overstated the scope of whatever degree of pagan revival occurred at the time, but Eugenius certainly reappointed a staunch pagan, Nicomachus Flavianus, to the office of praetorian prefect. He had held it at least as early as 390, but when Valentinian died Theodosius seems to have appointed another person to it.[28] Ambrose's old antagonist Symmachus made plans to attend a festival in honour of Vesta.[29] Eugenius was diplomatic enough to offer

---

28. *PLRE* 348 (Flavianus). In the preceding year, at the beginning of Eugenius' reign, Flavianus' son had been appointed prefect of the city of Rome (*PLRE* 346).
29. *Ep.* 2.59, assuming a late date for this letter; her festival was held on 9 June.

gifts to the church, but according to Paulinus these were rejected, and he was not admitted to common prayers (*VAmb.* 31.3). One understands why Ambrose's customary bravery deserted him.

But the doom of Eugenius was already being prepared. The demise of Valentinian opened the way for Theodosius to pass the empire on to his two young sons, referred to by Ambrose at the end of his private letter a few years earlier. On 8 November 392 he enacted in Constantinople stronger legislation against pagan worship (*cod.Theod.* 16.10.12), and in the spring of 394 led to Italy a large army, which included many barbarian troops. Alarming stories were told that Eugenius and Flavianus had taken an oath that if they defeated Theodosius their horses would be stabled in a basilica at Milan and clergy forced into the army, and Ambrose claimed that they threatened savage persecution against the churches (*ps.* 36.25). He was always inclined to exaggerate threats, and in view of the power which the church had come to enjoy such a plan would have been foolhardy. Nevertheless, the tide which had been flowing so strongly towards Christianity had, at least momentarily, turned. Ambrose returned to Milan at about the beginning of August, as his enemies were leaving to confront Theodosius. The armies met near the River Isonzo, in the area where many armies invading Italy from the East in late antiquity encountered its defenders. On 5 September the fighting went against Theodosius, and on the following day the battle again turned against him. Rufinus describes him throwing away his weapons and resorting to prayer, whereupon a strong wind sprang up from behind his army, and his cause triumphed (*HE* 2.33). Eugenius was beheaded, while Argobast took his own life.

Initially, relations between the triumphant emperor and Ambrose were awkward. His earlier dealings with Ambrose may well have made Theodosius resentful,[30] and he may have thought Ambrose's hands-off attitude towards the regime of Eugenius disloyal. Theodosius wrote him a cool letter. Ambrose replied, again suggesting a connection between

---

30. This would explain an order to the count of the Orient to restrain those who forbade Jewish meetings for worship and attempted to destroy and despoil synagogues (*cod.Theod.* 16.8.9, of 29 September 393).

the offering of the eucharist and the emperor: had he not held Theodosius' letter in his hand as he offered the sacrifice (*ep.ext.coll.* 2(=61).4f)? Paulinus told a story that Theodosius cast himself at the feet of Ambrose, attributing his success to the merits and prayers of the bishop, but his account is supported by no other evidence and merely reflects his desire to inflate the position of his hero (*VAmb.* 31.5). The victorious emperor acted towards his former foes with his customary mildness. But the cause of the pagans was now lost, and Flavianus committed suicide.

. . .

THE DEATH OF THEODOSIUS

Theodosius was not to enjoy his triumph for long. He was ill, and on 17 January 395 died while still in Milan, a city which knows cold winters. The body lay in state for forty days, after which Ambrose delivered an address, On the death of Theodosius (*De obitu Theodosii*). In some ways Ambrose's task was easy, for whatever difficulties he had had with the late emperor, the first mature and accomplished man to hold the office in the West since Valentinian I, his defeat of Eugenius and Argobast had, at the last, made it possible for him to be portrayed as a friend of the church. On the other hand, his decease created an awkward political situation. Theodosius left behind two sons, Arcadius, born in about 377, who would assume power in the East, and Honorius, a mere ten years old, who would govern in the West. There, effective power would be held by another of the great Germanic military commanders of the period, Stilicho. What was to stop him playing Arbogast to Honorius' Valentinian?

Ambrose's address on Theodosius is the most interesting of his four discourses on the dead. It begins in gloom, placing Theodosius' demise in a context of the cosmic events which, for centuries, had been thought fitting portents of the deaths of emperors. Yet the style is light. Always sensitive to his audience, Ambrose adopted a folksy tone, doubtless in the hope of influencing as wide a cross-section of the people as he could. His message is insistent: Theodosius' sons enjoy the grace of Christ and the faith of the army. Just as Theodosius had cast down the faithlessness of tyrants, his faith doing away with the worship of idols, the faith of the soldiers sufficed to provide a perfect age for an emperor, the faith of the emperor in turn supplying the strength of his soldiers. Turning towards the soldiers, Ambrose observes that the faith of Theodosius had gained them triumphs; old in years but strong in faith, he had given strength to all. The faith of Theodosius was their victory; their faith would be the strength of his sons, for faith supplies what is lacking in age. Ambrose proceeds to discuss examples of faith in the Bible, using the word fourteen times in a short passage. It occurs to him to describe the patriarchs of Genesis as having been involved in a 'warfare of faith', and from this he easily moved back to military matters. Now explicitly addressing the soldiers among his hearers, Ambrose alludes to the recent victory of Theodosius:

> You have heard, you soldiers standing around, that where there is misbelief there is blindness. The army of the faithless was deservedly blind, but where there is faith, there is an army of angels.

When Ambrose stressed the importance of faith, he was using the word in two senses. One of these was that of the orthodox Christian faith. Employed in this way, the word recalled a comment Ambrose made when he informed Gratian that victory came from the faith of the emperor more than from the strength of the soldiers (*fid.* 1 prol. 3; see too above, page 118). But the army which Theodosius had recently led to Italy included a large number of barbarians from the region of the Danube (Sozomen *HE* 7.24) whose faith was by no means Nicene. Paulinus termed the commanders of the army at this time 'Arians' (*VAmb.* 34), and many of the Germanic troops who were finding their way into the army were not Christians of any kind. If they were following Ambrose's address, they must have understood the word 'faith' in another sense, that of human fidelity or loyalty, as Ambrose had intended it to mean when speaking with Theodosius over the affair at Callinicum.[31] Less than a

---

31. *Ep.ext.coll.* 1(=41).28. He had also used the word in this sense when referring to the army of that emperor being made up of many untamed nations which God had caused to have faith, as if it were made up of one race (*ep.* 74(=40).22).

decade earlier, during the struggle over the churches of Milan, Ambrose had played on the antagonism aroused by Gothic troops in the entourage of Valentinian; now, in more straightened political circumstances, he optimistically spoke of the good faith of such people. It was a sign that the western empire was increasingly to depend on the attitude of Germanic soldiers.

After touching on Theodosius' virtues of goodness, mercy and faithfulness, Ambrose characteristically changes direction. He begins an exposition of the opening portion of psalm 116, placing the utterances made there, starting with the words 'I have loved', in the mouth of Theodosius. He then makes these words his own as he lists the good qualities which had made him love Theodosius, among them the humility with which he performed penance in public after the massacre at Thessaloniki. Ambrose envisaged a celestial imperial gathering, at which Theodosius embraced Gratian, who no longer grieved at his wounds, for he had found an avenger. Maximus and Eugenius, on the other hand, could now safely be seen as languishing in hell, and Valentinian II, whom Ambrose had located in heaven together with Gratian in an address delivered less than three years earlier, is not mentioned. But the heavenly company would include Constantine, the first Christian emperor whose times saw the fulfilment of the saying of the prophet 'On that day, that which is upon the bridle of the horse will be holy to the Lord Almighty' (cf. Zech 14:20). At this point Ambrose produces one of the most dazzling passages he ever wrote.[32]

Constantine's mother Helena, he states, wished to secure divine protection for her son. Ambrose sees her as having been an innkeeper. Little status attached to this job, but Ambrose made the most of its biblical possibilities:

> A good innkeeper, who so carefully sought out the Lord's stable [cf. Luke 2:7]! A good innkeeper, who was not ignorant of that innkeeper who cared for the wounds of the man wounded by robbers [Luke 10:35]! A good innkeeper, who preferred to be thought of as dung, so that she might gain Christ [cf. Phil. 3:8]!

32. I know of no earlier interpretation similar to that developed by Ambrose. Jerome found it pious but ridiculous (*PL* 25:1540), but the sixth-century hymnographer Romanos Melodos accepted it.

He tells how Helena went to Jerusalem and inspected the site of the Lord's passion. Digging, she found three crosses, but was unable to establish which was the Lord's. She then read the account in the gospel, according to which the inscription 'Jesus of Nazareth king of the Jews' had been placed above the cross which stood in the middle. She found the inscription, and so adored the King who, hanging on the cross, cried out to his Father like a scarab, asking him to forgive the sins of those persecuting him.[33] Having also found the nails which had been used at the crucifixion, she ordered that a bridle be made out of one of them, thereby fulfilling the prophecy of Zechariah, and that the other was to be placed in a diadem. Both these were sent to Constantine. Ambrose comments:

> A good nail for the Roman empire, which rules the whole world and clothes the forehead of princes, so that there might be preachers where there had been persecutors... A crown on the head, reins in the hand: a crown from the cross so that faith may shine, and reins from the cross so that power may rule.

Now, as even a nail used in the crucifixion came to be held in honour, the church rejoiced, while the Jew blushed and suffered torments. The language Ambrose uses to represent the Jews speaking is strong:

> We thought we had won, but we confess ourselves beaten... Now our struggle against him is greater, our battle more fierce. We have despised the one to whom kingdoms are subject and whom power serves. How shall we resist kings? Kings bend down before the nail which fastened his feet.

But why, Ambrose asks, did the prophet describe that which is upon the bridle as holy? This referred to the curbing of the insolence of emperors. Having left behind the muzzle of unbelief, the emperors took the bridles of devotion and faith; not only Constantine but the others too, all of whom were Christians except Julian.

The conclusion of the discourse is therefore reassuring. It had begun by responding to fears created by the death of

---

33. An implicit reference to Hab. 2:11, where LXX has a scarab speaking from the wood. Predictably, Jerome was hostile to the identification of the scarab with Christ; see Dölger (1930).

Theodosius, but these fell away as Ambrose expounded a 'whig' interpretation of fourth-century history. No longer were there emperors like Nero and Caligula! For the words of the prophet, 'kings shall walk in thy light' (Is. 60:3, LXX), had been fulfilled, most clearly in Gratian and Theodosius. Looking back from the vantage point of 395, Ambrose produced his final evaluation of the emperors with whom he had been so involved. Valentinian I, the ambiguous figure whom the pagan Symmachus had located in the starry arc of heaven, and the young Valentinian II were edited out of the sequence of good emperors. But whatever the changes in the line-up, Ambrose interpreted Roman history from the time of Constantine positively. Turning to Theodosius' younger son, Ambrose puns, describing Honorius weeping as his father's body, 'still dishonoured and lacking the honour of a tomb', began its long journey to burial in Constantinople. But his remains will not lack honour there, for his glorious return to that city will be accompanied by a band of angels and a throng of saints. How blessed Constantinople will be, concludes Ambrose, possessing the body of one who dwells in paradise and inhabits the city above.

. . .

LAST YEARS

The sentiment was a fine one. But power in Milan was in the hands of the general Stilicho, with whom Ambrose had to come to an accommodation. Stories told by Paulinus suggest that relations between them were awkward. On one occasion, a detachment of troops commanded by anti-Nicaeans went to a church where a criminal had taken sanctuary and, despite the protests of the clergy, took him to the amphitheatre where Honorius was staging games to mark one of his consulships. While Ambrose wept before the altar, prostrate in prayer, leopards attacked the soldiers. Stilicho spent some days making satisfaction to the bishop, and the criminal was exiled (*VAmb.* 34). When Stilicho complained to Ambrose that one of his slaves had taken to forging documents after being healed of a demon, the bishop delivered him over to Satan. To the astonishment of all, before he had finished speaking the man was seized by an unclean spirit (*VAmb.* 43).

Involvement with the court also occurred after more relics, those of the martyr Nazarius, had been discovered in a garden outside the city in July 395. Paulinus reports that the martyr's blood was so fresh it could have been shed that very day, his head was intact, and his hair and beard were fresh. There was a wonderful smell, sweeter than that of any spice. When his body had been lifted up and placed on a litter, Ambrose then went to pray at a place in the same garden where he had never prayed before, and where another martyr, Celsus, had been buried. The watchmen told Paulinus of their parents' advice never to leave the place, great treasures having been placed there. The body of Nazarius was taken to the basilica of the Apostles, which came to be named after him. While Ambrose was preaching, someone, filled by an unclean spirit, began to cry out that Ambrose was torturing him, but the bishop told him to hold his tongue, for it was not Ambrose who was torturing him, but the faith of the saints and his own envy at the sight of humans going up to heaven, whence he had been cast down. In any case, Ambrose announced, he did not know how to be puffed up (*VAmb.* 32f). The church was decorated with marble from Libya which Stilicho's fervently Christian wife, Theodosius' niece Serena, supplied in thanksgiving for favours she had received (*CIL* 6:6250). The court apparently found it worthwhile to seek the support of Ambrose.

But he was now old. His horizon became darker, the views on God's grace he came to express being more influenced by St Paul and Augustinian in their emphasis.[34] He began to refer to his words as those of an old man (*ep.* 28(=50).16; 32(=48).7), and a round of activities took its toll. He became involved in the election of a new bishop at Vercelli, and ordained a friend, Gaudentius, bishop of Brescia. After ordaining a bishop for Pavia in February 397 he fell ill and took to his bed. According to a tradition known to Paulinus, when Stilicho heard that Ambrose was not well he commented that if such a man were to leave the body Italy itself would be threatened with extinction, and sent leading men whom Ambrose loved to ask him to pray that his life would be extended. Ambrose's reply was brisk, and memorable: 'I have

---

34. Faust (1983): 136. See for example *Luc.* 7.27 ('*deus quos dignatur vocat et quem vult religiosum facit*', quoted several times by Augustine).

not lived among you so as to be ashamed to continue to live, and I am not afraid to die, because we have a good Lord' (*VAmb.* 45).

Ambrose had become concerned about the difficulty of finding men worthy of being bishops, and wept bitterly when he heard that a good one had died. It is therefore not surprising that he intervened when he overheard a group of deacons talking about who would succeed him in Milan. They would themselves have been potential candidates for the office, but one of them mentioned Simplicianus, whom Ambrose regarded as his father in grace. Hearing the name, to their alarm he cried out three times from his bed of sickness 'Old but good!' As he prayed, Ambrose saw the Lord Jesus approaching him smiling, and a few days after this he composed himself to die, stretching out his arms in the shape of the cross and praying so quietly that bystanders could not hear his voice as his lips moved. The bishop of Vercelli whom he had recently ordained gave him the sacrament and Ambrose died, early in the morning of 4 April 397. It was the day before Easter. His body was taken to the cathedral, where the Easter baptisms were carried out in its presence. On Easter Day it was taken to the Basilica Ambrosiana where, as he had planned, he was buried (*VAmb.* 46–8). Simplicianus duly succeeded him as bishop, to be succeeded in turn by Venerius, one of the deacons who had heard Ambrose approving Simplicianus.

At the end of his life Ambrose had been dictating a commentary on psalm 44 to Paulinus. In his biography, Paulinus asserted that, while he was taking down Ambrose's words, he suddenly saw a flame like a small shield cover his head and gradually enter his mouth, like a householder going indoors. Then his face came to look like snow, afterwards regaining its usual appearance. Paulinus was so surprised that he could not write down what Ambrose was dictating until the vision passed. As it turned out, this was the last day of Ambrose's work, and the commentary remained unfinished. The deacon Castus, to whom Paulinus confided the vision, explained it with reference to the Acts of the Apostles: what he had witnessed was the coming of the Holy Spirit (*VAmb.* 42.3; cf. Acts 2:3). Perhaps, although Paulinus' language hints at another biblical perspective, that of the appearance of Christ described in the narratives of the Transfiguration.[35]

Paulinus' story faithfully represents the way his subject had developed. Much of what Ambrose did cannot be admired. His personality and background combined to make him overly convinced of the rightness of his causes, hectoring in tone, a bad listener, and possibly hungry for power – respects in which he provided a malign example for later leaders of the church. In political affairs and other matters his relationship with the world around him was complex, for Ambrose often operated along the fault lines which separated this world from medieval Christendom, his ideas pointing beyond the environment in which they were articulated. In the midst of these tensions, Ambrose grew. While Paulinus' account of his life begins with the standard classical motif of bees entering his mouth, its end is unambiguously Christian. In the same way, Ambrose's religion came to touch deeper parts of his being. It is beyond the scope of this book to pry into this area, but the fire and snowy appearance mentioned by Paulinus reflect a sustained theme of the commentary on psalm 44 he was then dictating, which is packed with references to light (*ps.* 43.6–8, 12, 15, etc). Perhaps it was the very light to which he would shortly be admitted. For Ambrose believed that the shadow of the law, the darkness of night and the gloom of the Jews had already yielded to the gospel, which allowed an image of good things to be seen. A third stage lay in the future, when the image would pass away and the truth come:

> Go up into heaven, therefore, and you shall see those things of which there was a shadow or image here. You shall see, not in part and not in obscurity but in fullness, not behind a veil but in light. (*ps.* 38.25f)

---

35. On this occasion Christ's face shone as the sun (Matt. 17:2), and his clothing was whiter than snow (Mark 9:3).

Chapter 8

NACHLEBEN

Not all Ambrose's contemporaries were taken with his work. In a catty mood, Jerome once wrote that he would not comment on the works of Ambrose while the bishop was still alive, lest he be accused of flattery or of telling the truth.[1] But the reputation of thinkers often lies in the hands of those they influenced, and Ambrose was fortunate in the role he played in the life of Augustine, for whom he became more important early in the fifth century. This was a period when Augustine was involved in bitter controversy with the adherents of a point of view within Christianity labelled 'Pelagian', and he often found it worth his while to quote the unimpeachably orthodox Ambrose against his opponents. He sometimes did this in a cheeky fashion: after reproducing passages of Ambrose which contradict the teaching of Pelagius, Augustine quotes Pelagius to the effect that not even an enemy would question Ambrose's faith and his sure grasp of the Scriptures.[2] Augustine played on Ambrose having been not only his teacher but also the destroyer of his opponents,[3] which is precisely the way in which he is depicted in Paulinus' biography, with which Augustine was in some way connected. Paulinus introduced the figure of Ambrose to a wide readership, both directly and by way of the inclusion of much of his material in the immensely popular *Golden Legend* prepared by a Dominican of the thirteenth century, James

---

1. *PL* 23:751. As this chapter covers a wide area, and seeks to offer general perspectives, it is not extensively footnoted.
2. *Contra Julianum* 1.10f, 30 (*PL* 44:645–47, 661).
3. E.g. *Contra secundum Juliani responsionem opus imperfectum* 5.41 (*PL* 45:1478).

of Voragine. His work became a source of pithy sayings, to be misquoted by Charlemagne, according to his unreliable biographer Notker, and misquoted more interestingly by Bede, in the last weeks of his life.[4] By the tenth century it had been translated into Greek,[5] in which language Ambrose was also commemorated in a large number of hymns. His memory lingered in Milan, where early in the sixth century he was mentioned in the works of Ennodius. In particular, Ennodius alluded to Ambrose's success in his controversy with Symmachus in a witty epigram: Victory had taken the palm of eloquence from her friend and it passed to Ambrose. Data from various sources was later fused with legendary material to create the potent figure, larger than life, who emerged in the *History of Milan* written in about 1100 by Landulf.

The boldness with which Ambrose treated emperors, in particular Theodosius, was another reason for posthumous fame, and eastern authors elaborated with enthusiasm on this aspect of his activities from an early date. Sozomen, the Byzantine author of a church history who wrote between 439 and 450, found Ambrose noteworthy for his freedom of speech in the presence of the powerful (*HE* 7.25.2,13), while his contemporary, Theodoret, wrote an account of his dealings with Theodosius after the massacre at Thessaloniki which is more than half legend (*HE* 5.17). Whereas Sozomen has Ambrose grabbing Theodosius' robe and denying him entry to church, and explicitly states that Ambrose excommunicated the emperor, Theodoret describes Ambrose saying that Theodosius was like a dog, and relates with enthusiasm the humiliation endured by the emperor before he was readmitted to communion. Ambrose, he felt, was to be praised for his brave words and Theodosius for his docility. It was with menace that the African bishop Facundus informed Justinian that Theodosius had been chastized and excommunicated

---

4. Notker *Gesta Caroli* 2.10, where Louis the Pious is compared to Ambrose (ed. G.H. Pertz, *MGH Scriptores* 2). Cuthbert's letter on the death of Bede is in B. Colgrave and R.A.B. Mynors, ed. *Bede's Ecclesiastical History of the English People*, Oxford 1969, 581, but Cuthbert has '*deum*' for Paulinus' '*dominum*', revealing a misunderstanding similar to that of Augustine (above, p. 14).
5. McLure (1972f).

by Ambrose.[6] Ambrose's dealings with emperors have sometimes been interpreted by modern scholars as victories which made possible the later successes of the western church in its dealings with the state,[7] but this is implausible. The case of Ambrose can easily be parallelled in the East by that of his near-contemporary John Chrysostum, bishop of Constantinople, whose resistance to the state was at least as striking, and the early heightenings of the victories of Ambrose occur in texts written in the East, where another biography of Ambrose based on Theodoret's account was to be written, and not the West. The Latin chroniclers of the early middle ages seem not to have known of Ambrose's dealings with Theodosius, although Byzantine readings were mediated to the West through Cassiodorus' *Historia tripartita*, which follows Theodoret in providing a version of his election emphasizing the role of Valentinian and, more importantly, a long account of his dealings with Theodosius after the massacre at Thessaloniki. Cassiodorus' account of Ambrose, as well as that of Paulinus, was used by the author of a *Life* in the ninth century, and such traditions lie behind the use to which the precedent of Ambrose was put by Pope Gregory VII (1073–1085). Seeking to justify his excommunication of the Emperor Henry IV, Gregory cited Ambrose as an example of a bishop who had not merely excommunicated an emperor but also forbidden him to remain in the part of the church reserved for priests and, indeed, kept him out of the church, an interpretation which could be politely described as fanciful.[8]

Yet Ambrose's chief legacy to the following centuries was neither a starring role in a widely read biography nor the provision of a model of dealing with secular authorities which later ecclesiastics found to their taste, but the body of his writings. Of these, the hymns were the most widely known. Augustine, writing within a few years of Ambrose's death, states that the practice of singing hymns and psalms according to the custom of the eastern lands which he introduced

---

6. *CCSL* 90A:396.
7. As by Rahner (1992).
8. *Registrum* 4.2, 8.21 (ed. E. Caspar, *MGH Epp.sel.* 2). See further Schieffer (1972), who incidentally brings out how intermittently Ambrose's example was appropriated.

had been imitated in nearly all the world (*conf.* 9.7.15; cf. *VAmb.* 13.3). This is doubtless an exaggeration, but the hymns were certainly well known in Italy, where Pope Celestine (422–432) was aware that Ambrose had made the people sing words from a hymn on Christmas Day, from which he was able to quote four lines (*CCSL* 25:112), and an inscription in the mausoleum of Galla Placidia, who was buried at Ravenna in 450, contains verses from another (*CIL* 11:276). In the Rule he wrote for monks in the sixth century, St Benedict used the word '*ambrosianum*' for a hymn sung at some of the offices.

The more formal works met with varied fates. The fact that Augustine quoted from a wide variety of them indicates that some were being copied and diffused very early, and the respectable number of early manuscripts confirms this. Two manuscripts of the fifth century contain portions of the commentary on Luke, while one of the following century contains more than half the work. Three of the great Italian preachers of the early fifth century, Chromatius of Aquileia, who succeeded Ambrose's old ally Valerian as bishop in that city, Maximus of Turin and Peter Chrysologus of Ravenna made use of this commentary, although Leo of Rome apparently did not. In the early eighth century Bede drew on it heavily for his commentary on Luke, in the prologue to which he places Ambrose alongside Augustine, Gregory and Jerome, an early grouping of these four great fathers (*CCSL* 120:7). The earliest full manuscript of the commentary on psalm 119 dates from the ninth century, although the portion covering the letter cof is extant in a sixth/seventh-century manuscript. The series of commentaries on twelve psalms seems to have been slower to find copyists, and while Cassiodorus was aware that Ambrose had written on the psalms, he made no use of his writings in his own long commentary on them. The commentary which Ambrose never quite wrote on the Song of Songs was, as it were, reconstituted from discussions in his various works by a Cistercian author of the twelfth century, William of St Thierry (ed. *SAEMO* 27).

The most popular of Ambrose's works has been the *Exameron*. Part of it survives in a manuscript of the seventh century, and its appreciative readers included one in the ninth century who uttered words which could have been spoken by many: 'If you delight in the beauty of creatures you should keep going back to the Exameron of Ambrose, just for fun.'[9] The animal lore Ambrose presented overlaps with that contained in a bestiary, the *Physiologus*, and the fact that the textual tradition of this work is complex makes the direct influence of Ambrose's work hard to trace. However, references to the practices of animals in the letters Cassiodorus wrote in the sixth century seem to draw directly on the *Exameron*, while the author of a *Liber glossarum* preserved in a manuscript of the late eighth century used it as well, not for the moral and religious information it contained but also as a factual source for the habits of animals.[10]

Of Ambrose's non-biblical works, the *De officiis* was recognized by both Augustine and Cassiodorus as useful, but it was to face stiff competition from the *Regula pastoralis* of Pope Gregory the Great. It is not hard to see why Gregory's book became the more widely read: not only was it shorter and, it could be argued, possessed of greater psychological insight, but it owed less to a Roman world-view which medieval readers must have found alien. A Spanish bishop who wrote to Gregory after reading the *Regula pastoralis* quoted remarks of Hilary and Augustine which he felt were similar to Gregory's teaching, but did no more than allude in a general fashion to the *De officiis*,[11] and it is not clear that Gregory himself knew this work of Ambrose. Yet it continued to find readers, being quoted by Bishop Atto of Vercelli in the tenth century as well as Ailred of Rievaulx in the twelfth.

The oldest surviving manuscript of the *De fide* was written in northern Italy in the fifth century, while another, now in the library of the archbishop of Ravenna, was written at the turn of the sixth century, as was the oldest surviving manuscript of the *De Spiritu Sancto*; the Italian provenance of these manuscripts may reflect the concerns of Nicaeans when Italy was under anti-Nicaean governments in the immediate post-Roman period. The *De fide* had the honour of being cited at the four ecumenical councils which followed Ambrose's

---

9. *PL* 131:995A, a comment to be picked up by a monastic author of the twentieth century, Thomas Merton (1968): 296.
10. Barbero (1990), esp. 156f.
11. Gregory *Reg.* 1.41a (ed. L.M. Hartmann, *MGH Ep.* 1).

death, those of Ephesus (431), Chalcedon (451) and Constantinople II and III (553, 680f), and a complete, or at least substantial, translation of it into Greek may lie behind the volume of quotations from it in early Byzantine florilegia. A passage from the *De incarnationis dominicae sacramento* was quoted by the iconophil council of Nicaea in 787, the last ecumenical council according to the Orthodox reckoning, but a Carolingian author who wrote a response to that council, probably Theodulf of Orleans, queried the use to which it was put, claiming that the Byzantines had failed to understand the purport of Ambrose's Latin.[12] The *De sacramentis* has played an important part in the controversies on the eucharist which have occurred within western Christianity, having been drawn on by Paschasius Radbertus in the ninth century and both Berengar and Lanfranc in the eleventh. During the Reformation its authenticity was denied by Protestants who found what they took to be a catholic tendency in its theology distasteful, but it is now accepted as having been written by Ambrose. Even the *Apologia David*, scarcely one of Ambrose's major works, was to influence the portrayal of the Capetian King Robert the Pious by the eleventh-century author Helgaud.[13]

All this may suggest that Ambrose was a gigantic figure, whose works were destined to play a determining role in subsequent intellectual life. Yet later generations may have been attracted by his style as much as by the content of his works, for the sweetness of his writing was widely praised. Perhaps this judgment was already implicit in Paulinus' story of bees entering Ambrose's mouth when he lay asleep as an infant. In his *Institutes*, Cassiodorus draws attention to his style as much as the content of his writings, and the vocabulary is consistent, Ambrose being praised for being sweet, pleasant and eloquent, and having a 'milky' style. Scholars with intellectual agendas more demanding than that of Cassiodorus were less inclined to call on Ambrose's services. When Bede came to write his commentary on Genesis he found the writings of Augustine and Jerome served his purposes better than those of Ambrose, despite his voluminous output on the first book of the Bible, and Bede's commentary on Luke

12. *Libri Carolini* 2.15 (*PL* 98:1079f).
13. Hamilton (1997).

uses Jerome's commentary on Matthew more often than that of Ambrose on Luke itself. In his *Summa theologica*, Thomas Aquinas cites Ambrose somewhat less often than Jerome, less than half as often as Gregory, and a tenth as often as Augustine. The spread is less wide in the theological writings of Abelard, who seems to have found Jerome more useful than Gregory, but again Ambrose brings up the rear among the four great fathers of the Latin West. Thomas and Abelard, powerful thinkers who loved to wrestle with ideas, seem to have found relatively little to engage them in Ambrose. As Europe passed beyond the medieval period, perspectives changed in ways which were reflected in the works of Martin Luther. His literal approach to Scripture meant that, among the fathers, he referred far more frequently to Jerome and Augustine than Ambrose.

Yet Ambrose's position as a respected exegete was secure in the middle ages, and it may be the case that, in very broad terms, the relative degree of interest later scholars took in Ambrose and Augustine is an index of their general orientations. Many intellectuals in the medieval period were given to a meditative recycling of the works of their predecessors, in rather the same way that Ambrose had often been. In this respect, and a general taste for synthesis over analysis, the qualities of Ambrose's mind were akin to those of many scholars during the following centuries. For them, Ambrose's attractiveness may have lain in his having been an eloquent and orthodox spokesperson for an emerging catholic position on various issues, rather than for the degree of originality, insight and precision he possessed in working out that position. In addition, he may also have appealed to later readers because he offered them things which were not otherwise available.

When Ambrose disparaged non-Christian points of view, he was attacking ideas which were current in his time. But as Christianity became more central to intellectual life and the transmission of the texts on which this life was based, the works of non-Christians became less easy of access. For readers in later centuries, whose intellectual horizons were narrower than those of the mental world of the fourth century, Ambrose may have conveyed an air of the broad outdoors. Moreover, as we have seen, his thought was nourished on books written in Greek, which gave him access to an intellectual world more spacious than that at the command of many of the other Latin fathers (however much one may suspect that what he took from the Greek authors was less than what they had to offer) and still more broad than the restricted intellectual world inhabited by most scholars of the first half of the middle ages. The very respectable body of material already produced by Christian writers in Africa, which Augustine was to deploy to good effect, left few traces in the writings of Ambrose. Of his favourite Latin authors, Cicero stood outside the Christian tradition, as did Vergil, whom in any case Ambrose used as a source of poetic images rather than ideas, and Hilary of Poitiers was himself tributary to Greek thought. To an extraordinary extent, the major influences on Ambrose were writers in Greek; while his reading of poetry was predominantly in Latin, for theology and ideas he turned to Greek authors. Ambrose was thus superbly placed to present material which would find appreciative readers in the largely Greekless centuries which were to follow in the West. The authors he used were little known in the succeeding centuries, some of the works on which he drew being unknown even to modern scholarship. Most of them were never translated into Latin, and some of the translations which were made, such as those of Plotinus which Augustine read, were not to enjoy a wide readership.

Ambrose's posthumous stature therefore owed something to his having lived at the right time and enjoyed the right education. But we can be more precise than this, for it is not simply the case that Ambrose read books in a strange language. Secular Greek writers from the classical period are scarcely present in his works. Some of the later, Christian authors who are, such as Athanasius and Basil, were major thinkers in what we now see as the central, orthodox tradition, but it is noteworthy how many of those Ambrose drew on were, in one way or another, marginal to that tradition. Indeed, surprising as it may seem, the pivot of Ambrose's intellectual life may have been the thought-world of Hellenistic and Roman Alexandria. It seems to have been here that Jewish scholars composed the Septuagint, and it was in that city that Philo and Origen, respectively a Jew and a Christian of dubious orthodoxy, wrote. Among the other authors Ambrose used most, Plotinus was a pagan, Hippolytus a schismatic, and Eusebius stood at some distance from Nicene theology. The intellectual world of these writers of Greek, especially those in Egypt and Italy, to which Ambrose offered indirect access would have been immensely exotic by the standards of the Carolingian period, for example. Hence Ambrose's appropriation of Greek material, while its apparently unthinking nature earned him the scorn of Jerome, may have given his works a fascinating allure for readers in the medieval West. It has been plausibly suggested that the attractiveness of Ambrose to the ninth-century scholar John the Scot, who names him thirty-six times and textually cites him some twenty times, may have arisen from the closeness of both Ambrose and John to Greek thought,[14] but even those less attuned to such influences must sometimes have responded to the sheer unusualness of much they read in Ambrose.

Yet Ambrose did not only live at the end of a period in intellectual life. Just as he wrote shortly before the intellectual horizons of the West entered a period of contraction, so he stood towards the end of the Roman empire in the West. A century after he died, it had ceased to exist there, leaving the church, which had so prospered during the fourth century, to outlive its former patron, the state. Its leaders, the bishops, had a bright future in Europe, but the habits of class and of the exercise of leadership in a complex bureaucracy which Ambrose brought to the job of bishop and which defined the way he exercised it, did not. Few in future generations would think of the duties of the clergy in terms derived from Cicero, and the élan which bishops possessed would be derived from sources other than their having spent years sitting on a tribunal. Yet, as we have seen throughout our study, Ambrose cannot be seen as simply a figure of the ancient world, for his thinking and activities looked beyond that world. His attitudes to women, the Bible and other texts, the church and the secular state, as well as the authority he could command in his city, in varying degrees all pointed beyond the fourth century and firmly into the middle ages. It is this sense of pointing beyond the world in which he lived that gives Ambrose a lasting fascination.

14. Madec (1976).

BIBLIOGRAPHY

WORKS BY AMBROSE

Ambrose has been well edited. In addition to the versions given in *PL* (*Patrologia Latina*), which reprints a Benedictine edition of the late seventeenth century, most of his works are available in *CSEL* (*Corpus Scriptorum Ecclesiasticorum Latinorum*), each equipped with a superb critical apparatus. There is also a complete recent Italian edition, *SAEMO* (*Sancti Ambrosii Episcopi Mediolonensis Opera*) (Milan/Rome, 1977ff), which supplies facing Italian translations as well as introductions and commentaries, and this is the edition which I have generally had on my desk. The following list aims to combine concision with much information as possible. Arranged according to the abbreviated forms used to cite Ambrose's works in this study, it supplies full titles, indicates key editions, concerning which more detail is available in *Clavis Patrum Latinorum*, 3rd edn., Steenbrugis 1995 39–50, some translations, and for most works gives an idea, sometimes very approximate, of the date of composition; for some it has not seemed worthwhile to suggest a possible date of composition. The abbreviation 'Ramsey' is used for B. Ramsey, *Ambrose* (London and New York, 1997).

Abr. De Abraham CSEL 32, *SAEMO* 2 (c.382f)
apol.alt.Dav. Apologia David altera CSEL 32, *SAEMO* 5 (c.388)
apol.Dav. De apologia prophetae David CSEL 32, *SAEMO* 5
bon.mort. De bono mortis CSEL 32, *SAEMO* 3, *FC* 65 (c.391)
Cain De Cain et Abel CSEL 32, *SAEMO* 2, *FC* 42 (c.378)
ep. Epistulae CSEL 82, *SAEMO* 19–21, *FC* 26

exa. Exameron CSEL 32, SAEMO 1, FC 42 (late 380s)
exc.fr. De excessu fratris CSEL 73, SAEMO 18, FC 22 (377)
exh.virg. Exhortatio virginitatis SAEMO 14 (394)
expl.symb. Explanatio symboli CSEL 73, SAEMO 17
fid. De fide CSEL 78, SAEMO 15 (378–380)
fuga De fuga saeculi CSEL 32, SAEMO 4, FC 65 (c.394)
Hel. De Helia et ieiunio CSEL 32, SAEMO 6 (c.387–390)
Hymnes ed. and trans. J. Fontaine et al., Paris 1992, SAEMO 22
Iac. De Iacob et vita beata CSEL 32, SAEMO 3, FC 65 (386)
inc. De incarnationis dominicae sacramento CSEL 79, SAEMO 16, FC 44
inst.virg. De institutione virginis SAEMO 14 (393f)
interpell. De interpellatione Iob et David CSEL 32, SAEMO 4, FC 65 (388f)
Ios. De Ioseph CSEL 32, SAEMO 3, FC 65 (c.388)
Is. De Isaac uel anima CSEL 32, SAEMO 3, FC 65 (c.391)
Luc. Expositio euangelii secundum Lucam CSEL 32, SAEMO 11f (c.385–89)
myst. De mysteriis CSEL 73, SAEMO 17, FC 44; trans. Ramsey; ed. and German trans. J. Schmitz, Freiburg 1990
Nab. De Nabuthae historia CSEL 32, SAEMO 6 (386–390); trans. Ramsey
Noe De Noe CSEL 32 (c.377f)
ob.Theod. De obitu Theodosii CSEL 73, SAEMO 18, FC 22 (395)
ob.Val. De obitu Valentiniani CSEL 73, SAEMO 18, FC 22; trans. T.A. Kelly, Washington D.C. 1940 (392)
off. De officiis ed. and trans. M. Testard (*Les Devoirs*), Paris, 1984–1992, SAEMO 13 (388f)
paen. De paenitentia SC 179, SAEMO 17 (c.389f)
par. De paradiso CSEL 32, SAEMO 2, FC 42 (377f)
patr. De patriarchis CSEL 32, SAEMO 4, FC 65 (c.391)
ps. Explanatio psalmorum xii CSEL 64, SAEMO 7f (387–397)
ps.118 Expositio psalmi cxviii CSEL 62, SAEMO 9f (386–388?)
sacr. De sacramentis CSEL 73, SAEMO 17, FC 44; ed. J.H. Srawley and trans. T. Thomas, London 1950; ed. and German trans. J. Schmitz, Freiburg 1990
Spir.S. De Spiritu Sancto CSEL 79, SAEMO 16, FC 44 (381)
Tob. De Tobia CSEL 32, SAEMO 6; trans. L.M. Zucker, Washington D.C. 1933 (c.388)
vid. De viduis SAEMO 14 (377f)

virgb. De virginibus SAEMO 14 (377), trans. Ramsey
virgt. De virginitate SAEMO 14 (late 380s)

. . .

WORKS BY OTHER ANCIENT AUTHORS

This list excludes works by classical and Christian authors cited for background or by way of comparison.

Ammianus Marcellinus, trans. J.C. Rolfe, London 1950–52
Augustine, *Confessions*, ed. J. O'Donnell, Oxford 1992; trans. H. Chadwick, Oxford 1991 (*conf.*)
Augustine, *De Civitate Dei* (The City of God), ed. *CCSL* 47f, trans. H. Bettenson, Harmondsworth 1972 (*civ.dei*)
R.H. Charles, ed., *The Apocrypha and Pseudepigrapha of the Old Testament*, Oxford 1913
Julian, *The Works of the Emperor Julian*, ed. and trans. W.C. Wright, London 1913–23
Paulinus, *Vita di S. Ambrogio*, ed. M. Pellegrino, Rome 1961 (*VAmb.*); trans. Ramsey, *FC* 15
Philo, ed. and trans. F.H. Colson et al., London/New York 1929–62
Plotinus, ed. and trans. A.H. Armstrong, London 1966–88
Possidius, *Vita Augustini*, ed. M. Pellegrino, Alba 1955 (*VAug*); trans. *FC* 15
Scolies ariennes sur le concile d'Aquilée, ed. R. Gryson, Paris 1980 (=*SC* 267)
Symmachus, *Quae supersunt MGH AA* 6
The Theodosian Code, trans. C. Pharr, Princeton N.J. 1962 (*cod.Theod.*)
Zosimus, *New History*, trans. R.T. Ridley, Canberra 1982
The historians Socrates, Sozomen and Theodoret are available in SAEMO 24, and have been translated into English in the *The Nicene and post-Nicene Fathers* (the first two in 2/2, Theodoret in 2/3).

. . .

WORKS BY MODERN AUTHORS

The following list constitutes only a small proportion of relevant work; material on Ambrose himself is listed annually in *L'année philologique*, while the bibliography in McLynn (1994) is an excellent guide to general work on the period.

Arslan, E.A. (1982) 'Urbanistica di Milano Romana', *Aufstieg und Niedergang der Römischen Welt* II, 12/1, 179–210.
Aubineau, M. (1955) 'Les écrits de Saint Athanase sur la virginité', *Revue d'ascétique et de mystique* 31, 140–73.
Barbero, G. (1990) 'Contributi allo studio dal "Liber Glossarum"', *Aevum* 64, 151–74.
Blaise, A. (c.1994) *A Handbook of Christian Latin: Style, Morphology and Syntax*, trans. G.C. Roti, Turnholt/Washington D.C.
Bloch, A. and Bloch, C. (1995) *The Song of Songs*, New York.
Brown, P. (1967) *Augustine of Hippo*, London.
Brown, P. (1988) *The Body and Society: Men, Women, and Sexual Renunciation in Early Christianity*, New York.
Brown, P. (1992) *Power and Persuasion in Late Antiquity: Towards a Christian Empire*, Madison.
Buchheit, V. (1984) 'Hippolyt, Origenes und Ambrosius über den Census Augusti', *Vivarium Festschrift Theodor Klauser*, Münster, 50–56.
Cantalamessa, R. (1979) 'La concezione teologica della Pasqua in sant' Ambrogio', *Paradoxos politeia studi patristici in onore di Giuseppe Lazzati*, Milan, 362–75.
Chadwick, H. (1976) *Priscillian of Avila*, Oxford.
Chastagnol, A. (1960) *La préfecture urbaine à Rome sous le bas-empire*, Paris.
Colombo, O.P. (1974) *A doutrina de santo Ambrósio sobre o uso dos bens temporais*, Porto Alegre.
Consolino, F.E. (1982) 'Dagli *exempla* ad un esempio di comportamento cristiano: il *de exhortatione virginitatis* di Ambrogio', *Rivista storica italiana* 94, 455–77.
Corbellini, C. (1975) 'Sesto Petronio Probo e l'elezione episcopale di Ambrogio', *Istituto Lombardo Accademia di scienze e lettere rendiconti classe di lettere e scienze morali e storiche* 109, 181–89.
Courcelle, P. (1950a) 'Plotin et saint Ambroise', *Revue de philologie*, 29–56.
Courcelle, P. (1950b) *Recherches sur les 'Confessions' de S. Augustin*, Paris.
Courcelle, P. (1963a) 'Anti-Christian arguments and Christian Platonism: from Arnobius to St Ambrose', in A. Momigliano, ed., *The Conflict between Paganism and Christianity in the Fourth Century*, Oxford, 151–92.
Courcelle, P. (1963b) *Les Confessions de S. Augustin dans la tradition littéraire: Antécedants et postérité*, Paris.

Courcelle, P. (1965) 'Tradition platonicienne et traditions chrétiennes du corps-prison', *Revue des études latines* 43, 406–43.

Dassmann, E. (1966) 'Die Kirche und ihre Glieder in der Hoheliederklärung bei Hippolyt, Origenes und Ambrosius von Mailand', *Römische Quartalschrift* 61, 121–44.

Dassmann, E. (1975) 'Ambrosius und die Märtyrer', *Jahrbuch für Antike und Christentum* 18, 49–68.

Davidson, I.J. (1995) 'Ambrose's *de officiis* and the intellectual climate of the late fourth century', *Vigiliae christianae* 49, 313–33.

Dölger, F.J. (1930) 'Christus im Bild des Skarabäus. Der Text *scarabaeus de ligno* in Habakuk 2, 11 nach der Auslesung von Ambrosius und Hieronymus', *Antike und Christentum* 2, 231–40.

Duval, Y.-M., ed. (1974) *Ambroise de Milan*, Paris.

Faust, U. (1983) *Christo servire libertas est. Zum Freiheitsbegriff des Ambrosius von Mailand*, Salzburg.

Fenger, A.-L. (1982) 'Tod und Auferstehung des Menschen nach Ambrosius' *De excessu fratris II*' in *Jenseitsvorstellungen in Antike und Christentum Gedenkschrift für Alfred Stuiber*, Münster, 127–39.

Fischer, B. (1970) 'Hat Ambrosius von Mailand in der Woche zwischen seiner Taufe und seiner Bischofskonzekration andere Weihen Empfangen?', *Kyriakon Festchrift Johannes Quasten* 2, Münster, 527–31.

Fischer, B. (1984) 'Ist Ambrosius in Trier geboren?', *Vivarium Festschrift Theodor Klauser*, Münster, 132–35.

Fischer, B. (1988) 'Bonum dominum habemus – Wir haben einen guten Herrn. Ein Rhema des heiligen Ambrosius' in *Itinera Domini . . . Festschrift Emmanuel V. Severus*, Münster, 99–105.

Fontaine, J. (1982) 'Un cliché de la spiritualité antique tardive: stetit immobilis', *Romanitas-Christianitas Festschrift Johannes Straub*, Berlin.

Gibbon, E. (1896+) *The History of the Decline and Fall of the Roman Empire*, ed. J.B. Bury, London.

Gilliard, F.D. (1984) 'Senatorial Bishops in the fourth century', *Harvard Theological Review* 77, 153–75.

Goody, J. (1983) *The Development of the Family and Marriage in Europe*, Cambridge.

Grosso, G. (1983) 'La "Lettera alle vergini" Atanasio e Ambrogio', *Augustinianum* 23, 421–52.

Gryson, R. (1966) 'L'interprétation du nom de Lévi (Lévite) chez saint Ambroise', *Sacris erudiri* 17, 217–29.
Hagendahl, H. (1958) *Latin Fathers and the Classics*, Göteborg.
Hamilton, S. (1997) 'A new model for royal penance? Helgaud of Fleury's Life of Robert the Pious', *Early Medieval Europe* 6, 189–200.
Hanson, R.P.C. (1988) *The Search for Christian Doctrine: the Arian Controversy 318–381*, Edinburgh.
Heinen, H. (1985) *Trier und das Trevererland in römischer Zeit*, Trier.
Homes Dudden, F. (1935) *The Life and Times of St Ambrose*, Oxford.
Jenal, G. (1995) *Italia ascetica atque monastica*, Stuttgart.
Kaiser, E. (1964) 'Odyssee-Szenen als Topoi', *Museum Helveticum* 21, 109–36.
Kaster, R.A. (1988) *Guardians of Language: the Grammarian and Society in Late Antiquity*, Berkeley.
Klein, R. (1970) 'Die Kaiserbriefe des Ambrosius Zur Problematik ihrer Veröffentlichung', *Athenaeum* 48, 335–71.
Krautheimer, R. (1983) *Three Christian Capitals*, Berkeley.
Lamirande, E. (1979) 'Quelques visages de séductrices. Pour une théologie de la condition féminine selon saint Ambroise', *Science et esprit* 31, 173–89.
Lamirande, E. (1981) 'La datation de la "Vita Ambrosii" de Paulin de Milan', *Revue des études augustiniennes* 21, 44–55.
Lawrence, P. (1997) 'Les moniales de l'aristocratie: grandeur et humilité', *Vigiliae christianae* 51, 140–57.
Lazzati, G. (1955) 'L'autenticità del *De sacramentis* e la valutazione letteraria delle opere di S. Ambrogio', *Aevum* 29, 17–48.
Lazzati, G., ed. (1976) *Ambrosius episcopus*, Milan.
Lewy, F. (1929) *Sobria ebrietas: Untersuchungen zur Geschichte der antiken Mystik*, Geissen.
Lizzi, R. (1989) *Vescovi e strutture ecclesiastiche nella città tardoantica (L'Italia Annonaria nel IV–V secolo d.C.)*, Como.
McLure, R. (1972f) 'The Greek translation of the *Vita Ambrosii* of Paulinus of Milan', *Sacris erudiri* 21, 57–70.
McLynn, N. (1994) *Ambrose of Milan*, Berkeley.
Madec, G. (1974) *Saint Ambroise et la philosophie*, Paris.
Madec, G. (1976) 'Jean Scot et les pères latins', *Revue des études augustiniennes* 22, 134–42.

Madec, G. (1987) 'Le milieu milanaise philosophique et christianisme', *Bulletin de littérature ecclésiastique* 88, 194–205.
Markus, R. (1990) *The End of Ancient Christianity*, Cambridge.
Markus, R. (1996) *Signs and Meanings. Word and Text in Ancient Christianity*, Liverpool.
Matthews, J. (1975) *Western Aristocracies and Imperial Court A.D. 364–425*, Oxford.
Mazza, E. (1989) *Mystagogy. A Theology of Liturgy in the Patristic Age*, Engl. transl. New York.
Mazzarino, S. (1973f) 'Il padre di Ambrogio', *Helikon* 13f 111–17.
Mazzarino, S. (1989) *Storia sociale del vescovo Ambrogio*, Rome.
Mazzucco, C. (1980) 'Due visioni cristiane del mondo e due stile: Cipriano "ad Demetrianum" 3–5 e Ambrogio "Epistula" XVIII 23–29', *Civiltà classica e cristiana* 1, 219–41.
Merton, T. (1968) *Conjectures of a Guilty Bystander*, Garden City, N.Y.
Mohrmann, Ch. (1952) 'Le style oral du *De sacramentis* de Saint Ambroise', *Vigiliae christianae* 6, 168–77.
Moorhead, J. (1983) 'The Greeks, pupils of the Hebrews', *Prudentia* 15, 3–12.
Moorhead, J. (1997) 'Cooking a kid in its mother's milk: patristic exegesis of an Old Testament command', *Augustinianum* 37, 261–71.
Nauroy, G.G. (1998) 'Le fouet et le miel: le combat d'Ambroise en 386 contre l'arianisme milanaise', *Recherches augustiniennes* 23, 3–86.
Nauroy, G.G. (1990) 'Du combat de la piété à la confession du sang. Une interprétation chrétienne du martyre des Maccabées chez Ambroise de Milan', *Revue d'histoire et de philosophie religieuses* 70, 49–68.
Oppel, J. (1993) 'Saint Jerome and the history of sex', *Viator* 24, 1–22.
Opelt, I. (1968) 'Das Bienenwunder in der Ambrosiusbiographie des Paulinus von Mailand', *Vigiliae christianae* 22, 38–44.
Otten, R.T. (1963) 'Amor, caritas and dilectio: some observations on the vocabulary of love in the exegetical works of St. Ambrose', *Mélanges offerts à Mademoiselle Christine Mohrmann*, Utrecht, 73–83.
Paredi, A. (1960) *S. Ambrogio e la sua età*, 2nd edn, Milan.

Paredi, A. (1963) 'Paulinus of Milan', *Sacris erudiri* 14, 206–30.
Pellegrino, M. (1979) '"Mutus . . . loquar Christum" Pensieri di sant' Ambrogio su parola e silenzio', *Paradoxos politeia studi patristici in onore di Giuseppe Lazzati*, Milan, 447–57.
Perer, M.L.G., ed. (1995) *La basilica di S Ambrogio: il tempio ininterotto*, Milan.
Peters, F.E. (1990) *Judaism, Christianity and Islam* 2, Princeton, N.J.
Picard, J.-Ch. (1988) *Le souvenir des évêques: sépultures, listes épiscopales et culte des évêques en Italie du nord des origines au Xe siècle*, Rome.
Pietri, Ch. (1992) 'Aristocratie milanaise païens et chrétiens au IVe siècle', in G.S. Chiesa and E.A. Arslan (eds.) *Felix temporis ratio*, Milan, 157–70.
Piredda, A.M. (1991) 'Susanna e il silenzio. L'interpretazione di Ambrogio', *Sandalion* 14, 169–92.
Pizzolato, L.F. (1976) 'La coppia umana in sant' Ambrogio', in R. Cantalamessa (ed.) *Etica sessuale e matrimonio nel cristianesimo delle origini*, Milan, 180–211.
Pizzolato, L.F. (1978) *La dottrina esegetica di sant'Ambrogio*, Milan.
Poirier, M. (1979) '"Christus pauper factus est" chez Saint Ambroise', *Rivista di storia e letteratura religiosa* 15, 250–57.
Puech, H.-C. and Hadot, P. (1959) 'L'entretien d'Origène avec Héraclide et le commentaire de Saint Ambroise sur l'évangile de Saint Luc', *Vigiliae christianae* 13, 204–34.
Rahner, H. (1992) *Church and State in Early Christianity*, Engl. transl., San Fransisco.
Riggi, C. (1975) 'Lineamenti delle personalità di S. Ambrogio nel ricordo agostiniano', *Salesianum* 37, 3–37.
Roques, M. (1996) 'L'authenticité de *l'Apologia David altera*: historique et progrès d'une controverse', *Augustinianum* 36, 53–92, 423–58.
Rosso, G. (1983) 'La "Lettera alle vergini" Atanasio e Ambrogio', *Athenaeum* 23, 421–52.
Ruggini, L. (1961) *Economia e società nell' 'Italia annonaria'*, Milan.
Savon, H. (1977a) *Saint Ambroise devant l'exégèse de Philo le Juif*, Paris.
Savon, H. (1977b) 'Saint Ambroise et la philosophie à propos d'une étude recente', *Revue de l'histoire des religions* 173–96.

Seibel, W. (1958) *Fleisch und Geist beim heiligen Ambrosius*, Munich.
Steidle, W. (1984) 'Beobachtungen zu des Ambrosius Schrift *De officiis*', *Vigiliae christianae* 38, 18–66.
Steidle, W. (1985) 'Beobachtungen zum Gedankengang im 2. Buch von Ambrosius, *De officiis*', *Vigiliae christianae* 39, 280–98.
Testard, M. (1973) 'Observations sur la thème de la "conscientia"', *Revue des études latines* 51, 219–61.
Testard, M. (1989) 'Recherches sur quelques méthodes de travail de saint Ambroise dans le *De officiis*', *Recherches augustiniennes* 24, 65–122.
Thelamon, F. (1981) *Païens et chrétiens au ive siècle*, Paris.
Vasey, V.R. (1982) *The Social Ideas in the Works of St Ambrose. A Study in the 'De Nabuthe'*, Rome.
Vismara, G. (1987) 'Ancora sulla "episcopalis audientia" (Ambrogio arbitro o giudice?)', *Studia et documenta historiae et iuris* 53, 53–73.
Williams, D.H. (1995) *Ambrose of Milan and the end of the Nicene–Arian conflicts*, Oxford.
Wilmart, D.A. (1911) 'Transfigurare', *Bulletin d'ancienne littérature et d'archéologie chrétiennes*, 282–92.
Zelzer, M. (1987) 'Ambrosius von Mailand und das Erbe der klassischen Tradition', *Wiener Studien* 100, 201–26.

The late Roman world of Ambrose

INDEX

Aaron, priest 110 n. 13, 179
Abelard 216
Abraham 44, 57, 64, 115
Adam 40, 44, 45–8, 49, 92, 94, 106f, 138
Adrianople, battle of (378) 33, 104, 113, 118
Aesculapius 122
Aetius 114
Africa 21, 37
Agnes, virgin martyr 52, 135
Ahab, king 29, 130
Ailred of Rievaulx 162 n. 8, 214
Alaric, Goth 128
Alexandria 122, 133 n. 15, 144, 196, 217
Ambrose, works of (main references):
  Abraham 44, 57f
  Apologia David altera 82f, 194f
  De apologia prophetae David 82, 195, 215
  De bono mortis 173–6
  De Cain et Abel 61f, 72
  De excessu fratris 37–9
  De fide 113–18, 214f
  De fuga saeculi 73
  De Iacob 135–7
  De institutione virginis 40f
  De Isaac vel anima 172f
  De mysteriis 147
  De Nabuthae historia 130f
  De obitu Theodosii 202–6
  De obitu Valentiniani 197f
  De officiis 34, 60f, 134f, 157–214

  De paenitentia 191f
  De paradiso 45–7, 72
  De sacramentis 93f, 146f, 215
  De Spiritu Sancto 114–18, 214
  De Tobia 131
  De viduis 40
  De virginibus 40, 48–50, 65–9
  De virginitate 40, 53f
  Epistulae 7–9, 125–7, 137–40, 147–50, 150–5, 186–90, 192f, 199f
  Exameron 72f, 213f
  Exhortatio virginitatis 41, 51
  Explanatio super psalmos xii 73f, 208f
  Expositio de psalmo cxviii 109f, 213
  Expositio euangelii secundum Lucam 74, 88–90, 94–6, 97, 106f, 213
  Hymns 141–3
  Interpellatione Iob et David 73, 99f
Ammianus Marcellinus 168f
Anna, widow 43, 90
anti-Nicaeans ('Arians') 13, 17, 28, 111–22, 132f, 147–50, 152f, 169 n. 22, 203, 214
Antioch 122, 144, 196
Antiochus, king 135f
Apollo 122
Aquila, translator 79, 109
Aquileia 2 n. 1, 154, 186
  council of (381) 12, 119–22, 196
Aratus 176

229

Arbogast 197, 198–201, 202
Arcadius, emperor 193, 202
Arians *see* anti-Nicaeans
Aristotle 164, 165
Arius 16, 119f
Athanasius, bishop of Alexandria 20 n. 12, 53, 68, 103, 114, 133 n. 15, 217
  his *Life of Antony* 11, 29
Athena 128
Athenagoras 38
Athens 128
Attalus, priest 119
Atto, bishop of Vercelli 214
Augustine, bishop of Hippo 3, 10, 11, 14, 19, 27, 31, 49, 79 n. 17, 81, 83, 105, 124, 142f, 145 n. 34, 146, 162, 170f, 210, 212f, 214, 215f, 217
  his *City of God* 127
  his *Confessions* 12, 35f
  on Ambrose 35f, 76f, 115 n. 22, 141, 146, 150 n. 46, 152, 180
Augustus, emperor 63, 104 n. 3, 124
Ausonius 63, 168
Auxentius, bishop of Milan 16, 17, 24, 31, 111, 112, 121 n. 26
Auxentius Mercurinus, bishop 132f, 147–9
avarice 130f, 161f

baptism 22f, 28, 30, 37, 55, 93f, 99f, 144f, 146f, 167, 198
Basil, bishop of Caesarea 5, 72 n. 2, 73, 74, 109 n. 12, 114, 217
Bathsheba 82f, 107
Bauto, general 123
Bede 211, 213, 215
Benedict, St 213
Benivolus 134
Berengar 215
Bible, books of (main references only):
  Deuteronomy 84
  Ecclesiastes 84
  Ezekiel 118, 178
  Genesis 44, 45–8, 72f, 84, 106, 178, 184
  Hebrews 80
  Isaiah 4 n. 2, 68 n. 47
  Job 86
  John 84, 88
  Lamentations 198
  Leviticus 84
  Luke 42, 74, 78, 81, 84, 89f, 97, 104, 131 n. 12
  Mark 78, 84
  Matthew 78, 80, 84
  I Peter 80
  Proverbs 84
  Psalms 41, 73f, 79, 85, 87f, 141, 208f
  Song of Songs 52, 53f, 55, 56, 57, 84, 108–10, 172, 184, 198, 203
  Tobit 131
  Zechariah 204f
bishops 30–5, 158
blindness 50 n. 21, 151, 153, 203
body, the 55, 56–9, 173–7, 179, 184, 198
Bologna 100
Bonosus, bishop of Niš 196

Caligula 206
Calligonus, eunuch 140, 148, 155
Callinicum 185, 195, 203
Capua, council of (392) 196
Cassiodorus, his *Historia tripartita* 212, 213, 214, 215
Castus, deacon 208
Celestine I, pope 213
Celsus, martyr 153, 207
Chalcedon, council of (451) 215
Charlemagne 211
Chromatius, bishop of Aquileia 9, 213
church, the 47, 50 n. 20, 82f, 90, 94, 99f, 102f, 105, 106–10
Cicero 7 n. 9, 20 n. 11, 34, 38, 46 n. 13, 59, 62 n. 35, 158, 159, 162, 164, 165, 166f, 176, 177, 180, 217, 218
Claudian 125
clergy 33, 158, 159f, 161–3, 200
Concordia, Coelia, vestal virgin 123
conscientia 177

INDEX

Constantine, emperor 1, 17, 103, 132, 204, 205, 206
Constantinople 1, 30, 63, 119, 133 n. 15, 144, 187, 199, 201, 206
  basilica of the Holy Apostles 132
  councils of (381) 119, 133; (553) 215; (680f) 215
Constantius II, emperor 111, 124, 133 n. 15, 168
creeds 76, 118, 138, 147, 173
Cyprian, bishop of Carthage and martyr 49, 127 n. 37, 134 n. 18
Cyril, bishop of Jerusalem 146

Damasus, pope 124, 153
Daniel 136
David, king 73, 82f, 135, 141, 160, 164, 165, 167, 187, 189, 193, 194–6
  death 173–6
Deborah 31 n. 37
delight 46, 47, 58, 59, 60, 174
Delilah 61
demons 29, 151
Devil, the, Satan 46, 82, 154, 206
Didymus 114, 195
Diocletian, emperor 1
Dionysius, bishop of Milan 16
Donatists 118 n. 25
Donatus 77

Easter 133, 143–7, 208
ecclesia 183
Egypt 164, 165, 180
Eleazar, scribe 136, 182
elements, four 55, 89, 179
Elijah, prophet 29, 52, 73, 87, 93, 94, 105, 139
Elisha, prophet 94, 148, 151, 183
Elizabeth 43, 44
enjoyment 46, 47
Ennodius 211
Ephesus, council of (431) 215
Esdras 165
eucharist, mass 30, 85, 94, 138, 143, 145f, 147, 153, 167, 186, 189f, 193f, 202
Eugenius, usurper 198–201, 202, 204

Eunomius 114, 119
Euphrates, river 31 n. 37, 178
Eusebius 74, 217
Eusignius, praetorian prefect 137
Eve 40, 42 n. 4, 45–8, 49, 106f, 108, 109, 138

Facundus, bishop 211
Faenza 199
faith 202–4
Faustus, Manichean 35
Flavianus, Nicomachus 200, 201, 202
Florence 199
friends, friendship 8f, 160, 162f
Fritigil, queen of the Marcomanni 104

Galla Placidia, mausoleum of 213
Gaudentius, bishop of Brescia 150 n. 46, 207
Gervasius and Protasius, martyrs 150–4
Ghazali, Muslim theologian 100 n. 40
Gihon, river 178
Gog 105, 118
Goliath 194
Goths 33, 105, 112, 118, 151, 204
Gratian, emperor 2, 11, 63, 112f, 118, 119, 121, 123, 124, 125, 126, 127, 132, 154, 168, 198, 203, 204, 206
Greek language 21f, 75f, 78f, 80, 81, 91, 178, 197, 210
Gregory I, pope 3, 213, 214, 216
Gregory VII, pope 212
Gregory, bishop of Nyssa 146
Gregory of Nazianzus 22, 119

'handing over' (*traditio*) 137f, 140, 148, 149, 150
Hannah 77
Hebrew language 78, 107
Helena, mother of Constantine 66 n. 43, 204
Helgaud 215
Henry IV, emperor 212
Heraclitus 164
Herod, king 61, 139, 148, 171

Herodias 139
heretics 102, 155 (*see also* anti-Nicaeans)
Hilary, bishop of Poitiers 17, 74, 121 n. 26, 142, 214, 217
Hippolytus 73, 104, 109, 217
Hiram, king 113
Holophernes 61
Holy Spirit 85, 93f, 114, 115–17, 208
Homer 59, 79, 173 n. 29
Honorius, emperor 193, 202, 206
Horace 79 n. 17, 132, 136, 142
Hydra, the 168
hymns 141–3, 212f

Illyricum 192
Irenaeus 8 n. 12, 75
Isaac 41f, 64, 84, 188
Isaiah, prophet 4 n. 2, 68 n. 47, 83, 136
Isonzo, river 201

Jacob, patriarch 98, 135f, 184
James of Voragine 210f
Jephthah 61
Jeremiah 136, 180
Jerome 3, 54, 77, 162, 213, 215f
  his letters 21
  his *Life of Paul* 11
  on Ambrose 26, 31 n. 37, 73, 105 n. 5, 115 n. 22, 204 n. 32, 210, 218
Jerusalem 187, 205
Jesus Christ 53f, 82f, 86–8, 92–8, 106–10, 114–18, 171, 205, 208f
Jews, Judaism 34, 66 n. 43, 83, 86–8, 92, 102, 109, 121, 153, 182–9, 195, 205, 209
Jezebel 139
Job 73, 93, 105, 138, 165
John the Baptist 44, 105, 106, 139
John Chrysostum, bishop of Constantinople 212
John, disciple 108, 184
John, praetorian prefect 10
John the Scot 218
Joseph 42, 98, 130, 136, 155
Jovinian, heretic 196

Judith 61
Julian, emperor 64, 103, 124, 153 n. 49, 168, 186, 205
Julian Valens, bishop 112
Juliana, widow 51, 62, 65 n. 41
Jupiter 122
Justina, empress 42, 113, 133, 139, 149, 154
Justus, bishop 8 n. 12

Landulf 211
Lanfranc 215
Laurence, deacon and martyr 66 n. 43, 135
Lent 144
Leo I, pope 213
Leontius, senator 24
Levi 91
Liberius, pope 21, 68
Life of Martin 11
Livy 123
Lord's Prayer 147
lust 130
Luther, Martin 216

Maccabees 60, 135f, 183, 185
Macedonius, *magister militum* 11, 154
Manicheans 35f, 43, 63
manliness 61f
Marcellina, sister of Ambrose 7, 9, 21, 36, 52, 68, 69, 137, 150, 188
Marcus, son of Cicero 158, 162
Marcus Aurelius, emperor 1
Marius Victorinus 8 n. 13, 171
marriage 43–50, 51
Martha, sister of Lazarus 85
Martin, bishop of Tours 26
martyrs, martyrdom 69, 103, 134–7, 148, 153, 186, 187, 191 (*see also* Agnes, Cyprian, Laurence, Pelagia)
Mary, blessed Virgin 34, 43, 48, 68, 69, 70, 76, 90f, 99, 107f, 196f
Mary, sister of Lazarus 56, 81
Mary Magdalene 48
mass *see* eucharist
Maximus, bishop of Turin 213

Maximus, Magnus, usurper 123, 126, 140, 150, 154, 155, 182, 187, 197, 204
Melitus, bishop in Antioch 122
Menander Rhetor 38
Merton, Thomas 214
Milan 2, 65, 113, 126, 129–33, 137–40, 143, 188, 191, 192, 197, 199, 200, 201, 202, 204
  basilica Ambrosiana 28, 132, 151, 208
  basilica Apostolorum 132, 207
  basilica of Fausta 151
  basilica Portiana 133, 137f, 139
  cathedral 17, 137
  church of San Simpliciano 132
  council at (396) 196
  shrine of Felix and Nabor 151
mind 47, 55, 57, 58, 59, 60, 61
Miriam 52, 141
monks 33, 185, 190
Moses 34, 86, 87, 164, 165, 184
music 59, 140–3

Naboth 73, 130, 149
Nathan, prophet 105, 187, 189
Nazareth, alleged birthplace of Jesus 31 n. 37
Nazarius, martyr 153, 207
Nectarius, bishop of Constantinople 22
Neoplatonism 56, 58, 169–77
Nero, emperor 206
Nicaea, councils of (325) 16, 111, 113; (787) 215
Noah 42, 90
  his sons 166
Notker 211
Novatians 191

Origen 72 n. 4, 74, 83 n. 23, 104, 108, 110, 146, 174 n. 31, 195, 217
Ovid 38

'pagans' 15, 17, 32, 37f, 102, 121, 122–8, 155, 164–9, 191, 195, 197, 199
Palladius, bishop in Antioch 122

Palladius, bishop of Ratiaria 112, 113, 119–21, 122, 134 n. 18, 168
Panaetius 158, 164, 165
parables 70 n. 17, 94, 183f
  Good Samaritan 94–6, 134, 191
  Good Shepherd 92
  Great banquet 102
Paschasius Radbertus 215
Passover 144
Paul, St, apostle 41, 48, 51, 61, 80, 83 n. 21, 95, 107f, 144, 174, 175, 176, 184, 185, 207
Paulinus, deacon, his *Life of Ambrose* 9–12, 13, 18f, 20, 21, 23f, 24f, 27, 28, 111, 112, 141f, 150 n. 46, 152, 162f, 194, 198f, 200, 203, 206–9, 210, 215
Paulinus, senator 64
Pavia 207
Pelagia, virgin martyr 69, 105, 134
Pelagius, heretic 10, 210
penance, penitence 30, 191f, 194
Peter, St, apostle 45, 85, 115, 148, 184
Peter Chrysologus, bishop of Ravenna 213
Philo 8, 45 n. 11, 57, 72f, 80, 87, 111, 146, 159, 164, 166, 169, 177, 217
Phison, river 178
Photinus 119, 169–77
Photius 133 n. 15
Physiologus 214
pietas 66f
Plato 20, 165, 180
Pliny 7, 20 n. 12
Plotinus 58, 80, 136, 146, 169–76, 181, 217
Pompey 131
Pontius Pilate 27f
Porphyry 169, 170
Possidius, biographer of Augustine 170
Praetextatus 15, 123
Priscillian, heretic 154
Probus, praetorian prefect 20, 22
Pythagoras 140, 164

Quintillian 79 n. 17

Rachael 107 n. 7
Ravenna 139, 214
Rebekah 41, 107 n. 7, 188
Rhaetia 123
Rimini, council of (359) 111, 133
Robert the Pious, king 215
Roman empire 1, 20, 104f
Romanus melodos 204 n. 32
Rome 2, 122, 124f, 127, 144, 160, 166, 187, 191, 196
 church of Sta Maria Maggiore 15
 curia Iulia 124
 first stone theatre 131
Rufinus, his *Ecclesiastical History* 9, 17, 18, 20 n. 12, 145, 194, 201

Sabinus, bishop 34
sacerdos 182
Salim 93
Samson 61
Sarah 44, 107 n. 7
Satan *see* Devil, the
Satyrus, brother of Ambrose 7, 22, 36–9, 111
Saul, king 141
Scipio 34, 160
Scylla 168
Secundianus, bishop of Singidunum 119
Seneca 38, 159
senses 47, 49f, 54–6, 57, 89
Septuagint 78f, 109, 136, 183, 185, 217
Serena, wife of Stilicho 207
Servius 77
Shechem 98–100
silence 22 n. 19, 33 n. 42, 34, 36, 69, 76f, 158
Simeon 90
Simon the Pharisee 188f
Simplicianus 8, 31, 170f, 207
Sirens 59f, 141, 174
Siricius, pope 196
Sirmium 2, 22, 111 n. 16, 113
 council of (357) 111

Sixtus, pope 66 n. 43, 135
Socrates, historian 12, 19 n. 10
Socrates, philosopher 164
Solomon, king 99, 113, 141, 179
Soteris, virgin and martyr 21 n. 17, 52
soul 56f, 58, 59, 61, 172–4, 184
south, Queen of the 113
Sozmonen, historian 12, 19 n. 10, 211
Stilicho, general 202, 206f
suicide 69 n. 50, 134, 202
Susannah 77
Symmachus, Quintus Aurelius, senator and prefect of the city 12, 32, 37, 123–8, 160 n. 6, 200, 206, 210
Symmachus, translator 79, 109

tears 37, 143, 197
Tertullian 109
Theoderic, king 150
Theodoret, historian 12, 211, 212
Theodosian Code 12
Theodosius I, emperor 7, 22, 113, 118f, 121, 122, 154f, 176 n. 36, 182, 185–91, 192–6, 197, 199, 201f, 202–4, 206, 211
Theodotion, translator 79
Theodulf of Orleans 215
Theophilus 81
Theotimus 50
Thessaloniki 154, 182, 192, 193, 195, 204, 212
Thomas Aquinas 216
Tigris, river 31 n. 37, 178
Timasius, general 190
Titans 167
Tobias 73
Trier 1, 2, 20f, 123, 154
Trinity 115f, 143

Ulfilas, bishop 132
unclean spirits 152, 153, 185, 206, 207
Uranius, alleged father of Ambrose 21 n. 16
Uriah 82f
Ursinus 112

INDEX

Valens, emperor 111, 118
Valentinian I, emperor 17, 23, 24, 111, 112, 125, 202, 206, 212
Valentinian II, emperor 11, 22, 105, 112f, 121, 123–7, 139, 140, 143, 150, 154, 168, 182, 197f, 200, 201, 204, 206
Valentinians, heretical group 185
Valerian, bishop of Aquileia 119, 213
Vandals 170
Venerius, deacon and bishop 208
Vercelli, bishop of 207, 208
Vergil 63, 67, 93 n. 34, 126, 165, 168f, 217
Verona 192
Vesta 200

vestal virgins 70, 123, 125, 127
Victor, martyr, shrine of 37
Victory, altar of 124–8
Vienne 197
virgins, virginity 40, 43, 50, 51–4, 62, 64–70, 90, 144, 161, 174, 196f
virtue, virtues 60, 61
virtues, cardinal 159, 172, 178f
Vitalis and Agricola, martyrs 199

widows, widowhood 43, 62, 90, 161, 174
William of St Thierry 213
wives 43–50, 51, 62f, 90, 196

Zacharias 42, 44, 158
Zarephath, widow of 107 n. 7